THE LAST DAYS OF HITLER

THE MACMILLAN COMPANY
NEW YORK · BOSTON · CHICAGO
DALLAS · ATLANTA · SAN FRANCISCO

MACMILLAN AND CO., LIMITED
LONDON · BOMBAY · CALCUTTA
MADRAS · MELBOURNE

**THE MACMILLAN COMPANY
OF CANADA, LIMITED**
TORONTO

HITLER AND HIMMLER
(Captured photograph from *S.S. Hauptamt*)

THE LAST DAYS
OF HITLER

by

H. R. TREVOR-ROPER

New York

THE MACMILLAN COMPANY

1947

PRINTED IN THE UNITED STATES OF AMERICA
BY H. WOLFF, NEW YORK

AUTHOR'S PREFACE

SINCE the completion of the original investigation into the circumstances of Hitler's death, I have been indebted to many friends, both British and American, who have helped me in the composition of this book, and whom I would here like to thank for their assistance; but since some of them are still serving, I am sure that the others will forgive me for including all alike in this general and impersonal acknowledgment, and for mentioning only one name, already familiar to most of them. My friend Dick White was brigadier commanding the Intelligence Bureau at the time when Hitler's death was still a mystery. He conceived the idea of this enquiry; and in Bad Oeynhausen in September 1945, he invited me to carry it out. Since then he has encouraged me to write this narrative, and has given me continual help in every problem (and there have been many) which I have referred to him. He is thus both the first parent and the ultimate midwife of this book; and I dedicate it to him.

H. R. T.-R.

Christ Church,
Oxford.
25th October 1946

CONTENTS

Chapter One

HITLER AND HIS COURT   I

True nature of Nazi government and of Nazism—The Eastern
policy—Party and Army—Growth of the court—Struggle for the
succession—The flight of Hess—Bormann—Goering—Goebbels—
Himmler—The rise of Himmler—Schellenberg and his ambitions—
German intelligence—The Plot of 20th July 1944 and its effects—
Decline of Himmler and rise of Bormann—Bormann and Goebbels—Hitler remains undisputed master of all

Chapter Two

HITLER IN DEFEAT   42

The break-through at Avranches—Policy of Nazi leaders in face
of defeat—Collapse of organisation and discipline—"Resistance
movements"—The "Werewolves"—The intervention of Goebbels
—Ideological nihilism—Hitler after the Plot—Hitler's "Diary"—
Change in Hitler's habits: he becomes a neurotic recluse—Hitler's
doctors — Professor Morell and his drugs — Decline in Hitler's
health—Crisis among the doctors—Dismissal of Morell's rivals—
Appointment of Dr. Stumpfegger—Hitler's hypnotism and blood-
lust

Chapter Three

THE COURT IN DEFEAT   74

Albert Speer and nihilism—The technocratic philosophy and its
limitations—Speer's detachment from Hitler—Himmler and Schellenberg—Schellenberg saps Himmler's loyalty to Hitler—Schellenberg proposes liquidation of Hitler—Indecision of Himmler—
Hitler despairs of the succession—Hitler in Berlin—Eva Braun—
Count Schwerin von Krosigk and his diary—Carlyle and astrology in the Bunker—Death of Roosevelt—The fools' paradise of
Nazism—Ribbentrop—Schellenberg, Schwerin von Krosigk, and
Himmler—Schellenberg's self-deception

Chapter Four

Chapter Five

Chapter Six

Chapter Seven

THE DEATH OF HITLER (30TH APRIL–1ST MAY)   196

ILLUSTRATIONS

FOREWORD

By Marshal of the R.A.F., Lord Tedder G.C.B.
Deputy Supreme Commander, Allied Expeditionary Force
1943–1945

THERE used to be a school of historical thought which held that the course of human history was determined largely by political and economic factors rather than by the characters and actions of individuals. My own experience during this last war has emphasised to me the immense, and in some cases decisive influence exercised on the course of events by individual personalities. In the past it has rarely been possible for the effects of the personality and character of individual leaders to be assessed other than by the study of documents. Their writings may have been recorded; their words may have been memorised; but the life had gone out of them. History written on such a basis is inevitably liable to distortion due to point of view or due to incomplete evidence.

Here on the other hand we have history written from living material. Mr. Trevor-Roper, as an intelligence officer, was given the task of uncovering step by step the events of Hitler's last few weeks of life. In discharging this duty he has produced a piece of history which is as living as it is accurate, and as monumental as the scale of events he recalls. Although Hitler is dead, the agonies he brought on mankind are still alive, and however much mystery he attempted to weave around his personal activities, they have been laid bare by the flood of living testimony and documentary material which has become available since Germany's capitulation. There is no possibility of distortion in this case. Mr. Trevor-Roper's story sets the seal on Nuremberg.

Hitler was not one who was prepared to allow history to follow any pre-determined political or economic course. In a megalomania fired by almost hypnotic personality he set himself to determine the pattern of the history of Europe for a thousand years. Here was a man who by ordinary standards would be judged insane, yet it took the combined might of the British Commonwealth, of the United States and of the Soviet Republic to pull Hitler's lunatic structure to the ground.

It is not for me to attempt to point lessons to be drawn from the horrid madhouse which was Hitler's court, or from the fantastic debacle which is depicted in this record. I can only be unutterably thankful that the lunatic devotion of the madman's judgment pervaded every aspect of German activity. Never before has the truth of the old saying been so conclusively borne out, "Whom the Gods wish to destroy they first make mad." May no nation in the world ever again allow itself to be led by a megalomaniac.

21st October 1946

THE LAST DAYS OF HITLER

Chapter One

HITLER AND HIS COURT

Now THAT the New Order is past, and the Thousand-Year Reich has crumbled in a decade, we are able at last, picking among the still smoking rubble, to discover the truth about that fantastic and tragical episode. It is a chastening as well as an interesting study; for we discover not only the true facts, but the extent of our own errors. If we are to understand the extraordinary tale of Hitler's last days, and appreciate the true character of Nazi politics, it is essential that we should first dispose of those errors. We must recognise that Hitler was not a pawn; that the Nazi state was not (in any significant use of the word) totalitarian; and its leading politicians were not a government but a court,—a court as negligible in its power of ruling, as incalculable in its capacity for intrigue, as any oriental sultanate. Further we must know the true political significance of the Nazi doctrine, and the extent to which it retained its purity and determined events in these last days; and the nature of Hitler's struggle with the Army General Staff,—the one dissident group which he could neither dissolve nor eliminate, and which, at one time, might have eliminated him. Unless such political facts and relations are understood, the events of April 1945 will be quite incomprehensible, and the labour of collecting and arranging that complicated mass of evidence will have been, in one sense, in vain: for while solving one mystery of fact, it will have added a greater mystery of interpretation.

Some of these statements may seem paradoxical. How many people, in the past years, were unconsciously seduced by

Nazi propaganda into believing that Nazi Germany was organised as a "totalitarian" state,—totally integrated, totally mobilised, centrally controlled! Had this been true, Germany might yet have won the war, for its advantages in time, resources, and preparation were enormous; but in fact the totalitarianism of Germany was something quite different from this. Only policy, not administration, was effectively controlled at the centre. Total war, to the Nazis, did not mean, as it meant to us (and perhaps only to us), a concentration of all efforts upon the war, and a corresponding suspension of all irrelevant industry, for in Germany the production of many inessential luxuries was continued; it meant indiscriminate war by all methods and in all elements. In Nazi Germany neither war production, nor man-power, nor administration, nor intelligence, was rationally centralised; and Ribbentrop's protest at Nuremberg that foreign intelligence was not supplied by the Foreign Ministry but by thirty competing agencies is substantially true. The structure of German politics and administration, instead of being, as the Nazis claimed, "pyramidal" and "monolithic," was in fact a confusion of private empires, private armies, and private intelligence services. In truth, irresponsible absolutism is incompatible with totalitarian administration; for in the uncertainty of politics, the danger of arbitrary change, and the fear of personal revenge, every man whose position makes him either strong or vulnerable must protect himself against surprise by reserving from the common pool whatever power he has managed to acquire. Thus there is, in the end, no common pool at all. Irresponsibility of the ruler causes irresponsibility of the subject; the conception of the commonwealth no longer exists outside propaganda; and politics become the politics of feudal anarchy, which the personal power of an undisputed despot may conceal, but cannot alter.

And how wrong many of us were about that despot too, who has often been represented as a tool, but whose personal power was in fact so undisputed that he rode to the end above the chaos he had created, and concealed its true nature,—even presiding from his grave over his weak and worthless subordinates in the dock at Nuremberg! If this absolutism was unchecked, uncontrolled, by any external force, it is vain to suppose that any internal resistance could have corrected it. No man can escape the corruption of absolute power. The inhibitions, the cautions, the introspections which may influence the exercise of power when it is limited by insecurity or competition do not survive those limitations; and in Hitler's last years it will be futile to look for the diplomacy and concessions of his more tentative days, or the reservations and occasional humilities of *Mein Kampf*.[1]

Then there is Nazism itself, the religion of the German revolution, which underlay and inspired its temporary but spectacular success, and was as important an element in its politics as was Calvinism in earlier convulsions. Many worthy scholars have examined this vast system of bestial Nordic nonsense, analysing its component parts, discovering its remote origins, explaining its significance, and disposing of its errors; but of all the works on that dispiriting subject, the best, the most illuminating, the most valuable, seem to me to have come not from the conscientious scholars, nor from the virtuous victims of the movement, but (since failure is often a better political education than either industry or virtue) from one disappointed Nazi. Hermann Rauschning, an East Prussian magnate, was one of those military aristocrats who joined the movement in its early days, hoping to use it for their own ends, and who, having made their contribution to its success, and been cheated of their reward, saw the final ruin of their class in the purge of 1944. More intelligent than the rest, Rauschning escaped early from the movement which he

[1] Some of the contrasts between Hitler's theory, as published in *Mein Kampf*, and his practice during the war will be noticed as they become relevant. *e.g.* pp. 48 53, 64.

could neither control nor stop, and in two books[2] exposed, with terrible clarity, the true significance of the Nazi movement. His motives had not been pure, either in joining or in leaving the Party. He was no democrat, no pacifist, no martyr (if these are pure professions); and the intellectual clarity he achieved was the clarity not of suffering but of disillusion. But truth is independent of the stimulus that has provoked its discovery, and the conditions that have guided its expression; and to say that Rauschning is no better than his class is an irrelevant criticism of his books. In those books he demonstrated, as none other has done, the essential nihilism of the Nazi philosophy. This nihilism, the expression of frustration by the existing world, had inspired the Nazi movement in its early days; it was obscured in the days of power by other, more positive interests which became parasitical upon it; but in the last days, with which this book is concerned, when all hope and profit had departed, when all rivals had been eliminated or had fled, and the Party, in undisputed power, had nothing positive to offer any more, it was to this nihilism that it returned as its ultimate philosophy and valediction. The voice that issued from the doomed city of Berlin in the winter of 1944 and the spring of 1945 was the authentic voice of Nazism, purged of all its accessory appeals, its noonday concessions, and welcoming once more the consequences of its original formula, World Power or Ruin.

[2] *Die Revolution des Nihilismus*, 1938 (English translation, *Germany's Revolution of Destruction*, 1939), and *Hitler Speaks*, 1940 (Published by G. P. Putnam's Sons, New York, under the title, *The Voice of Destruction*). The latter volume is a collection of conversations with Hitler from the period 1932 to 1934, the period when Rauschning, who was President of the Danzig Senate, was one of Hitler's intimate circle. I make no apology for recommending it, although Professor Norman Baynes, in his *Short List of Books on National Socialism*, published for the Historical Association in 1943, shows considerable distrust of its authenticity. Professor Baynes' list (in which he mentions with praise Rudolf Olden's *Hitler the Pawn* and Mr. Arthur Bryant's "deeply sympathetic" study of Nazism) is based on the public beliefs of 1943, which represent a very inaccurate knowledge of the true nature of the Nazi Government. The vast mass of intimate matter since available has shown Rauschning to be completely reliable.

For by the winter of 1944 the positive alternative of the formula had failed, as all knew except a few still blinded devotees. That positive alternative was described in general terms as "world power," or "historical greatness"; more particularly defined, it meant one thing only,—the conquest of Russia, the extermination of the Slavs, and the colonisation of the East. This was the real message of Nazism. It is the burden of *Mein Kampf;* [3] obscured by the more general terminology of destruction, it rings through the conversations recorded by Rauschning; [4] and in Hitler's last written message, composed when the Russians were already at the gates of the Berlin Chancellery, the last and only positive aim which he bequeathed to his people was still "the conquest of territory in the east." [5] This Eastern policy was essential to Nazism; all other positive aims—the conquest of France or Britain—were subsidiary and incidental to it. The offence of France was its traditional policy of Eastern alliances, which had enabled it, for three centuries, to intervene in Germany. The offence of Britain was its refusal to be content with a maritime supremacy, its insistent tradition of preventing the domination of Europe by a single continental power. But the offence of Russia was the existence of Russia. As these offences were different, so the German response to each was different,—at least until Hitler, in the intoxication of success, abandoned all discrimination and diplomacy. France was to be finished as a great power; it was to be reduced to second-rate status, and, thus reduced, might survive as a western Croatia or Slovakia, independent, but incapable of a European policy. Britain was to become a purely maritime power; it need not sink to second-rate status,—Hitler was always prepared to "guarantee the

[3] *Mein Kampf*, chap. xiv, p. 933. All references to *Mein Kampf* are to the 1939 edition published by Reynal & Hitchcock, N. Y., copyright, 1939, by Houghton Mifflin Company.

[4] *The Voice of Destruction*, chap. III, p. 30 ff. (Darré's war-time speeches fully confirm this account by Rauschning of his earlier utterances.)

[5] See below, p. 195.

British Empire,"—but it must never intervene in Continental politics again. Thus the Nazi policy in respect of the West would ensure to Germany freedom to deal unhindered with the fundamental problem of the East. For Russia there was no such indulgent solution. As Russia's crime was its existence, so its judgment was extermination. The war in the West was a traditional war, a war of diplomatic aims and limited objectives, in which some residue of international convention was regarded; the war in the East was a crusade, "a war of ideologies," in which all conventions were ignored. It is essential that we remember the basic anti-Russian significance of Nazism. All the general concepts of that terrible creed conceal a particular anti-Russian significance. Racialism means the supremacy of Germans to Slavs; "living space" and "geopolitics" mean the conquest of their territory; the rule of the "master race" means the enslavement of their surviving population. Crusades require crusaders; and again it is in the anti-Russian character of Nazism that we find the significance of the S.S., the most fanatical, most mystical missionaries of the new gospel. It was they who preached racialism and "living space," and practised extermination and enslavement; it was they who emphasised the crusade by organising "Germanic" foreigners into anti-Russian legions; they carried Nordic mysticism to lengths which even Hitler ridiculed; and in the end they were prepared to carry on the Eastern crusade at a price which even Hitler rejected—surrender in the West. It was not Hitler but Himmler, the high-priest of the S.S., who expressed the Nordic gospel in its most outrageous form; and it was particularly in respect of Russia that he expressed it.[6] An appreciation of this anti-Russian character of Nazism is not only necessary to the understanding of Nazism itself; it will also explain, in part, the most significant opposition to Hitler inside Germany,—the opposition of the Army General Staff.

[6] Compare his speeches quoted below, pp. 19 note, 23-24, 27.

Hitler's struggle with the Army General Staff is one of the most interesting features of Nazi history during the war, for the General Staff was the one centre of opposition which Hitler, though he succeeded in ruining it, was never able to conquer. In 1924, when Hitler wrote *Mein Kampf*, he looked back on the German General Staff as "the mightiest thing the world has ever seen"; [7] but once he had attained power, he discovered, with disgust, that the General Staff was not content to be a mighty instrument of his policy,—it had a policy of its own. Just as it had dictated terms to the Kaiser, so it sought to dictate to the Fuehrer. Hitler liquidated the trade unions without a blow; he frightened the middle-classes into submission; he bribed the industrialists; he had no trouble from the Churches; and the Communists, since they had long surrendered their independence, supplied the easiest converts of all. But the Army refused to be converted or bribed or frightened; and since Hitler needed it, he could not ignore or liquidate it,—rather, he had to increase it. At one time, in 1934, the Army even forced Hitler to crush his own radical wing and publicly to disown the Revolution of Destruction.[8] In 1938, at the time of the Munich crisis, the General Staff, under Halder, decided to remove the demented government; but the sudden news that Chamberlain had accepted the invitation to Munich knocked the weapons from their hands as they were preparing to strike.[9] Hitler's success at Munich was temporarily fatal to the Army leaders. They never had any outside support; they represented only themselves; and they were powerless against a dictator who could achieve triumphs such as this. For a time, the opposition of the General Staff

[7] *Mein Kampf*, p. 308.

[8] In a speech to the Reichstag after the liquidation of Roehm and his followers on 30th June 1934, Hitler condemned those who regarded revolution as an end in itself; but this was only a tactical condemnation forced upon him by the temporary ascendancy of the Army.

[9] The account of this abortive plot, first revealed by Halder, and since confirmed by other generals (*e.g.* Mueller-Hillebrandt), has been accepted as genuine by the authorities who examined it.

became again insignificant. Besides, the policy of the German Government for the next three years was not inconsistent with their own.

The leaders of the German Army believed in a policy of limited conquest. They wished Germany to be a great power, capable of supporting an efficient, well-paid, and privileged army. Such a position could be achieved by a mere reversal of the events of 1918; in fact, a restoration of imperial conditions. In so far as Hitler was likely to gain for them that external support which they lacked, they were prepared to support him, and to connive at some of the incidental vulgarities of his movement; but as practical men, organisers and calculators, not mystics or prophets, they were opposed to any unlimited venture of which they could not foresee or control the consequences. In particular, they were opposed to any conquest which would alter the social structure of Germany, and submerge their own privileged but precarious class in a new millenary Nazi Reich. Thus they were consistently opposed to war with Russia. Russia was the traditional ally of the German Junkers, whose prejudices, though swamped in the middle-class officers' corps, still dominated the General Staff. The Bolshevik Revolution did not alter this alliance, for they were practical men, above mere ideological conceptions; and in fact it was through an agreement with Bolshevik Russia that they had contrived to keep a shadow army in existence during the dark days after Versailles. Thus the interest of the German Army leaders was satisfied by the conquest of Poland and France, and in 1940 they would gladly have called a halt and stabilised the position on the basis of their gains. Unfortunately, what had satisfied them had merely inspired the confidence and excited the appetite of Hitler. The imperial frontiers of Germany were to him a contemptible ambition.[10] What was an end to them was only a means to him. In June 1941, flushed with success, and intoxi-

[10] *Mein Kampf*, pp. 944 ff.

cated by the propaganda which hailed him as "the greatest strategic genius of all time," he set out to achieve the fundamental aims of the Nazi movement,—the colonisation of the East.

With the opening of the Russian campaign in 1941, the opposition of the German General Staff began again. Its ultimate achievement was the abortive Plot of 20th July 1944; but it had passed through long underground channels before it broke out in that sudden, spectacular cascade. At first the generals had merely advised and protested. A Russian war was against their political interest; but their political interest no longer mattered. They had launched themselves on the brown Nazi current without making sure of its direction, and now they were adrift. It was against their military knowledge too; but that too was brushed aside, for now they were faced by the greatest strategical genius of all time, who of all things most resented the suggestion that there were "experts" who knew more than he. That Russia could resist the German armies seemed to him a ridiculous belief. "You have only to kick the front door," he declared, "and the whole house will tumble down." When the chief of the Army General Staff produced figures of Russian tank production, Hitler flew into a rage and ordered the technical department which had compiled such "defeatist" figures to be silenced.[11] So the generals meekly gave in, as the *burgeoisie* had given in, as everyone (according to Hitler's philosophy) would ultimately give in, before a superior will-power; and the Russian adventure began. It is true the house did not tumble down at the first kick, but that was explained away. Just as Britain was only apparently unbeaten, so Russia was only apparently standing up. For practical purposes, Hitler announced in October 1941,

[11] Halder, who witnessed it, has described this scene, when Hitler "went off the deep end,—he was no longer a rational being . . . he foamed at the mouth and threatened me with his fists. Any rational discussion was out of the question." The offending department was the *OKH Wehrwirtschafts-amt*, under General Thomas. Speer has also described the incident.

the war was over; "the Russians no longer *exist!*" he would shout at doubting generals; [12] or in a more compromising mood he would explain that the Russian bear was dead,—it merely refused to lie down; and to advertise his confidence, he ordered the dissolution of forty divisions of the Army, the return of man-power to industry, and the cessation of armament production, all without reference to the Army Command. Nevertheless, the generals continued to doubt. In November 1941 Hitler took over the high command of the German Army. A few months later Halder, chief of the Army General Staff, by common consent the ablest of German generals, the only successor in the great tradition of Moltke and Schlieffen, was dismissed. Meanwhile the OKW, or Combined General Staff,[13] had become a new political directorate of the Armed Forces, and suitable generals had been exalted within it,—the grovelling Keitel, who believed in Hitler's strategical genius,[14] and the industrious Jodl who applied it. From the Fuehrer's Headquarters in deep underground

[12] This phrase, according to Halder, was Hitler's "theme-song," and the idea became a monomania with him.

[13] The OKW (*Oberkommando der Wehrmacht*), originally a coordinating committee of the three branches of the Armed Forces, was gradually developed by Hitler into an instrument of political control, which he used particularly to impose his will upon the OKH, or Army General Staff, the stronghold of military opposition. I have translated OKW throughout as "Combined General Staff," as this gives a more accurate idea of its functions under Hitler than would a literal translation. Keitel was Chief OKW, Jodl *Chef OKW Fuehrungsstab* (operational staff).

[14] Keitel said at Nuremberg that "every professional soldier would confirm that Hitler's grasp of strategy and tactics commanded admiration. Nights of the war were passed at his headquarters in study of all the General Staff books by Moltke, Schlieffen, and Clausewitz, and his remarkable knowledge not only of all the armies, but of the navies of the globe, amounted to genius. Far from the chief of the OKW (*i.e.* Keitel) advising Hitler, it was Hitler who advised him" (5th April 1946). Hitler certainly showed an astonishing grasp of military detail, but such knowledge has not hitherto been understood to constitute strategical genius. A more critical judgment is that of Halder, that Hitler showed an extraordinary grasp of technical detail and a capacity for unlimited generalisation, but that nearly all decisions of strategy must be taken in the middle region between these two categories,—and there Hitler was deficient.

bunkers in Berlin and Rastenburg the war was directed by somnambulist decisions; the control of the Party over the Army was complete; and the opposition of the Army General Staff continued underground.

The existence of serious opposition to Hitler in the Army General Staff during the years 1941 to 1944 has sometimes been doubted. Hitler never made that error. It was the greatest mortification to his otherwise complacent spirit that the one instrument on which he must always rely was secretly but fundamentally opposed to him. He often said so. Often he declared that in 1941 the generals had lost their nerve, and only his iron will, his military genius, had saved the German armies in that first terrible Russian winter. Often he openly envied and praised the power, the foresight, and the thoroughness of Stalin, who had liquidated his General Staff by a wholesale purge before undertaking the risk of war. Often he raged at his own indignant officers, calling them liars and traitors to their faces, until, as some believed, resentment drove them to conspiracy. Personal antipathies increased his hatred of the whole class. However shrilly he might protest his strategical genius, however complacently he might listen to the flattering echo of his protestations, he could never convince himself of its universal acceptance. With his inner ear he always listened for the voice of mockery; and if anyone at court wished to ruin the career of an officer, he had only to whisper, in the right quarter, that his intended victim had referred to Hitler as "the corporal." [15] Nevertheless, though this opposition to the war existed since 1941, and though its leaders were planning the assassination of Hitler from January 1942 onwards, it could not, owing to the unrepresentative character of its leaders, express itself in action until the myth of Hitler's omnipotence had been shaken by defeat. By 1944 that condition seemed to have been fulfilled; but in 1941 the Party was triumphant as never before.

[15] Statement by Keitel.

If 1941 marks the triumph of the Party over the Army, it also marks a further stage in the change within the government,—the change from a cabinet to a court. Absolute power brings its own corruptions, and after the successes of 1940, a marked deterioration became apparent in the characters of all the Nazi leaders. There were also important changes in personnel. The ascendancy of Hitler, indeed, remained unchallenged within the Party till the end; even in the last days of all, when all power to compel or reward, all machinery to enforce his decisions, all hope of success or relief, all glory of achievement had departed, that demonic character, by mere force of personality, and perhaps the habit of control, reigned undisputed over his followers. But if he should die, who, among his eager flatterers, could hope to succeed to that vertiginous position? "Relations between the various high leaders can only be understood," says the ablest and least corrupted member of the court,[16] "if their aspirations are interpreted as a struggle for the succession to Adolf Hitler. The 'War of the Diadochi'[17] started very early behind the scenes." At first the succession had been vested, by a decree of 1st September 1939, in Goering, who, though politically a coward, was still an able and important functionary,—the founder of the Luftwaffe, the architect of the four-year plan, head of the Hermann Goering Werke, originator of the Gestapo and concentration camps,—a man who had assumed responsibility for bloodshed before which even Hitler had quailed. After Goering, the next in succession, by the same decree, was Rudolf Hess, a harmless, simple-minded crank, unstable in his decisions and absurd in his beliefs. But in 1941 Hess had flown to Scotland on his crack-brained mission, and the question of the succession had to be reconsidered.

[16] Speer.
[17] The War of the Diadochi was the war between the successors of Alexander the Great.

Albert Speer, who was present at Hitler's chalet at Ober-salzberg on the day of Hess's flight, has described how Hitler received the news of his deputy's eccentric gesture. Two of Hess's adjutants arrived at the chalet and announced that they had a personal letter from Hess to Hitler. One of them was called in and delivered the letter. Standing in the passage, Speer heard the loud voice of the Fuehrer raised in command; Martin Bormann, Hess's indefatigable assistant, who was already beginning to overshadow his nominal chief, was ordered to make immediate telephone connexion with the satraps of the Court, Goebbels and Ribbentrop, Goering and Himmler, who were all summoned to the presence. Hitler then called Udet, the air-ace of the Luftwaffe, and asked whether Hess had any chance of reaching Scotland, flying alone in a twin-engined aircraft, without navigational aids. The reply of the Luftwaffe was a categorical negative; Hess, the experts were agreed, would come down in the sea, short of his destination. Encouraged by this, there were some who advocated that the whole affair should be hushed up: Hess would perish, and no one need ever know. But Hitler was un-convinced. He despised experts, and he knew Hess's ability as a pilot; he had sometimes remonstrated with him about his in-dulgence in these dangerous sports.[18] Lest the British should get in first with their version, and exploit the propaganda value of the incident, he at once issued a communiqué. Hess's two adjutants were arrested, and in 1945 were still in prison, although hitherto, observes the caustic Speer, "the custom of punishing the bearers of bad news had been known only in Asiatic countries."

When Hess flew to Scotland, he was already a back num-ber in the Fuehrer's *entourage*, from which he was gradually being ousted by the persistent Bormann. This mole-like crea-

[18] An incident described by Rauschning contains a pleasant element of dramatic irony. Hess had just been a successful competitor in a flying com-petition. "You must give that sort of thing up in future," Hitler told him. "There are better things in store for you." (*The Voice of Destruction*, p. 8.)

ture, who seemed to avoid the glare of daylight and publicity [19] and to despise the rewards and trimmings, was nevertheless insatiable in his appetite for the reality of power; by his invariable presence he gradually became indispensable to Hitler; and by his well-timed insinuations he succeeded ultimately in removing all rivals about his master's throne. At first, though private adviser and financial administrator to Hitler, he was nominally responsible to Hess; but his work inevitably drew him into the personal circle of the Fuehrer. Entrusted with the building of the Berghof, Hitler's chalet, and with the purchase of pictures for his collection, he soon found himself among the privileged favourites of the court, and lost no time in discarding his former associates; and Hitler, thinking he had found an industrious and reliable servant, did not detect, or at least never distrusted, in this unobtrusive secretary, the consuming ambition which thus innocently disguised itself. By 1941 Bormann, now personal secretary to the Fuehrer, had almost replaced Hess in the inner council. He was permanently there, while Hess emerged less and less frequently from embittered seclusion.

On the flight of Hess, Bormann was therefore a powerful candidate for his position as head of the Party Chancery. Goering, sensing a rival and personally detesting Bormann, warned Hitler against him, but in vain. A fortnight later, on opening his morning paper, he read that Bormann had been appointed to the vacant post. To the greater position, of second in succession to the Fuehrer, he could not yet aspire. By a decree of 29th June 1941, the succession was vested in Goering alone, and no other heir was mentioned. From now on, Goering was Bormann's greatest enemy, his next-intended victim, in the Byzantine palace-politics of Berlin, Berchtesgaden, and the mobile Fuehrer's Headquarters.

Nevertheless, though Goering thus still occupied the greatest position in the state under Hitler, the real position bore

[19] Photographs of Bormann are regarded as a rarity.

little correspondence with its formal expression. From 1941 onwards, the corruption of power and the complacency of the *arriviste* began to consume, and ultimately to obscure, the once vigorous abilities of that formidable character until, at the end, he was popularly regarded as a mere voluptuary, a scented Nero fiddling while Rome burned. For by 1941 Goering had achieved everything that he had ever sought. He was Grand Vizier; he was Reich Marshal; enormously rich; and contented. The war (it was agreed) was won; there was no need of further effort. So Goering began to take his ease among his flatterers and neglect his offices. The Luftwaffe failed, the bombers came through, German industry creaked, but Goering came only rarely to Berlin. He was in Karinhall, his vast country palace in the Schorfheide, dressed (says an eye-witness) now like an Oriental Rajah, now in a light-blue uniform with a bejewelled baton of pure gold and ivory, now in white silk, like a Doge of Venice, only studded with jewels, with the emblematic stag of St. Hubertus on his head, and a swastika of gleaming pearls set between the antlers. There, in scenes of Roman luxury, he feasted and hunted and entertained, and showed his distinguished guests round the architectural and artistic wonders of his house,—a study like a medium-sized church, a domed library like the Vatican library, a desk twenty-six feet long, of mahogany inlaid with bronze swastikas, furnished with two big golden baroque candelabra, and an inkstand all of onyx, and a long ruler of green ivory studded with jewels. Meanwhile his art-gangsters came continually in from Paris and Rome, from Athens and Kiev, and some also from the museums of Germany, with their tribute of jewels and statuary, of old masters and *objets d'art*, of Gobelin tapestries and altar-pieces, of goldsmiths' work and Augsburg work, and old Roman bishops' staves, from the looted museums and gutted palaces of more ancient, famous states.

There, for the time, we may leave Goering; for whatever

pose he may have been able to strike at Nuremberg, he was in fact, by the end of the war, a totally discredited figure, as will be evident in this narrative. He had taken Hitler at his word and behaved as if the war was won; and it was not. The Russian bear refused to lie down; the British refused to admit defeat; and soon there were the Americans to consider too. Doubts grew about the Fuehrer's somnambulist strategy; under defeat in the East, and bombing in the West, and a universal mental perplexity, the brief unity of Party, Army, and People began to decompose; and other figures rose to prominence in place of the too soon contented Reich Marshal. To resolve the mental doubts, to refute the whispered heresies, the voice of the prophet Goebbels was once more raised after a long silence; for in times of victory, prophets are unnecessary distractions. To prevent heresy from hatching into plots and conspiracies, the power of Himmler began that rapid growth by which it ultimately seemed to overshadow even the authority of Hitler himself.

Joseph Goebbels was the intellectual of the Nazi Party; perhaps its only intellectual. The prize-pupil of a Jesuit seminary, he retained to the end the distinctive character of his education: he could always prove what he wanted. Unlike most of the Party leaders, who sprang with monotonous uniformity from Saxony, Bavaria, and Austria, he was a West German, from the Latin Rhineland; and it was this Latin lucidity of mind, this Jesuit suppleness of argument, which made him so much more successful as a preacher than the froth-blowing nationalists of the South. As the Jesuit persuades his penitent that all is well, that he has not really sinned at all, and that the obstacles to belief are really much less formidable than they appear, so Goebbels persuaded the Germans that their defeats were really victories, that the enemy was only apparently superior, and that new weapons would make all old problems obsolete; until in the end his constructive propaganda became ridiculous and of no effect. "I often had occasion to notice," observes Speer, "that Goebbels' style was 'Latin,' not 'Germanic.' His propagandist principles were also essentially Latin. For example, it would have been much better if Goebbels had given the people the same watchword as Churchill gave his people, *Blood, Sweat, and Tears*. This was a hard and honest watchword, and it would have suited the German people well. But Goebbels always caused false hopes among the people which merely resulted in discrepancy between his propaganda and the trend of popular opinion." In fact, Goebbels' position did not depend solely on his propaganda. He was respected for his intelligence, his administrative efficiency, and his personal integrity; he neither believed palpable nonsense, nor performed ludicrous antics, nor exhibited indecent opulence; he wielded no engines of terror or oppression; and he was a radical, who preached not only total war but total mobilisation, which those (like Goering) who prized their privileged standard of living would never advocate. And whatever else history may say of Goebbels, it will credit him with one contribution to the science of politics,—a terrible but a positive contribution, which, like the atom bomb, may be deplored but cannot be undone. As the Jesuits created a system of education aimed at preventing knowledge, so Goebbels created a system of propaganda, ironically styled "public enlightenment," which successfully persuaded a people to believe that black was white. Certainly Hess and Goering and Bormann could claim no achievement comparable with this.

On Hitler's other side, the sinister figure of Himmler grew daily in stature. In the public imagination Himmler is a real and terrible figure, a cold-blooded inhuman ogre ruthlessly exterminating millions of helpless prisoners by every refinement of sadistic torture; not a man, but an impersonal abstraction, a creature to whom the weaknesses of pity and forgiveness are unknown; an inexorable monster whose cold, malignant rage no prayers, no human sacrifices can ever for one moment appease. Certainly Himmler was implacable. His power seemed as unlimited as his ambitions of destruction. In the calmest, most dispassionate manner he ordered the destruction of whole races, the extermination of Jews and Slavs. He was quite pitiless; nothing horrified him. The thought of hundreds of thousands of men and women stuffed into "humane" gas-waggons—incidents which frequently drove the criminal attendants mad,—the knowledge that the torture-chambers of Europe were peopled by his victims, and that at every hour of the day his name was being execrated by dying people in a whole continent,—these things (if he thought of them) never interrupted the regularity of his meals, never disturbed the routine of his office, never disconcerted the puffy smoothness of that cold complacent expression. But Himmler was not a sadist. There was nothing terrible or volcanic in his character. His very coldness was a negative element, not glacial, but bloodless. He did not delight in cruelty, he was indifferent to it; and the scruples of others were to him not contemptible, but unintelligible. "But they are animals," or "criminals," he would say, with ingenuous deprecation, when foreign ambassadors, or even his own subordinates, sometimes remonstrated at some particularly savage holocaust. In this monster there were many curious qualities, which have made him to some an incredible, enigmatical figure. He was extraordinarily ignorant and naïve. The man who, after such a career, culminating in total defeat, still regarded himself as a fit negotiator to meet the Allied commanders, and hoped to be continued in office by their permission, cannot have been a man of diabolical subtlety. He was also beloved by all of his subordinates,—men of neuter conscience indeed, but in other respects apparently of only normal weakness. His adjutants and advisers remained, even after his death, unconditionally loyal to him. No one in the S.S. conspired against him. To the end he was its *Reichs-fuehrer*; and its members spoke of him with affection as

"Reichsheini." Brutality? his subordinates exclaim in naïve chorus, there were no signs of brutality in his private nature; hesitation seemed to them his most obvious characteristic. Himmler himself could never understand the reputation which he had acquired. In the end he despaired of understanding it; it was some strange foible of foreigners, he concluded; and he satisfied himself with making little jokes about it in his private circle.[20]

Nevertheless the character of Himmler is not as mysterious as these facts may suggest to those unfamiliar with the variety of the human mind. In a civilised world, it is true, such men are seldom tolerated; but if we look back at the cataclysmic periods of society, at periods of revolution and violent social change, his prototype is there. It is the Grand Inquisitor, the mystic in politics, the man who is prepared to sacrifice humanity to an abstract ideal. The Grand Inquisitors of history were not cruel or self-indulgent men. They were often painfully conscientious and austere in their personal lives. They were often scrupulously kind to animals,[21] like the blessed Robert Bellarmine, who refused to disturb the fleas in his clothes. Since they could not hope for theological bliss (he said), it would be uncharitable to deny them that carnal refreshment to which alone they could aspire. But for men who, having opportunities of worshipping aright, chose

[20] Some such jokes are mentioned in Count Bernadotte's book, *The Curtain Falls*.

[21] In what has been described as "one of the most monstrous documents ever penned," Himmler vividly illustrates this extraordinary trait. In a speech delivered to S.S. generals on the war in Russia he said: "What happens to a Russian or a Czech does not interest me in the slightest. . . . Whether these nations live in prosperity or starve to death interests me only in so far as we need them as slaves for our *Kultur*. Whether 10,000 Russian females fall down dead from exhaustion while digging an anti-tank ditch interests me only in so far as the anti-tank ditch for Germany is finished. We Germans, who are the only people in the world who have a decent attitude towards animals, will also assume a decent attitude towards these human animals but it is a crime against our own blood to worry about them and give them ideals." (*The Times* (London), 12th December 1945.)

wrong, no remedy was too drastic. So the faggots were piled
and lit, and the misbelievers and their books were burned, and
those gentle old bishops went home to sup on white fish and
inexpensive vegetables, to feed their cats and canaries, and
to meditate on the Penitential Psalms, while their chaplains
sat down in their studies to compose their biographies and
explain to posterity the saintly lives, the observances and
austerities, the almsgivings and simplicity, of those exemplary
pastors, knowing (as Cardinal Newman said) that it is better
that all humanity should perish in extremest agony than that
one single venial sin should be committed.

Such a comparison perhaps seems fanciful; but nature is
fanciful in designing the human mind, and times of revolution
do throw up into positions of eminence men who, in stable
periods, remain unobserved in gaols and monasteries. Himmler
himself, everyone is agreed, was an utterly insignificant man,
common, pedantic, and mean. He was greedy of money and
incapable of thought; and yet he could not resist the tempta-
tion to speculate, to lose himself in the *O Altitudo*, and en-
tangle himself in the theological minutiae, of the pure Nazi
doctrine. Hitler himself, in one sense, was not a Nazi, for the
doctrines of Nazism, that great system of teutonic nonsense,
were to him only a weapon of politics; "he criticised and
ridiculed the ideology of the S.S."; [22] but to Himmler they
were, every iota of them, the pure Aryan truth, which if a
man keep not pure and undefiled, he shall without doubt
perish everlastingly. With such a narrow pedantry, with such
black-letter antiquarianism, did Himmler study the details of
this sad rubbish, that many have supposed, but wrongly, that
he had been a schoolmaster. He gave Speer the impression of
being "half schoolmaster, half crank." During the war, while
Goebbels was demanding total mobilisation, Himmler was
employing thousands of men and millions of marks in the
projects of a religious maniac. In one department of his foreign

[22] Speer.

intelligence service, a school of eager researchers studied such
important matters as Rosicrucianism and Freemasonry, the
symbolism of the suppression of the harp in Ulster, and the
occult significance of Gothic pinnacles and top-hats at Eton.[23]
The S.S. scientific laboratories laboured infelicitously to
isolate pure Aryan blood. An explorer was sent to Tibet to
discover traces of a pure Germanic race believed to preserve
the ancient Nordic mysteries in those unvisited mountains.
Throughout Europe excavators sought for relics of authentic
German *Kultur*. When the German army prepared hastily to
evacuate Naples, Himmler's only demand was that it should
not omit to carry with it the vast stone tomb of the last
Hohenstaufen Emperor. Meanwhile, rich business men, if
they wished to join his exclusive Circle of Friends,[24] had to
buy admission by subscribing perhaps a million marks to the
Ahnenerbe, a "scientific" institute that made expensive re-
searches into Aryan origins.[25] Even in April 1945, when the
whole Reich was tumbling in ruins, Himmler was contemplating the colonisation of the Ukraine with a new religious sect
recommended by his masseur,[26] and in conversation with
Count Bernadotte (having just maintained that he was the
only sane man left in Germany), interrupted the discussion
of war and peace to digress for an hour on runes. He was
particularly interested in runes, the uninterpreted script of the
Northmen of the Dark Ages. Studied with the eye of faith,

[23] The department was *R.S.H.A.* (*Reichssicherheitshauptamt*) *Amt VII*.
[24] The *Freundeskreis des RfSS*, a group of mystical financiers, headed by
one Wilhelm Keppler (see below, p. 70 note), who formed themselves into
an "exclusive" club under this name.
[25] It was the *Ahnenerbe* whose fine collection of human skulls was
described at Nuremberg. Himmler welcomed the Russian war (among other
reasons) because it would enable him to enrich this collection with the
hitherto unobtainable skulls of that sub-human species "the Jewish-Bolshevik
commissar," and elaborate instructions were given to ensure that commissars
should be killed without damage to their skulls. (Letter from Dr. Wolfram
Sievers, head of the *Ahnenerbe*, to Himmler's secretary Dr. Brandt, read at
Nuremberg, 8th August 1946).
[26] Information from Schellenberg.

they might, he believed, yield resemblance to Japanese ideo-
grams, and thus prove the Japanese to be Aryans after all.[27]

In such a character no grain of subtlety is discernible.
Himmler was an elementary believer. His fanaticism was not
the difficult birth of fear and weakness, nor his hesitation the
consequence of doubt. Doubt had not yet nibbled at the in-
fantile serenity of his cosmic acceptances. It was because he
could not follow the intellectual processes or the labyrinthine
plots of his subordinates that he would not become involved
in them; because he was assured of their ultimate loyalty to
him that he did not interfere with what must have seemed,
and sometimes certainly were, their treasonable dabblings.
For two years this *"treuer Heinrich,"* this "faithful Heinrich,"
who really believed that he was unconditionally loyal to
Hitler, allowed his favourite adviser to indulge in absurd, but
serious, attempts at peacemaking. He cannot have been altogether ignorant of the plans to substitute himself for his
master; but he would neither condemn these activities nor
accept their implications. His followers wrung their hands
in despair at his interminable vacillation. In fact he simply
turned a blind eye. The true believer can afford to let others
speculate, provided their final loyalty is assured.

Of course if Himmler had been only a crank, we should
have heard less of him. He was also, in an executive capacity,
very efficient; and he had a capacity for choosing useful subordinates. It is true that his personal court contained some strange
figures; that he took political advice from his doctor Gebhardt,
the sinister adviser whom many regarded as his evil genius;
that (like Hitler and Wallenstein) he was unduly influenced
by his astrologer, Wulf; that his masseur, Kersten, had attained the position which more orthodox believers entrust to
a father-confessor; and that his relations with Hitler depended
on the illiterate jockey, Fegelein; but these were all personal
advisers. On a purely executive level Himmler chose well,—

[27] Speer.

as far as it was possible to choose well in a world of illusion. In return, he was well served; followed even to his squalid grave by the devotion of his subordinates.

This dual character of Himmler, his impersonal efficiency as an executor, and his oceanic credulity as a thinker, is, I believe, the key to his fantastic career. Animated by an unconditional loyalty to Hitler, to whom, as he often protested, he owed everything, and inspiring, as such simple characters do, a similar loyalty among his own followers towards himself, both competent to execute and too unoriginal to conspire, he was, as long as this harmony continued, an ideal chief of police to a revolutionary leader. It is said that soon after his rise to power, Hitler once called, in Munich, on the aged philosopher Oswald Spengler, in order to receive the blessing of that disreputable sage. The reply of the oracle was unusually laconic. "Beware," he said, "of your praetorian guard." On 30th June 1934 Hitler took the necessary precautions. After that, the praetorian guard was in the hands of the stupid, devoted, ruthless, efficient, mystical Himmler; and Hitler felt safe. Safe, that is, until the delicate balance of Himmler's personality had been fretted away; and then it was Himmler's unexpected defection that decided Hitler to end the tedious drama. Only if this dual character of Himmler is appreciated, can the extraordinary events of April 1945 be understood.

From the opening of the Russian campaign, the power of Himmler had continued to rise; for the Russian campaign, while it alienated the regular army, or at least the General Staff, was the consummation of the long ambition of the S.S. While Hitler and Goering, intoxicated with pride and assurance, "cut up the giant cake" of European Russia, promising themselves the Volga and the Crimea, Bialystok and Baku, and awarding the unvalued scraps to their Balkan satellites, Himmler was fixing his more mystical eyes on a vaster, remoter horizon. He was demanding "an open road to the east,

the creation of the German Reich this way or that, the fetch-
ing home of thirty million human beings of our blood, so that
even during our lifetimes we shall be a people of 120 million
Germanic souls." [28] The defeat at Stalingrad, which chastened
more realistic thinkers, did not affect the transcendental views
of Himmler (for facts do not trouble the bigot and the
crank); and his practical activity as a policeman became only
more necessary than ever. Throughout 1943 and 1944 his
power continually grew. Already head of the S.S., the Armed
S.S.,[29] the Secret Police, and the Criminal Police, in 1943 he
became Minister of the Interior, and the entire police system
of Germany became united under his command. In 1944 he
achieved a further signal triumph. The German Foreign Intelligence Service or *Abwehr* had hitherto been part of the
Combined General Staff. Under the negligent rule of Admiral
Canaris, an enigmatical figure, more interested in anti-nazi
intrigue than in his official duties,[30] for the first two
years of the war it had been borne along, a happy para-
site, on the success of the German Army, and its well-
paid agents had been able to enjoy the café and cabaret life
of Madrid and Estoril, and to speculate profitably in the black
markets of Belgrade and Sofia, with an easy conscience. But
when the military initiative had passed to the Allies, the Party
began to expect something more; it expected intelligence
which might restore the failing balance of power; and since
none came, it began to criticise. The criticism came loudest
and most insistent from the S.S., whose own foreign intelli-

[28] Statement by Himmler quoted at Nuremberg, *The London Times*,
15th February 1946. The scene in which Hitler, Goering, Keitel, and Rosenberg "cut up the giant cake" at the Fuehrer's Headquarters in July 1941 is
described in a minute by Bormann, quoted in *The Times*, 18th December
1945.
[29] *Waffen S.S.*
[30] The account of Canaris as "a personality of pure intellect," and the
Abwehr as "a spiritual organisation," which was given at Nuremberg on 30th
November 1945 by Colonel Lahousen (one of its members) is highly ideal-
ised. The *Abwehr* can claim a few martyrs, but no saints or thinkers.

gence service was already growing in establishment and ambition under the control of Walter Schellenberg.

Among the universally parochial minds of the S.S., Schellenberg, its youngest general, enjoyed an undeserved reputation. He was credited with understanding foreign affairs. It is true that his notions were a little less extravagant than those of some of his rivals, and the fact that he began to work his passage home as early as 1942 separates him from the crasser intellects of the Party. A North German, he was also exempt from the ideological gibberish of the Austrian and Bavarian Nazis. He believed not in force, nor in nonsense, but in subtlety; and he believed that he was subtle. This was perhaps his greatest mistake, for he was in fact a very trivial character; but he made other mistakes too. Like so many of Himmler's subordinates, he believed in Himmler, and aspired to be the good genius of his master, a counter-influence to monsters like Kaltenbrunner and Ohlendorf,[31] and tempters like Gebhardt, who also shared the confidence and perverted the judgment of the Reichsfuehrer. He believed that Himmler alone was capable of purging the administration of its inveterate ignorance and corruption, and of rectifying the disastrous, arrogant foreign policy of Hitler and Ribbentrop. If only Himmler would be guided by him, if only the master of the greatest, most efficient organisation in Germany would be directed by the subtlest and best-informed intelligence, then (so Schellenberg naïvely believed) there would be an authority which might yet rival the fatal maniac of Berchtesgaden, and, with a little good fortune and some careful preparation, might yet save Germany by negotiating a compromise peace.

Such, as they ultimately developed, were the plans of Schel-

[31] Ernst Kaltenbrunner succeeded Heydrich as *Chef R.S.H.A.*, and was nominally Schellenberg's superior, although Schellenberg's direct access to Himmler reduced the significance of this subordination. Otto Ohlendorf was head of *R.S.H.A. Amt III* (also called S.D. or *Sicherheitsdienst*), and also *Ministerialdirektor* in the Reich Ministry of Economics.

lenberg, the Gestapo officer who, in 1941, had taken over the
control of Himmler's foreign intelligence service. To achieve
them, two things were necessary. Firstly, he must create an intelligence service superior to all rivals in power and efficiency;
secondly, he must build up some capital of goodwill in the
Allied camp and among neutral powers, and seek, where
possible, to mitigate the odium which clung, throughout the
world, to Himmler's name. These two objects Schellenberg
set himself conscientiously to attain. For two years he negotiated with Swedish and Swiss friends, arranged the escape
of Jews and condemned prisoners of war, and sought to reduce the severity of Himmler's judgments and frustrate the
savagery of Kaltenbrunner.[32] As time passed, he became more
ambitious, more fanciful than ever. Like Hess, he believed
that English public figures would listen to his overtures. He
sent emissaries through neutral countries with tales so extravagant that they were dismissed with humiliating ridicule; he
even discovered a cracked psychologist who believed that, by
ingenious psychotherapy, he could bring about "the psychological revival of the Christian soul in the German people."
What better qualifications could be found for a peace emissary
to the devout English? So Schellenberg planned to send the
psychologist on a mission to Archbishop Temple.

At the same time he was building up his foreign intelligence
service. Like so many Germans, he was an admirer, a despairing admirer, of the British Intelligence Service,—an organisation of which indeed he knew very little, but of which he
had evidently read much in those amazing novelettes which

[32] Schellenberg's motives, in thus saving life, were of course purely
opportunist; for he was too "realistic" to indulge any humanitarian fancies.
As he explained to a friend, the extermination of the Jews would have been
unexceptionable if it could have been carried out completely; but since two-
thirds of the Jews were out of reach, such a policy "was worse than a
crime; it was folly" ("da aber nur ein Drittel in unserer Hand war, die
übrigen aber ausserhalb unseres Machtbereiches lebten, sei die Art der
Behandlung der Juden schlimmer als ein Verbrechen, es sei eine Dummheit
gewesen."–Schwerin von Krosigk's diary, *s.d.* 15th April 1945).

filled the reference library of the Gestapo. From these he had
learnt much about that all-pervasive, incessant engine which,
founded by Edward III and perfected by Oliver Cromwell,
has secured the otherwise unaccountable success of British
diplomacy and politics, and which, operating through the
Y.M.C.A., the Boy Scout Movement, and other dependent
organisations, has overthrown dynasties, altered governments,
and assassinated inconvenient ministers throughout the world.
To create such a universal, "totalitarian" intelligence service
in Germany was the ambitious dream of Schellenberg. The
first stage towards it would consist in the liquidation of the
existing intelligence service, the *Abwehr*; and this, after two
years of competition, during which he exploited every error,
every failure of his rival, he secured. The *Abwehr* was well
aware of the doom that was prepared for it; but it was helpless.
Rotten with corruption, notoriously inefficient, politically
suspect, it could do nothing; and the spasmodic efforts of certain conscientious staff officers to achieve some internal re-
form led only to disillusion and resignation. Meanwhile Schellenberg's service, if hardly more efficient, enjoyed all the advantages of attack. In February 1944, his bankruptcy demonstrated by a succession of glaring failures, Canaris was dismissed. In May Himmler took over. The surviving directors
of the old firm were summoned to the Kursalon at Salzburg,
and there they were met by Himmler with Schellenberg at
his side. In a bombastic speech Himmler outlined his programme. The name *Abwehr*, he said, was un-German; it implied defence. He was going to create a new, aggressive,
totalitarian and pure-Aryan intelligence service instead. And
then, his imagination warming as he left the tedious details of
organisation for the mysterious generalities in which his idealist
spirit was at home, he described the events which were about
to follow. There was no room for defeatism now, he said;
great things were coming. The Fuehrer was inspired as never
before; his statesmanship, skill, and intuitive wisdom were yet

to exhibit their masterpiece. He prayed that the infatuated plutocrats of the West might be foolish enough to invade the Continent. They would be hurled back and "drowned in the seas of their own blood." Then it would be the turn of the East. Within a year the Russians were to be chased headlong across the Volga, over the Urals, and into Asia, their barbarian home, whence a Chinese Wall, built by Slavonic slave-labour, would prevent them from ever returning. A fortnight later the Western Allies landed in Normandy. Two months after that occurred the most spectacular political event since 1934; the Generals' Plot of 20th July 1944, which showed that the leaders of the German Army regarded the war as lost, and were at last prepared to break their alliance with the Party.

Many of the details of the Generals' Plot are already well known. Its importance cannot be over-rated. After long preparation, a small section of the German people had at last taken the initiative. Ignoring, or overriding, the fumblings and hesitations of more timorous conspirators, it had made a positive, determined, and nearly successful effort to destroy the Nazi régime. That section was the East German aristocracy (appropriately it was in their home, in East Prussia, that the blow was struck), the rulers once of the German Army, now only of the General Staff, the colleagues of Rauschning who had thought it possible to bend the angry spirit of Pan-Germanism to their will by accepting the Nazis as junior partners, and who now sought, by this desperate blow, to undo their disastrous error. It was too late; their error was irreparable; as a class the Junkers are now gone for ever, as obsolete as the mammoth and the mastodon.[33]

---

[33] It should be emphasized that the men of 20th July, Beck, Tresckow, Olbricht, Stauffenberg and a few other General Staff officers, were a radical group among the opponents of the Nazi Government, and were not necessarily supported by the numerous other groups whose ineffective opposition is often discernible. Had Stauffenberg succeeded in killing Hitler, the other groups would doubtless have followed his lead; his failure, by frightening them back into mutual distrust and hostility, enabled the government, by prompt action, to destroy them all. The equal retribution which fell

Nevertheless the conspiracy had been well planned and was nearly successful. Several times the explosive charge had been sent to Hitler's Headquarters, and had returned unused through some technical hitch, before Count von Stauffenberg finally introduced it, concealed in a brief-case, into the conference room at Rastenburg. When Hitler had taken his place, and the conference had begun, von Stauffenberg laid his brief-case against the table-leg and made an excuse to slip out of the room. As he crossed the outer compound, he heard the noise of detonation. Then he climbed into his plane, flew to Berlin, and confidently announced the death of Hitler and the successful usurpation of a new government. It was a premature announcement. In the meantime Providence (as all good Nazis agreed) had intervened. How Hitler escaped is still not quite clear. Either he had moved away from his place in time, or the peculiar construction of the table had diverted the blast from him. When the dust and turmoil of the explosion had subsided, it was clear that the plot had failed. Hitler's ear-drums were pierced, his right arm was bruised, his uniform was tattered, and he had fallen, dazed, into the arms of the ever-obsequious Keitel; but while four men lay dead or mortally wounded around him, he was alive. Had the conference taken place in the usual concrete bunker, instead of in a wooden hut, not one of the participants could have survived.

Almost every element in the German political situation was affected by the Plot of 20th July. From that time onwards Hitler knew that the Army, as an institution, was in opposition; he knew that if he won the war, it would be in spite

---

upon all groups alike, has given them the semblance of a unity of purpose and policy which they certainly never had. Thus the civilian groups of Goerdeler and von Trott zu Solz seem to have been separate from the Army group, which was itself subdivided. Rommel, for instance, while agreeing with the purpose of the plot, seems to have been genuinely shocked at Stauffenberg's methods. The whole plot ought to be examined as a study in political conspiracy.

of the generals, not because of them. More and more, from that moment, he surrounded himself with officers from the Navy and the Luftwaffe. The German Navy might not have played a conspicuous part in the war, but it was untainted by treachery; the Luftwaffe might not have come up to expectations, but the blame for that belonged not to it but to Goering. As for the Army,—the common soldiers were doubtless loyal, and Hitler came more and more to identify himself with them to the exclusion of their officers. If he trusted in any generals at all, it was in a few toadies only, in Keitel and Burgdorf;[34] as a class, he regarded them all as traitors, and their treachery was always in his mind and often in his mouth. Whenever an army retreated or a stronghold fell, he cried treachery; telegrams of hectic recrimination and angry strategic lectures issued ceaselessly from the Fuehrer's Headquarters; and the sedulous Bormann screamed treble to his master's bass. At his last full-scale conference, Hitler accused the generals to their faces of deceiving him; and in his last written documents, the testaments that were to recommend him to posterity, he could not omit a last sidelong condemnation of the treachery of Army officers and the Army General Staff.

Drawing thus away from his generals into the safer company of his intimate admirers, Hitler inevitably hastened the conversion of his headquarters from a war cabinet to an oriental court of flatterers and toadies. How far the process had already gone is clear from eye-witness accounts of the scene shortly after the detonation. That same day, 20th July, Mussolini, now the puppet-ruler of Lombardy, was due to arrive at Rastenburg on a visit to his protector. His train reached the station early in the afternoon, and Hitler, white as a sheet, was there on the platform to receive him. As they

---

[34] General Wilhelm Burgdorf was *Chef Personalabteilung OKW* and *Wehrmacht* adjutant at the Fuehrer's Headquarters. He associated himself completely with the views of Hitler, Bormann, and Goebbels.

left the station, Hitler explained the miracle of his escape, only a few hours ago; and arriving at his headquarters, he took his guest to see the scene of the incident. The room was a mass of debris, for the walls had caught fire after the explosion and the ceiling had fallen in. After wandering through the smoking shambles, they withdrew for a tea-party. As so often, it is over the teacups that Hitler is seen in his most outrageous postures.

It was five o'clock when the tea-party began, and the whole court assembled in the Fuehrer's headquarters. Conversation was naturally about the Fuehrer's escape, but it quickly deteriorated into recrimination. Voices were raised in high-pitched and bitter argument; and everyone in turn was blamed because the war had not yet been won. Ribbentrop and Doenitz raved against the generals because they had betrayed Germany to England, and the generals raved in reply against Ribbentrop and Doenitz. All this time Hitler and Mussolini sat quiet and reserved, as if mere spectators of the scene, while Graziani told them of his African adventures. Then, quite suddenly, someone mentioned that other famous "plot" in Nazi history—the Roehm plot of 30th June 1934, and the bloody purge which followed it. Immediately Hitler leapt up in a fit of frenzy, with foam on his lips, and shouted that he would be revenged on all traitors. Providence had just shown him once again, he screamed, that he had been chosen to make world history; and he ranted wildly about terrible punishments for women and children,—all of them would be thrown into concentration camps—an eye for an eye, and a tooth for a tooth—none should be spared who set himself against divine Providence. The court fell silent as the Fuehrer raged for a full half-hour; the visitors thought he must be mad,—"I don't know," said one of them, "why I didn't go over to the Allies there and then." Mussolini looked embarrassed, and said nothing; Graziani sought feebly to break the spell by beginning a technical discussion with Keitel; and all the time footmen, dressed in white, circulated with their tea-pots among the gaping worshippers.

This scene was interrupted by a call from Berlin, where order had not yet been restored. Hitler seized the telephone and shouted his orders into the mouthpiece, giving full orders to shoot anyone and everyone. Why hadn't Himmler arrived yet? Then came the portentous statement of the megalomaniac: "I'm beginning to doubt whether the German people is worthy of my great ideals."

These words broke the spell of silence. At once the entire court competed to speak, each protesting his loyalty. In grovelling terms Doenitz sang the praises of the German Navy. Goering began a violent quarrel with Ribbentrop and made a pass at him with his field-marshal's baton; and the voice of Ribbentrop was heard above the tumult protesting, "I am still Foreign Minister and my name is *von* Ribbentrop." Only Hitler was silent now. The parts in the comic opera had been reversed, and the *prima donna* ceased while the chorus discordantly sang. He sat still; in his hand he had a tube of brightly coloured pastilles which he continually sucked; [35] only at intervals, like a still spluttering volcano, would he utter some savage phrase, the residue of his unexpended emotion, about blood, and Providence, and concentration camps.

This scene, as it is described to us, is perhaps overdrawn; but not improbably. Absolute power corrupts absolutely, and we have too many accounts of life in that exotic court to doubt the authenticity, in its main lines, even of this. When a staid German general compared Goering to Elagabalus, he was not exaggerating. In the absolutism, the opulence, and the degeneracy of the middle Roman Empire we can perhaps find the best parallel to the high noonday of the Nazi Reich. There, in the severe pages of Gibbon, we read of characters

[35] The reader who will persevere as far as p. 66 will learn more about these pastilles.

apparently wielding gigantic authority who, on closer examination, are found to be the pliant creatures of concubines
and catamites, of eunuchs and freedmen; and here too we
see the *élite* of the Thousand-Year Reich a set of flatulent
clowns swayed by purely random influences. Even Mussolini
was embarrassed; but then Mussolini had after all, like Goebbels, a Latin mind; he could never be at home among these
cavorting Nibelungs. Goebbels, incidentally, was not present
at this Mad Hatter's tea-party; he was in Berlin, giving orders
for the suppression of the revolt.

The effect of the Generals' Plot on the career of Himmler
was also decisive. It was both personal and political. Personally
the Plot achieved a notable success; it brought Himmler to
God. In April 1945 he described to a friend this signal conversion. "I know," he said, "that I am generally regarded as
a heedless pagan, but in the depths of my heart I am a believer; I believe in God and Providence. In the course of the
last year I have learnt to believe in miracles again. The
Fuehrer's escape on the 20th July was a miracle; and a second
I have experienced in my own life, this very spring. . . ."
The second miracle was the convenient thaw on the river
Oder, when Himmler commanded an Army Group there, and
the Russians were about to break across the ice.[36]

Politically the Generals' Plot marked the beginning of
Himmler's decline. To the outer world indeed Himmler never
seemed so powerful as in the months immediately after the
Plot, the months when many supposed that he had actually
assumed control of the state, Hitler having been either killed
by the explosion or imprisoned by the usurper. Certainly,
after the Plot, Himmler increased his authority; for the policeman is never so necessary as when a widespread conspiracy
has been disclosed. One of his first acts was to complete his
victory over the old Army Intelligence Service, whose former
chiefs figured largely among the conspirators and had actually

[36] Schwerin von Krosigk. Cf. below p. 103.

supplied the explosive charge from their captured supplies. They had already been proved inefficient; now Himmler could show that they were disloyal. Against Admiral Canaris the evidence was inconclusive; he disappeared into prison, and nine months later was executed with medieval barbarity.[37] His successor, Colonel Hansen, was executed. General Freytag von Loringhoven, who, as head of the sabotage department, had supplied the explosive, committed suicide to avoid a more painful end. His predecessor, Colonel Lahousen, and some others escaped miraculously to tell the tale at Nuremberg and mortify Goering by their survival. But the old intelligence service was merely a department of the old General Staff; and the whole General Staff was involved, or suspected, in this extensive conspiracy. In the great blood-purge which followed—a purge more drastic even than the purge of 1934—over fifty General Staff officers perished, and hundreds of lesser figures were inconspicuously removed. General Halder, its now deposed chief, was thrown into a concentration camp on mere suspicion, and for four months never saw the light of day. Zeitzler, his successor, was dismissed. Stauffenberg and three other conspirators were shot at once on the orders of Fromm, who thus sought to conceal his own guilt,—but in vain; for he too was hanged. Stuelpnagel, commanding the armies of occupation in France, who had rashly obeyed the orders of the usurpers and had imprisoned the Gestapo in Paris, shot himself in a wood near Verdun. Misfiring, he only blinded himself, and was executed instead. Kluge, the commander in the field, also took his own life. Witzleben was executed; so was Fellgiebel,—a philosophical general, he followed the best examples, and spent his last hours discussing with his adjutant the immortality of the soul. To Rommel, once Hitler's darling general, whose prestige had been deliberately and (as it now seemed) dangerously enhanced by propaganda, Hitler sent General Burgdorf, his most assiduous sycophant, with

[37] He was strangled, in six stages, with a noose of thin wire, in Flossenbuerg concentration camp on 9 April 1945.

a revolver and a poison capsule. He was told that if he would commit suicide quietly, there would be no publicity and no reprisals on his family![38] and he obeyed. One general, who was killed soon afterwards, was about to receive a state funeral when his complicity was discovered; the plans were changed at once, and he was hustled unattended to a criminal's grave. No wonder Hitler withdrew into a long privacy; no wonder he shrank from the company of his most competent military advisers, and listened only to the bombastic amateurs of the S.S.; he could no longer be sure of the loyalty of any officer. And no wonder Himmler seemed in those months to enjoy an extravagant measure of power. On the day of the Plot he succeeded Fromm as commander-in-chief of the Reserve Army. Shortly afterwards he took over from the Armed Forces the control of all prisoner-of-war camps. Within a few months this former sergeant-major was himself in command of an Army Group, vainly resisting the Russians on the Vistula Front.

Nevertheless, in spite of these apparent accessions of power, Himmler was in fact in decline. Though the attempt on Hitler's life made him for a moment more necessary than ever, the narrowness of its failure was proof that he too had failed. After all, it had been a very near thing. It was Providence (as Himmler himself agreed), not the police, that had saved Hitler's life. There were even some who maintained that so extensive a conspiracy could not possibly have been developed over so long a period without Himmler's knowledge; it was against nature, or at least against all precedent.[39]

[38] This account of Rommel's death is given by Jodl and Keitel, and confirmed by several other sources.

[39] In fact it seems very unlikely that Himmler had any exact previous knowledge of the Plot, but the antipathy between the S.S. and the Party was already so strong that many would-be conspirators thought that they could enlist him, and his ambiguous behaviour encouraged these illusions. In fact, Himmler's opposition to the Party was paralysed by his personal loyalty to Hitler; his subordinates, being free from the second sentiment, could more easily entertain the first.

Such doubts were not left unexploited by the patient, persistent Bormann. This "evil genius of the Fuehrer," this "Brown Eminence, sitting in the shadows," as one of the court [40] described him, "Hitler's Mephistopheles," as he was more generally known, had by now achieved an undisputed supremacy such as had never been previously known in the immediate *entourage* of his master. Hitherto it had been, or at least it had seemed, Hitler's policy never to allow any of his ministers to attain to any singularity of position in his counsels. He had seemed always to play off one minister against another, and so himself to hold the balance among them. But now Martin Bormann, who, like Holstein in the cabinets of the Kaiser, had "realised from the beginning the importance of representing his position as insignificant," had won the reward of his infinite patience. Never away from his master's side, even keeping the same eccentric hours as he, —rising at midday and retiring at 4.30 or 5 in the morning,— in sole control of the vast machinery of the Party, indispensable, indefatigable, and ubiquitous, he was now the sole custodian of Hitler's secrets, the sole channel for his orders, the sole method of approach to that ever more inaccessible presence. During the years of war every development had strengthened his authority. The Gauleiters were subordinate to him alone; he had increased their subordination and altered their character. The original Gauleiters had been old Party hacks who, having thumped their tubs and blown their trumpets obstreperously in the early days of the movement, had been rewarded with these lucrative and not too exacting offices. Bormann had changed that. One by one the old Gauleiters had gone, and new men had replaced them, younger, more energetic, more fanatical men, who owed everything not to the impersonal Party in the days when Bormann was unknown, but to Bormann himself. Throughout the war the Party machine, like the S.S., had grown; like

[40] Schwerin von Krosigk.

the S.S., it had encroached on the functions of the Armed Forces, especially in matters of administration and supply, fortification and evacuation; like the S.S., it had become more formidable, and more indispensable, with every defeat of German arms. Observers who watched the parallel development of these twin engines of power wondered what would happen when they began to conflict, when Himmler and Bormann, having absorbed or conquered all independent bodies, at last met face to face. In 1943, when Himmler was made Minister of the Interior, that interesting moment had come. Till then the relations between the two men had been excellent; thereafter sharp conflicts broke out. The slightest attempts by Himmler to exercise authority outside the S.S. were openly resented by Bormann. In the provinces, several Higher S.S. and Police Leaders [41] thought they could presume on Himmler's new authority and trespass on the preserves of the Gauleiters; they were quickly undeceived. "Bormann immediately reported such cases to Hitler, and exploited them to fortify his own position. To our surprise [it is Speer who is speaking] it did not take him long to stalemate Himmler as Minister of the Interior." [42] Such are the advantages of a central position.

In the same way, after the Plot of 20th July, Bormann was again quick to exploit the errors or omissions of his rival. While Himmler naïvely believed (since Goering was plainly out of favour) that he was the obvious heir-apparent to the throne, and took every promotion as confirmation of such a certainty, Bormann was in fact seeing to it that he was moving not upwards and towards the centre of power, but outwards and away from it. In the dark days of the last winter of war, Bormann achieved a further triumph; he secured the appointment of Himmler as Commander-in-Chief of Army Group

[41] *Hoeherer S.S. und Polizei Fuehrer;* these were Himmler's regional deputies in Germany and occupied countries.
[42] A similar account has been given by Goering.

Vistula, a new formation fighting a desperate battle against the Russians east of Berlin. Thus Himmler was moved away from Berlin, where he might still attract the favour of Hitler or interfere with the influence of Bormann; and Bormann, remaining safely in possession, indeed monopoly, of the Fuehrer's ear, did not omit to ascribe the irresistible advance of the Red Army to the incompetence, perhaps even treachery, of his rival.

Nevertheless Bormann, though powerful, was not quite alone, not quite omnipotent, at Hitler's headquarters. Firstly, there remained Goebbels. Over all (or perhaps all but one) of Hitler's subordinates Goebbels enjoyed one indisputable advantage; he was able. Even Bormann recognised that to quarrel with Goebbels might prove fatal; and Goebbels, in his turn, recognised that Bormann had an undeniable vantage-post through the regularity of his attendance upon Hitler. Between these two, therefore, though they differed to the end on many matters of policy, there subsisted, to the end, a working agreement. As an intimate personal friend, Goebbels always had direct access to the Fuehrer; nevertheless he thought it prudent to conciliate Bormann by using him as an intermediary in inessential matters, and only using his own special position on special occasions. And Bormann, on his side, recognising this concession, did not seek to interfere with the occasional independence of Goebbels. In the last days of all, the actions of Goebbels and Bormann were symbolical of this practical compromise between the two surviving high-priests of Nazism. Their advice was different, their ambitions were different, their personal plans were different, but in the decisions of the Fuehrer, and in the mummery of his court, they agreed; and both officiated together at his last pagan sacraments of marriage and funeral before pursuing their separate courses to different fates.

The second character whose personality limited the empire of Martin Bormann was Hitler himself. Liberal refugees, theoretical Marxists, despairing reactionaries have pretended, or persuaded themselves, that Hitler was himself only a pawn in a game which not he but some other politicians, or some more cosmic forces, were playing. It is a fundamental delusion. Whatever independent forces he may have used, whatever incidental support he may have borrowed, Hitler remained to the end the sole master of the movement which he had himself inspired and founded, and which he was himself, by his personal leadership, to ruin. Neither Roehm nor Himmler, neither the Army nor the Junkers, neither high finance nor heavy industry, ever controlled that demonic and disastrous genius, whatever assistance they may at times have given or received, with whatever hopes or credulities they may have solaced their occasional misgivings, their frequent disappointments. And certainly, whatever ascendancy he may have gained over Goering, Hess, and Himmler, Bormann never controlled the uncontrollable will of Hitler, by whose favour alone he held office. His last political advice,—to leave Berlin for Obersalzberg in April,—was rejected; his dearest wish,—to retain power after Hitler's death,—was ignored. In 1939, when Sir Nevile Henderson suggested to Goering that he might use his influence to alter Hitler's mind, Goering had answered that once the Fuehrer had made up his mind, "all the rest of us are no more than the ground under his feet." It was a universal truth, as true of Bormann as of Goering, as true in 1945 as in 1939. Admittedly, says Speer, Bormann was to the end in complete control of all internal affairs; but at any time Hitler could have resumed direct control had he wished. "He had always carried out the old principle, *Divide and rule*. There were political groups who were always ready to do away with others. A few critical words from Hitler, and all Bormann's enemies would have jumped at his throat." If Bormann in fact exercised his power to the end, it was not in his own right, but by the sufferance of the formidable dictator whose incredible will-power, whose hypnotic influence, compelled even his critics to worship and obey. "Was Hitler, as an historic phenomenon, a product of the years after the first World War? Was he a sequel of the Versailles Treaty, the Revolution, and the events that followed? Was he a figure which these events would inevitably have produced?" So Albert Speer reflected in the philosophic leisure of the rock-perched fortress in which he was interned. But seeking to answer these questions, he was forced to re-envisage the character of the man whom he held responsible for Germany's downfall; and re-envisaging it, he replied that he was more than this. "It is true that without these events Hitler would never have found the soil on which his activities could bear such rapid and prolific fruit; but the whole demonic figure of the man can never be explained simply as the product of these events. They could just as easily have found expression in a national leader of mediocre stature. For Hitler was one of those inexplicable historical phenomena which emerge at rare intervals among mankind. His person determined the fate of the nation. He alone placed it, and kept it, upon the path which has led it to this dreadful ending. The nation was spellbound by him as a people has rarely been in the whole of history."

This conception of Hitler as a phoenix, rare in human centuries, a cosmic phenomenon exempt from ordinary laws, was not universally accepted inside Germany. It was not accepted by the generals, those hard-headed, unmystical, military engines. To them he was never more than a vulgarian of extraordinary power who fell short of their idea of genius. "When I was working with him," says Halder, the ablest of that class, "I was always looking for signs of genius in him. I tried hard to be honest and impartial, and not to be blinded by my antipathy to the man. I *never* found genius in him, only the diabolical." But one man accepted it completely, and his acceptance of it was the basis of its success. "At long intervals in human history," he wrote, "it may occasionally happen that the practical politician and the political philosopher are one. The more intimate the union, the greater his political difficulties. Such a man does not labour to satisfy the demands that are obvious to every philistine; he reaches out towards ends that are comprehensible only to the few. Therefore his life is torn between hatred and love. The protest of the present generation, which does not understand him, wrestles with the recognition of posterity, for whom he also works."

The author of that description is Hitler himself; and it is a self-portrait.[43] He had written it in prison, long before he had attained to the power he contemplated. His own firm belief in his messianic mission was perhaps the most important element in the extraordinary power of his personality, which lasted long after the external reasons for its survival had disappeared; and the acceptance of this myth even by the intelligent Speer is the best evidence of its power.

[43] *Mein Kampf*, p. 286.

Chapter Two

HITLER IN DEFEAT

SUCH WAS the setting of the stage, such the cast of the players, when the Allied break-through at Avranches in August 1944 opened the last act in the tragedy of Germany. The rest of the drama,—the pace of the catastrophe, the interrelation and concatenation of events,—was determined by an external, uncontrollable force: the advance of the Allied armies. With every new crisis, with the fall of each great fortress, the passage of each great river, a fresh fever seemed to break out in Rastenburg, Berlin, or Bad Nauheim; but these were merely stages in the development of the drama, not changes, or factors, in its course. Though strange errors still persisted in the politically illiterate court, though Himmler envisaged himself as a new colossus, and Ribbentrop to the last believed in an inevitable split between the Allies, in fact only two questions remained to which the answer was in any doubt: when would the end come, and how would the Nazi Party in general, and Hitler in particular, face it? For since the failure of the Generals' Plot, it was he alone who would decide the matter. By that last victory he had gained, not indeed the salvation or even the reprieve of Germany, but at least the power to ruin it in his own way.

To the first of these questions, no answer could rationally be made in Germany, for the answer no longer depended on Germany alone. The Party, of course, had an official answer: it would not come at all,—at least not in the form of a defeat for Germany. Never was the protest, "We shall never capitulate!"—that cry which had already punctuated Hitler's utterances in 1933,[1]—raised so frequently, so shrilly, and so unconvincingly, or repeated so obediently, as in the last winter of the war. Such an answer, had it really been admitted, would have rendered the second question irrelevant; but in fact not everyone, not even the Party leaders themselves, could really believe in it; many of them were already making their plans for escape, or at least survival. Nevertheless, it was the official answer; no other answer was allowed; and a curious but inevitable consequence ensued. With slogans of victory on their lips, everyone was preparing for defeat; and since no official preparation could be envisaged, a total breakdown of discipline and organisation became apparent. Plans for collective resistance, or even collective survival, were rendered impossible, because everyone, or almost everyone, was individually engaged in secret negotiations for surrender, or secret plans for desertion. Loud boasts were made of an impregnable bastion in the south, an Alpine Redoubt in the sacred hills of Nazi mythology, hills charged with legends of Barbarossa and sanctified by Hitler's residence; but when no one, except Hitler himself and a few over-heated schoolboys, believed in such resistance, and everyone else was preoccupied with personal projects of surrender or disappearance, all such designs remained in the already overcrowded realm of German metaphysics. The same fatal flaw condemned the so-called German resistance movement from the start. In fact, there was never any such movement. A "resistance movement," as defined by the circumstances of the war, is a movement of unconquered people in a conquered country. But it was the official doctrine of the Nazi Government that Germany not only would not, but could not be conquered. Indeed, since it had this implication, any mention of a German resistance movement was absolutely forbidden. Schellenberg has told us how, in these darkening days, a certain Major-General von Gehlen, who had long been busy studying the

[1] Rauschning, *The Voice of Destruction*, pp. 5, 121.

Polish underground movement, drew up a careful plan for German resistance on similar lines; but how, when Schellenberg forwarded these plans to Himmler, their reception made him tremble for his life. "This is complete madness!" was Himmler's answer. "If I were to discuss such a plan with Wenck,[2] I should be denounced as the first defeatist in the Third Reich. The fact would be served up to the Fuehrer piping hot!"; and he went on to denounce "high-class staff officers" who sat safely in evacuation areas nursing post-war plans instead of fighting. Even in February 1945, when the writing on the wall (one would have thought) needed no highly trained interpreters, General Staff officers received a circular reminding them of the severe penalties for defeatism, and naming three General Staff officers who had already been shot for that crime. Like the Roman augurs, who used to wink to each other over the obsolete religious ceremonies which they solemnly celebrated, many German Staff officers, whose secret plans had long ago been completed, must have smiled inwardly as they initialled, and passed on, this now meaningless document.

What then of the Werewolves? someone will ask. The answer is simple. The Werewolves do not contradict, they illustrate these facts. For a long time the facts were incomprehensible, because they seemed to conflict. It was known that an organisation for guerrilla warfare, the so-called Undertaking Werewolf, had been secretly set under the authority of the now ubiquitous Himmler; and then the German radio announced the desperate character, the invincible determination, and the expected results of this formidable movement. It was assumed, naturally enough, that this was to be a resistance movement comparable to the underground armies which had fought against the German armies of occupation in Poland and France, in Italy, Denmark, and the Balkans. At

[2] General Wenck was G.O.C. German 12th Army, fighting on the Elbe. This army is of importance later in this history. See below p. 122.

the same time it was surprising to find that the leader of the Werewolves, S.S. Obergruppenfuehrer Hans Pruetzmann, was engaged, together with the Gauleiter of Hamburg and others, in negotiating, or seeking to negotiate, with the British, through the Danish underground movement, for a peaceful surrender. And when the surrender came, and the operations of the Werewolves should have begun, the reverse happened. In a broadcast speech, Admiral Doenitz, the new Fuehrer, ordered all the Werewolves in the West to cease their activity. He was obeyed. Of all the conquered countries of Europe, Germany alone produced no resistance movement.

The explanation of these facts, at first obscure, is now clear. In May 1945 Pruetzmann, the head of the Werewolves, surrendered himself at Flensburg. Unfortunately he succeeded in committing suicide before full interrogation; but the story which he knew has since been learned from other sources. The Werewolves were never intended to operate after defeat; since the mention, or suggestion, of defeat was forbidden, that was out of the question. They were intended as a para-military formation, an auxiliary arm, to fight behind the Allied lines as diversionary forces, and thereby to assist the German armies. Thus their activity was parallel to that of the regular armies, not in succession to it. They were never intended to operate independently of the German High Command. Indeed, the Werewolves themselves never expected to have to fight in civilian clothes; they assumed they would fight in uniform, and thus, when captured, be entitled to the treatment of prisoners of war; and the discovery that this was not so was responsible for many desertions.

Why then were the Werewolves ever regarded as a serious menace? Here again we must appeal to later information to solve an old riddle. On 1st April 1945 a new development occurred which both obscured the real issue and vividly illustrates the condition of jungle war which made nonsense of so many Nazi plans and organisations. As the controlling centre of a wide organisation, Pruetzmann's office, according to all who knew it, was inefficient and uninspiring. Pruetzmann himself was vain, idle, and boastful. The organisation of his headquarters, says Schellenberg, corresponded with the mental capacity of its members,—it was weak; and he adds that he personally remonstrated with Himmler about the whole business, as "criminal and stupid." But on 1st April a new instrument of centralisation appeared. This was the Radio Werewolf, which first published the hitherto secret organisation, and turned the name "Werewolf" from a mysterious symbol into a public slogan. But this Radio Werewolf was in fact quite independent of Pruetzmann's organisation; for the propaganda of the movement had been seized by Goebbels, who, still struggling, even at this eleventh hour, for the dwindling fragments of authority, thus hoped (it seems) to gain control of the whole organisation. Goebbels had no relations with Pruetzmann whom he evidently thought insufficiently radical; but his use of Radio Werewolf, far from curing the defects of the movement, only made it more chaotic,—for he used it to preach an ideological nihilism which had no connexion with the real and limited aims of the Werewolf organisation, and which often discredited and discouraged its members. The usurpation of Radio Werewolf by Goebbels is responsible for many of the popular misconceptions about the Werewolves, and for the ridiculous difference between their supposed aims and their actual achievements. It did the Nazi cause no good; if anything, by discrediting the movement, it probably hastened its collapse.[3]

Nevertheless Radio Werewolf is of importance; for in it

[3] The facts given in this paragraph are given independently by Ohlendorf and Schellenberg. At Nuremberg both Speer and Fritzsche said that they understood the Werewolves to be controlled by Bormann—*i.e.* the Berlin group who had usurped the name and tried to control the policy—although Fritzsche added that Bormann had under him an Obergruppenfuehrer whose name he had forgotten—*i.e.* Pruetzmann. In fact Pruetzmann was always responsible to Himmler, and remained on his personal staff to the end.

is to be found the answer to our second question: how would the Nazi Party face the defeat which, openly, it refused even to contemplate? Because of this refusal there was, of course, no official, no direct answer, though it was always understood that Hitler would remain true to his original programme, *Weltmacht oder Niedergang*,—world-power or ruin. If world-power was unattainable, then (it was agreed by all who knew him) he would make the ruin as great as he could, and himself, like Samson at Gaza, perish in the cataclysm of his own making. For Hitler was not a figure of Western Europe, however he sought to pose as its champion against Asiatic Bolshevism; nor did his melodramatic character respond to the Confucian ideal of a tidy, unobtrusive death. When he envisaged himself against an historical background, when his imagination was heated, and his vanity intoxicated, with flattery and success, and he rose from his modest supper of vegetable pie and distilled water to prance upon the table and identify himself with the great conquerors of the past, it was not as Alexander, or Caesar, or Napoleon that he wished to be celebrated, but as the re-embodiment of those angels of destruction,—of Alaric, the sacker of Rome, of Attila, "the scourge of God," of Genghis Khan, the leader of the Golden Horde. "I have not come into the world," he declared in one of these messianic moods, "to make men better, but to make use of their weaknesses"; [4] and in conformity with this nihilistic ideal, this absolute love of destruction, he would destroy, if not his enemies, then Germany and himself and all else that might be involved in the ruins. "Even if we could not conquer," he had said in 1934,[5] "we should drag half the world into destruction with us, and leave no one to triumph over Germany. There will not be another 1918. We shall not surrender"; and again: "We shall not capitulate—no, never! We may be destroyed, but if we are, we shall drag a world

---

[4] Rauschning, *The Voice of Destruction*, p. 281.
[5] *The Voice of Destruction*, p. 121.

with us—a world in flames." [6] Now, in his positive hatred of
the German people, who had failed him in his megalomaniac
designs, he returned to the same theme. The German people
was not worthy of his great ideas; therefore let it perish
utterly. "If the German people was to be conquered in the
struggle," he told a meeting of Gauleiters in August 1944,
"then it had been too weak to face the test of history, and was
fit only for destruction." [7]

Such then was Hitler's answer to the challenge of defeat.
In part, it was a personal answer, the vindictive gesture of a
wounded pride; but in part it derived from another, more
rational feature of his terrible philosophy. For Hitler believed
in the *Myth*, as recommended by the irrationalist philosophers
Sorel and Pareto whose precepts he so faithfully followed
and so eloquently ratified.[8] Further, he despised, with an
overwhelming contempt, the Kaiser and his ministers, "the
fools of 1914–18" who feature so largely in his limited vocabulary of abuse. He despised them for many reasons; he
despised them for many errors into which he also fell, such
as undervaluing his enemies, and making war on two fronts,[9]
and for many which he avoided, such as being too mild in
their politics and too scrupulous in their methods of war; and
he despised them in particular for their failure to understand
the importance of the myth and the conditions of its growth
and usefulness. In 1918 the Kaiser had surrendered; weakly

[6] *The Voice of Destruction*, p. 5.

[7] Speer.

[8] Although it is improbable that Hitler had read either of these baleful
philosophers, there are many striking similarities between their principles
and his. Pareto's statement that the art of government lies in "taking advantage of sentiments, not wasting energy in a futile effort to destroy them"
(*Treatise on General Sociology*) is an exact parallel to the remark of Hitler
just quoted; and Hitler's theory (*Mein Kampf*, p. 787) that a people or a
class, that has once yielded to one threat, will go on yielding forever, is
exactly foreshadowed by Sorel.

[9] In *Mein Kampf* (p. 244) Hitler attacks the Kaiser's propagandists for
representing the enemy as contemptible. His "guarantees" that there would
never be another war on two fronts need no specification.

despairing, he had thrown in his hand (such was the official
Nazi version), without waiting for defeat. From such weakness, such despair, no flourishing myth could grow, whatever
useful lies might be invented. Myths require a dramatic, an
heroic end. Though its champions are overwhelmed, the idea
must continue to live, that when the winter of defeat is over,
and the cherishing airs return, it may put forth new flowers
and blossom again in apparent continuity. Therefore on form,
as the racegoers say, it had long been agreed by the experts
(even when such speculations seemed remote and ridiculous)
how Hitler and his apostles would face disaster. In the winter
of 1944–5 the time for the corroboration of this theory was
obviously near; and as in other dark hours, the prophet Goebbels came forth once more to corroborate it.

All his tricks had now been played out, and had failed, or
their temporary success had contributed too little to make
that last necessary difference. He had tried the glory of militarism, and failed. He had tried "true socialism," and failed.
He had tried the New Order, and failed. He had tried the
advancing crusade against Bolshevism, and failed. He had
tried the defence of Europe against the invading hordes of
Asia, and that had failed too. As the days darkened, he had
tried (as Speer said he should have tried) the appeal of blood,
sweat, and tears. But propaganda is subject to the law of
diminishing returns; what had worked in England in 1940
would not work in Germany in 1944, after the failure of so
many incompatible promises; and that had failed too. Then
he had tried the Frederican war. The German people were
reminded how, in the eighteenth century, even the great
Frederick had seemed doomed, when his allies fell away, and
his enemies closed in, when the Russians took Berlin, and he
was outnumbered on all sides and alone. Yet he had survived
and triumphed in the end, thanks to his oriental endurance,
his brilliant strategy, and the certain favour of Providence,
which had sown dissension among his enemies. Since the

Germans of 1944 were ruled by a leader of no less resource, the greatest strategical genius of all time, no less favoured by Providence (as events had recently shown), might not they too hope, if only they showed the same endurance, for a similar delivery? But even this appeal seemed inadequate in the winter of 1944–5. What then was left for the prophet to prophesy?

Goebbels was equal to the occasion. If all additional appeals had failed, if all supernumerary adherents had fallen away, at least there was still the original slogan of revolutionary Nazism, the slogan which had inspired the *déclassés* and the propertyless, the outcasts and casualties of society who had made Nazism before the Junkers and generals, industrialists and civil servants had joined it, and which might yet inspire them again, now that these fair-weather allies could no longer be counted on. From Radio Berlin, and later from Radio Werewolf, that slogan was heard again: the slogan of destruction; the authentic voice of Nazism uninhibited, unaltered by all the developments of the interim; the same voice which Rauschning had heard, with timid aristocratic dismay, ringing suddenly out among the tea-cups, the cream buns, the cuckoo-clocks and Bavarian bric-à-brac of the original Berchtesgaden. It was the doctrine of class war, of permanent revolution, of purposeless but gleeful destruction of life and property and all those values of civilisation which the German Nazi, though he sometimes tries painfully to imitate them, fundamentally envies and detests. The trials of war, the horrors of bombardment, now acquired a new significance for the exultant Dr. Goebbels: they were instruments not of fearful but of sanitary destruction, and he welcomed them. "The bomb-terror," he gloated, "spares the dwellings of neither rich nor poor; before the labour offices of total war the last class barriers have had to go down." "Under the *débris* of our shattered cities," echoed the German Press, "the last so-called achievements of the middle-class nineteenth century have been finally buried." "There is no end to revolution," cried Radio Werewolf; "a revolution is only doomed to failure if those who make it cease to be revolutionaries"; and it too welcomed the bombs which now fell nightly with ever more devastating effect on the industrial cities of Germany: "together with the monuments of culture there crumble also the last obstacles to the fulfilment of our revolutionary task. Now that everything is in ruins, we are forced to rebuild Europe. In the past, private possessions tied us to a bourgeois restraint. Now the bombs, instead of killing all Europeans, have only smashed the prison walls which held them captive. . . . In trying to destroy Europe's future, the enemy has only succeeded in smashing its past; and with that, everything old and outworn has gone." The virtue of Goebbels lay in his lucidity, the Latin clarity of his thought and style. The German language, especially in the mouths of its philosophers, is often cloudy and obscure; and such sentiments, uttered by Hegel or Spengler, Rosenberg or Streicher, would have been oracular but ambiguous and might be misinterpreted. There is no such danger with the language of Goebbels. There is no mistaking his jubilation.

Meanwhile, what of Hitler himself? After the Generals' Plot of 20th July he had withdrawn from publicity,—withdrawn, or been withdrawn, so effectively that many believed him dead, or imprisoned by the all-powerful Himmler. As nothing but silence answered these suggestions, rumour and exaggeration quickly extended their scope, and supplied the circumstantial detail which so often passes for evidence. Resourceful journalists described, with the exact relish of Dante or Baedeker, the medieval catacombs in which the deposed Fuehrer was now immured; or demonstrated, from the folds of his ears, that the Fuehrer portrayed in German photographs was a double, foisted upon the German people to conceal the death of their authentic master. In fact there is perhaps no period of Hitler's life with which we are more familiar, in its daily details, than the five months from October 1944 till the end of February 1945; over which period we possess the diary kept for him by his personal servant, Heinz Linge. This diary, picked up in September 1945 in the ruins of the Chancellery by a British officer, is in the form of a manuscript engagement-diary; but the reference to such unpredictable interruptions as air-raid alarms shows that the entries were made after, not before, the events they summarise. These are inscribed, hour by hour, on the left-hand page. The right-hand page, besides the regular signature of Linge, contains only the address of the Fuehrer's headquarters at the time,— until 20th November "*Wolfschanze*," [10] at Rastenburg, where the Plot had occurred; thence till 10th December at Berlin; from 11th December till 15th January "*Adlershorst*," [11] at Bad Nauheim in the Taunus hills, whence Hitler directed the Ardennes offensive; and finally, from 16th January till the end at Berlin, in the Reich Chancellery, which he never left.

This diary, though its entries are concise and factual, consisting only of interviews and meals and engagements, is nevertheless of value to the historian of Hitler. It shows the routine of his daily life, the nature of his court and visitors, the deviations of his health, and the increasing regularity of his engagements. Awakened daily at about noon, all his appointments have a corresponding eccentricity, and every day consists of a series of interviews with politicians and generals, adjutants and liaison officers, doctors and secretaries, punctuated only by belated meals, an occasional half-hour stroll in the garden, and an evening nap, until his last reception, a non-political tea-party between 2 and 3.30 in the morning, followed, some two hours later, by his retreat to bed. The strain which these eccentric hours put upon others can be

[10] Literally, "Wolf-fortress."
[11] Literally, "Eagle's nest."

imagined; for the interviews sometimes go on till 3.30 in the morning, and the other parties may not always have been able, like Hitler, to sleep through the following morning. In the last months they became even more eccentric; for by that time Hitler had reduced his hours of sleep to three.[12] But one man at least was equal to all such demands. The persistent Bormann determined never to lose sight of the master upon whom his whole power depended, or to allow another to monopolise that profitable ear; and he adjusted his own hours according to the same outrageous time-table. He at least was always on call.

Apart from this diary there are, of course, many other sources of evidence on Hitler's personal life during these final months. One is again the indispensable Speer, who has described the gradual change which came over Hitler's habits and character during the war, and, in particular, after the Plot of 20th July 1944. It was not only the obvious corruption of power, which led him to resent criticism, to feed on flattery, and to surround himself with spineless toadies; [13] not only the growing conviction that he alone had the will-power to continue the struggle, he alone still believed in ultimate victory and his own divine mission, while all others had abandoned hope and would capitulate; it was a fundamental change in his manner of life, which these secondary developments did but illustrate and intensify. For Hitler (Speer insists) was by nature an artist, averse from those methodical hours, that unremitting labour, which is so clearly reflected in the diary of the last months. In the days of peace he had found, in the irregular habits, the film-going and fantasies, the delays and holidays, the truancies and picnics, the tours of inspection

[12] Speer. Cf. Himmler's statement below, p. 88.
[13] The servility of Hitler's court makes a melancholy contrast to the ideals of *Mein Kampf* (pp. 323–324), in which he denounces as "grave-diggers of the monarchy" the flatterers who surrounded the Kaiser, when an honest man would "seriously admonish and seek to persuade even His Majesty, the wearer of the Crown himself."

and week-ends at Obersalzberg, the tea-parties and social gatherings of fellow "artists," that relief which the intolerable pressure of revolutionary politics demanded. Speer's account of Hitler's peace-time life is almost idyllic; for Speer had a vested interest in romanticising the past. After all, he had shared that life, and in its personal haven had completely forgotten the price at which it had been bought, the cruelties and concentration camps upon which it was based, and the sanguinary politics which it supported, but which, to him, the happy technocrat, seemed irrelevant distractions. Nostalgically, he has described those more care-free days in which Hitler listened to criticism, laughed and gossiped with his associates, and, whenever the weight of regular politics became too oppressive, disappeared to Obersalzberg with unpolitical friends and Eva Braun. There he would make up his mind on problems too vast to be considered in the hubbub of the Reich Chancellery, walking up and down in the Alpine summer, visiting small inns where he found (he said) "the inner calm and assurance necessary to his world-shattering decisions"; there he occupied himself more intensively with artistic things, with architecture, and continual films; there he would recover from the exhaustion of politics: his eyes would brighten again, his reactions would quicken, his enthusiasm for making decisions would revive; there his conception of life would become almost bourgeois: he would behave as a hospitable Austrian paterfamilias, good-natured and jocular, friendly and affable with all. While Goering and others would cover themselves with "tin-shops" of medals, he would exhibit a simplicity of manner and dress that brought him credit among his people and reconciled them to unpopular political decisions. "I suspect," says Speer, "that he was not happy with his 'mission'; that he would rather have been an architect than a politician. He often clearly expressed his aversion from politics, and even more from military matters. He disclosed his intention of withdrawing after the war from state affairs, to build himself a large house in Linz,[14] and there to end his days. He insisted that he would then completely retire. He did not wish to embarrass his successor in any way. He would then be soon forgotten and left to himself. Possibly some of his former colleagues would visit him occasionally, but he would not count on that. Apart from Fraeulein Braun he would take no one with him; nor would anyone stand living with him of his own free will for any length of time. . . ." Such were Hitler's day-dreams in 1939; and they are not reported by Speer only. On 25th August 1939, Sir Nevile Henderson had an interview with Hitler in Berlin. "Among various points mentioned by Herr Hitler," reported the ambassador, "were, that he was by nature an artist, not a politician, and that once the Polish question was settled, he would end his life as an artist and not as a war-monger." [15]

A naïve judgment, pathetically naïve. It is surprising that the otherwise sagacious Speer could be so elementary a psychologist, and suppose that this aesthetic *cri-de-cœur* was of absolute, and not merely of relative significance. But it is a not infrequent error. How many historians have been subject to it, who have defended corrupt politicians, weak governors, and bloodthirsty tyrants by appealing to their domestic virtues, their artistic tastes, the amiable simplicity of their personal lives! It is the error common to those who, like Speer, suppose politics irrelevant, and, in so doing, insensibly judge politicians by unpolitical standards. In this at least Rauschning showed more judgment than Speer. Less interested in art and the artist, he at least was not deceived by this bourgeois *bonhomie*. Above the crunch of the cakes and the tinkle of the tea-cups he heard, if not the cry of the tortured in the prison camps, at least the blood-curdling paean of universal destruction; and drew the consequences.

Though Speer's account of Hitler's life before the war

[14] Hitler always regarded Linz as his home town. Cf. below, pp. 57. 181.
[15] *Documents concerning German-Polish Relations* (Cmd. 6106), p. 128.

is of only partial validity, it is nevertheless valid within the limits of its incidence; and the statements of fact are certainly true. But during the war, he explains, all this changed. When he became the great war-lord, the greatest strategical genius of all time, Hitler's company changed, his hours of work became monotonously regular, the pressure of events gave him no release, he had no relaxations, no safety-valves, for the harmless discharge of his pent-up dynamism. Defeat intensified the process. If the German people must cut down their pleasures, he must sympathetically cut down his; and his were not only pleasures but the necessary conditions of his political life. Then came distrust and its attendant neuroses; the corruption of power reinforced by the fear of treachery. There were no more films, no more visits to Obersalzberg. Hitler surrounded himself not with artists and friends, but with illiterate soldiers, whom, in the height of his vainglorious disdain, he despised not merely socially and politically, but militarily, too. Conversation, instead of being a relief, became confined to the tedious trivialities of the barracks and the mess. Nor were there any compensating advantages. It had once been the tradition of the German Army to allow free criticism from subordinate officers. As the Party increased its control, this criticism was steadily reduced; after the 20th July 1944, it ceased altogether. A universal suspicion suppressed all healthy conversation and multiplied the effects of every setback. More and more the once sociable Fuehrer became an isolated hermit, with all the psychological repressions inherent in that dismal condition. He was isolated from persons, isolated from events. Convinced that only he could lead the German people out of defeat to victory, and that his life was therefore of cardinal importance; and yet convinced that every man's hand was against him, and assassination awaited him around every corner; by a logical consequence, he seldom left the protection of his underground headquarters, or the banal society of his quack doctor, his secretaries, and the few spiritless generals who still pandered to his inspiration. He seldom visited the front, never knew the true extent of the disasters to his armies, his towns, his industries; never in the entire war did he visit a bombed city. He remained a frustrated recluse, restless and miserable. More and more he dreamed of an elegant retirement in Linz. While Germany was crumbling in ruins, he occupied himself with ever more elaborate architectural plans. He was not (as his enemies said) redesigning Buckingham Palace for his own use; he was envisaging a new opera-house and a new picture gallery for Linz.[16] And as his contempt and distrust grew for the rest of mankind, so he thought more and more of Eva Braun, who was exempt from the otherwise universal vice of treachery. Only Eva Braun, he said, and his Alsatian dog Blondi were faithful to him. He had only one friend, he repeated, who would remain loyal to him in the last decisive hour, and that was Eva Braun. "We would never believe it," says Speer; "but this time his intuition had not failed him."

The effects of such a life on Hitler's physical condition can easily be imagined. "Up till 1940," says Dr. von Hasselbach, the most critical and reliable of his doctors,[17] "Hitler appeared to be much younger than he actually was. From that date he aged rapidly. From 1940 to 1943 he looked his age. After 1943 he appeared to have grown old." In his last days, says Speer, he was positively senile; and those were not yet the last days of all, the last days of April 1945, when all who saw him described him as a physical wreck. This rapid deterioration in Hitler's health has often been attributed to the effects of the bomb explosion of the 20th July 1944; but this is wrong. The wounds which Hitler received on that occasion

[16] When I visited the Bunker in September 1945, Goebbels' room was still full of illustrated books on opera-house architecture.

[17] Von Hasselbach is thus described by his interrogators, and by Drs. Geising and Brandt (see below pp. 59, 63) who add that von Hasselbach was "probably one of the few people associated with Hitler who did not fall under his spell."

were trivial and temporary. The real damage to his health
in the last months of his life proceeded from two causes: his
manner of life, which has been described, and his doctors.

Whatever Hitler's psychological condition may have been,
—and on such a subject, and in so unique a character, it would
be imprudent to speculate,—there can be no doubt that his
physical stamina was exceptionally strong. It could not have
been otherwise, to have endured, for so long, the tenancy of
that violent personality. Before the war, his only recorded
distemper was of the throat. In 1935, at the time of the Anglo-
German Naval Treaty, Hitler became alarmed at the condition of his voice, and sent for a specialist, Professor von
Eicken, of the Charité Hospital in the Luisenstrasse in Berlin,
who had previously attended one of his adjutants.[18] Von
Eicken diagnosed a polyp on the vocal cords and removed
it; after which Hitler recovered, and apart from an occasional
tingling in the ears, in consequence of general overstrain, and
a tendency to stomach cramps, continued in good health until
1943. He believed indeed that he had a weak heart, and after
1938 avoided all forms of exercise. On a mountain-top above
Berchtesgaden he had built a gazebo, the Kehlstein, whence
he could overlook the fabulous Bavarian Alps, and conquered
Austria, and the beautiful lake of Koenigsee. A lift, built in
the entrails of the mountain, would take him and his visitors
up to this eyrie; but Hitler soon ceased to make use of this
expensive observation post. In that rarefied atmosphere, 5400
feet above sea-level, he felt a tightening of his chest, which
he ascribed to the weakness of his heart; but his doctors found
no evidence of such a condition, and satisfied themselves that
these symptoms, like his epigastric pains and cramps, were of
hysterical origin.

All this time Hitler was attended, in the main, by three
doctors: Brandt, von Hasselbach, and Morell. Professor Karl

[18] The adjutant was Brueckner, and the incident the same which led to
the appointment of Brandt.

Brandt was his principal surgeon, and had been with him since 1934. A fortunate accident had made the career of Brandt, and of other doctors too, including von Eicken. Brandt belonged to the circle of notoriously Nazi doctors who surrounded Professor Magnus, and had their Berlin head-quarters at the clinic in the Ziegelstrasse. In August 1933 Brandt, then twenty-nine years old, was spending the summer in Upper Bavaria, when Hitler's niece and his adjutant Brueckner were injured in a serious motor accident at Reit-im-Winkel. Brandt was one of the doctors summoned to treat them; the impression he made was favourable, and next year he was invited by Brueckner to travel to Venice as personal surgeon to the Fuehrer. This was the beginning of a career at court. Brandt became official surgeon to Hitler and his staff. But since this immobilised him for long periods, prevent-ing him from the practice of surgery (for in fact Hitler never required his skill), Brandt introduced in turn two other mem-bers of Professor Magnus' circle to deputise for him at court, —firstly Professor Haase, who retired soon afterwards to the Ziegelstrasse for reasons of health and will appear again at the close of this narrative, and secondly, as successor to Haase, Professor Hans Karl von Hasselbach. Brandt and von Hassel-bach remained with Hitler until the great inter-medical battle of October 1944 which will shortly be related, Brandt being gradually promoted to the post of Reich Commissioner for Health and Sanitation; and their evidence is included in this summary of Hitler's health.

Professor Theodore Morell was Hitler's physician. If Brandt and his friends were not, technically, among the first flight of surgeons; if they owed their success to that element of chance which, after all, determines the majority of personal appoint-ments; they were nevertheless not altogether disreputable. At least, under Brandt's treatment, Brueckner recovered from his motor accident; and if Hitler had been similarly injured, he would doubtless have received competent attention. But of Morell it is difficult to speak in the measured terms and discreet vocabulary proper to his profession. He was a quack. Those who saw him, after his internment by the American forces, a gross but deflated old man, of cringing manners, inarticulate speech, and the hygienic habits of a pig, could not conceive how a man so utterly devoid of self-respect could ever have been selected as a personal physician by anyone who had even a limited possibility of choice. But Hitler not only chose him; he kept him for nine years, in constant attendance, preferring him above all other doctors, and, in the end, surrendering his person, against unanimous advice, to the disastrous experiments of a charlatan. From 1936 to 1945, Morell, in his own words, was Hitler's "constant companion"; and yet the health of his patient was to him only a secondary consideration. From all the evidence, it is perfectly clear that Morell's god was mammon. He was totally indifferent to science or truth. Rather than study the slow methods of patient research, he preferred to play with quick drugs and fancy nostrums; and when critics hinted at the inadequacy of his qualifications, he merely extended his claims in the empire of lies. He was, he maintained, the true discoverer of penicillin; but after he had devoted long years of single-minded research to its discovery, the ubiquitous British Secret Service had stolen the secret, and a British doctor had claimed the credit. Actually it was not necessary for Morell to make such defensive claims; for his position with Hitler depended upon his weaknesses, not his skill. Hitler liked magic, as he liked astrology and the assurances of somnambulism. "He had little respect for physicians," says one of that profession,[19] and believed in a kind of mystic medicine, which was akin to Christian Science." And so, when this ship's doctor, who had set up as a specialist in venereal disease among the artistic demi-monde of Berlin, came to Berchtesgaden as a necessary attendant on Hitler's photographer, Hoffmann, his fortune

[19] Professor Gebhardt.

was soon made. And fortune does not mean the modest opulence of a successful practitioner. Morell's financial ambitions
were far larger than that. He built factories and manufactured
patent remedies. As court physician, he secured lucrative approval of his manufactures. Sometimes he had their purchase
made compulsory throughout Germany; sometimes he secured a monopoly for his own brands. His vitamin chocolates
were a particularly successful venture. By an order from
Hitler, Morell's "Russia" lice-powder was made compulsory
throughout the armed forces, and no priorities were allowed
to interfere with the construction of factories for this important manufacture. "Ultraseptyl," the sulphonamide produced by Morell's company in Budapest, was condemned by
the pharmacological faculty of Leipzig University as harmful
to the nerves, and worse than the corresponding German
product. The report of the faculty was shown to Hitler, but
without effect. Morell's proprietary product obtained the
necessary political sanction, and priorities were granted to
enable him to increase still further its production.

These drugs were not so lucratively dispersed among the
German people without preliminary trial. The experiments
were made on Hitler. An *almost* complete list of the drugs
used by Morell upon Hitler, compiled from his own account
(which is unlikely to exaggerate on such a topic) and excluding the morphia and hypnotics which were also used, contains the names of twenty-eight different mixtures of drugs,
including the proprietary "Ultraseptyl" condemned by the
pharmacologists, various fake medicines, narcotics, stimulants,
and aphrodisiacs. The way in which Morell made use of these
drugs is thus described by Dr. Brandt:

"Morell took more and more to treatment by injections,
until in the end he was doing all his work by this method.
For instance, he would give large doses of sulphonamides for
slight colds, and gave them to everyone at Hitler's headquarters. Morell and I had many disputes about this. Morell

then took to giving injections that had dextrose, hormones,
vitamins, etc., so that the patient immediately felt better; and
this type of treatment seemed to impress Hitler. Whenever he
felt a cold coming on, he would have three to six injections
daily, and thus prevent any real development of the infection.
Therapeutically this was satisfactory. Then Morell used it as
a prophylactic. If Hitler had to deliver a speech on a cold or
rainy day, he would have injections the day before, the day of
the speech, and the day after. The normal resistance of the
body was thus gradually replaced by an artificial medium.
When the war began, Hitler thought himself indispensable,
and throughout the war he received almost continual injections. During the last two years he was injected daily. When
I asked Morell to name the drugs employed, he refused. Hitler
came to depend more and more on these injections; his dependence became very obvious during the last year. With the
exception of General Jodl, all the members of Hitler's staff
were treated from time to time by Morell."

By the time Brandt was interned, he had good reason to
hate Morell, and his opinion might therefore seem at first to
be biased against him; but there can be no doubt of its accuracy. It is supported by every other doctor who had opportunities of knowing the facts; and the professional verdict
of the faculty is supported by intelligent lay observers. Speak-
ing of the mental overstrain to which Hitler subjected himself, Speer says: "I believe that anyone who does a great deal
of intellectual work can understand this condition of mental
over-exertion; but there can hardly be another person who
has endured such an ever-increasing strain over so many
years, and who has further found himself a physician who
tried out completely new drugs on him, in order to keep him
capable of work, and, at the same time, to carry out a unique
medical experiment. It would be interesting to analyse Hitler's
handwriting during the last months; it had the uncertainty of
an old man. By his stubborn ways, his sustained outbursts of

anger, he often reminded me of a senile man. This condition became permanent after 1944, and was only seldom interrupted." "For purely physical reasons," says the same authority elsewhere, "most other men would have broken down under the strain of such a life, and after an enforced relaxation would have regained the capacity for work; or else nature would have come to the rescue with an illness. But Hitler's physician, Morell, managed to cover up his exhaustion by means of artificial stimulants, a method which, as is well known, ends by completely ruining the patient. Hitler became accustomed to these means of keeping up his endurance, and kept on demanding them. He admired Morell and his methods, and was in some sense dependent on him and his remedies." [20]

Under the combined pressure of such a life and such remedies, only a powerful constitution would have preserved Hitler's health from a much earlier collapse. In 1943 the first symptoms of physical alteration became apparent. Hitler's extremities began to tremble, especially the left arm and the left leg; his left foot dragged upon the ground; and he developed a stoop. The nature of this tremor was never satisfactorily explained. Some doctors thought that it might be due to Parkinson's disease; [21] but others supposed an hysterical origin, and no certainty could be achieved. At all events this tremor was not, as has often been stated, a consequence of the explosion of the 20th July 1944; it had already been obvious for some time, and the visible decline of the Fuehrer's health had even been the subject of an emotional birthday broadcast by Dr. Goebbels, who, in April 1942, had drawn a pathetic picture of the now lined and haggard Fuehrer, "the face of

[20] This account given by Speer is almost identical, in its main points, with another account by Heinz Lorenz. Hitler's signature may be seen in his will (p. 180).

[21] This view was more widely held among those doctors who had no direct connexion with Hitler (e.g. de Crinis; see below, p. 88); but it was not excluded as a possible interpretation by Brandt.

an Atlas, bearing the whole world on his shoulders." [22] In
fact, all the doctors are agreed that, after the shock of the explosion, the tremor, which had been becoming regularly
worse, ceased altogether; but later it began again in aggravated
form, and continued to grow worse until the end.

The events of the 20th July 1944, therefore, though they
represent a military, political, and psychological crisis, had
little physical significance in the life of Hitler. The first doctor
to be summoned on that occasion had been Dr. Erwin Giesing,
ear, nose, and throat specialist at a nearby military hospital;
and he was followed by Professor von Eicken, who had
previously operated on Hitler. They found that the tympanic
membranes of nearly all the officers present had been broken.
Hitler's tympanic membranes were broken on both sides. He
was also suffering from irritation in the labyrinths of the
ears, which caused a lack of balancing power; and a sub-
cutaneous haemorrhage in the right arm.[23] He was sent to bed,
and in about four weeks had completely recovered from the
immediate effects of the explosion.

The cumulative effects of his overstrained life and Morell's
treatment were not so easily cured. When Hitler resumed his
working life at Rastenburg, it was a life of eccentric hours in
an underground bunker in the damp, unhealthy climate of
East Prussia. He never left the bunker, for his phobias were
multiplying on him: he shunned the air, feared exercise, and
suspected danger everywhere. Professor von Eicken, who had
remained in regular attendance, urged him again and again
to leave that insanitary dug-out with its dank air and disturb-
ing associations. It was still summer: a week or two in the

---

[22] This broadcast makes another contrast with *Mein Kampf*. Hitler
speaks with great contempt of the foolish propaganda which sought to gain
support for the Kaiser by giving pathetic accounts of his long working hours
and frugal meals. "Nobody grudged him a square meal or the necessary
amount of sleep . . . the legends helped him little and harmed him much."
[23] It was observed that the photographs of Hitler greeting Mussolini after
the Plot showed him shaking hands with his left hand.

Obersalzberg would cure him; but Hitler refused to go. Then Keitel added his representations; but although ultimately, in November, Hitler yielded to his pressure and returned to Berlin, it was after a long resistance. "I am staying in Rastenburg," Hitler would reply. "If I leave East Prussia, then East Prussia will fall. As long as I am here, it will be held." So he stayed on, a sick man, spending a few days in bed at intervals, but always getting up for the daily Staff conference, though his health was plainly low, and his voice, usually so loud, energetic, and passionate, had become weak and faint. In September, and again in October, von Eicken treated him for infection of the maxillary sinus; he also found that he was suffering from swollen glands in the neck. In October he removed another polyp from the vocal cords. During this time Hitler was also in pain from continual headaches and stomach cramps which Morell was treating with drugs. These stomach cramps were not new; he had suffered from them intermittently for some years. But now they had become serious, and Hitler was forced to return to bed for a fortnight.[24]

It is clear that in the autumn of 1944 the long-concealed effects of Hitler's declining health were becoming manifest; and the diary, which begins on 14th October, registers the coming and going of a continual series of doctors. Besides von Eicken and the daily Morell, there is Dr. Weber, the heart specialist, and Professor Blaschke, the dentist, and several other medical men, whose visits continue until the end of November; then all is peace again, and an undisputed empire for Morell. Externally at least, and for a time, Hitler had weathered the crisis. When von Eicken revisited him, after a month's absence, on 30th December, in his headquarters at Bad Nauheim, Hitler seemed in good health once more; his voice was completely restored, and he seemed relatively strong and well. Nevertheless this period of illness had not passed without

[24] The facts in this paragraph come from Keitel and von Eicken.

leaving its trace in the history of the court; for in it, as a direct consequence of Morell's treatment, occurred the great medical row.

The crisis occurred in September. Hitler's stomach cramps were then at their worst; and Dr. Giesing, the ear, nose, and throat specialist who had been summoned after the Plot, had made an interesting discovery.[25] He discovered that, in order to relieve these pains, Morell had, for at least two years, been giving Hitler a proprietary drug known as Dr. Koester's Antigas Pills,[26] compounded of strychnine and belladonna. The dose which Hitler had been receiving was allegedly two to four pills with every meal, although the maximum dose which could safely be prescribed was said to be eight pills a day. Nor was this the worst. Morell did not himself administer the pills, but gave them, in gross, to Heinz Linge, Hitler's personal servant; Linge then gave them to his master as demanded, without medical supervision; and it was in Linge's drawer that Giesing had casually found these incriminating poisons. Shocked by his discovery, Giesing consulted Dr. Brandt, the surgeon. Together they agreed that under Morell's treatment Hitler was being slowly poisoned; and that this chronic poisoning was of itself quite enough to account not only for the stomach pains which it was designed to relieve, but also for the progressive discoloration of Hitler's skin which had become noticeable. Brandt consulted further with his deputy, von Hasselbach, who agreed; and Brandt and Giesing then told Hitler that he was allowing his health to be ruined by systematic poisoning at the hands of Morell. But the time had passed when Hitler would listen to reasons and arguments. For a while there was an uncertain silence, while the deity

---

[25] Giesing was technically an ear, nose, and throat-specialist, but he had experience in other fields also. His interrogators considered him to be a very competent doctor who had examined Hitler more thoroughly than his personal doctors.

[26] The prescription is given as Extr. Nux Vom.; extr. Bellad. a.a.o.5; extr. Gent. 1.0.

remained wrapped in blue smoke; then the thunderbolt was launched. Brandt was suddenly dismissed from all his political offices and from the appointment which he had held for twelve years; von Hasselbach followed into the wilderness; and Giesing was summoned no more to the Fuehrer's head-quarters. The fate of a fallen minister under an oriental tyrant is proverbially death; and if Brandt escaped this final punishment for his temerity, it was not through any remorse on the part of his enemies. On the 16th April 1945, when the final phase of the battle for Berlin was about to begin, and the doomed tyrant was crying for more blood before it was too late, Brandt found himself arrested on personal orders from Hitler and brought before a summary court. He was accused of having sent his wife to a place where she would fall into the hands of the advancing Americans. The court had received a personal letter from Hitler which charged Brandt with having lost faith in victory. He was condemned to death. "Your way of thinking is not our way of thinking," declared Artur Axmann, the spokesman of the court; "you will have to take the consequences"; and on Bormann's orders Brandt was removed to a condemned cell in Kiel. But events were now moving too fast for the Nazi leaders, and the procrastination of his friends saved Brandt until his capricious patron was dead.

The removal of Brandt and Hasselbach caused a vacancy for a surgeon at Hitler's court. To fill this vacancy Hitler applied to the faithful Himmler. In the days of universal treachery there were few others whom he could trust. Could the Reichsfuehrer S.S. recommend an absolutely reliable man? On this important matter Himmler decided to take the best professional advice. He therefore summoned his own doctor, Professor Karl Gebhardt.

Professor Gebhardt had been an intimate friend of Himmler since their early days, and there is a surprising unanimity of opinion about him. He was universally regarded as Himmler's evil genius. Schellenberg calls him "detestable." Ohlendorf, another of Himmler's subordinates and himself no squeamish character (at Nuremberg he confessed to the mass-murder of ninety thousand Jews), describes him as a corrupt and selfish intriguer, animated solely by personal expediency. Others knew him as an unscrupulous dabbler in politics, concealing his intrigues behind the innocent cloak of medicine. As a doctor he carried out experimental operations on Polish girls in the concentration camp at Auschwitz, and was rewarded by Himmler with the post of President of the German Red Cross. Speer's experience of him was curious. When suffering from a long illness in 1944, Speer accepted from Himmler the medical services of Gebhardt; but his health did not respond to the treatment, and his friends, being suspicious, called in another doctor, Professor Koch of the Berlin Charité Hospital, to observe Gebhardt's method. Professor Koch declared that Gebhardt's method was designed to aggravate rather than cure the ailment. Doctors disagree, and the incident may have been insignificant; but Gebhardt's reputation was enough to ensure the most sinister interpretation, and from that time Speer reduced his relations with Himmler to the minimum. Such was the appropriate adviser whom Himmler now consulted; such the sponsor who recommended his own most promising pupil, Ludwig Stumpfegger, a competent orthopaedic surgeon who had worked at his clinic at Hohenlychen and specialised in the regeneration of bones.

Whatever motives may have inspired Himmler and Gebhardt to send Stumpfegger to East Prussia as Hitler's new surgeon,—and those who knew Gebhardt could not believe that he lacked a selfish purpose,—they certainly gained nothing thereby. Possibly they sought nothing; for Himmler at least was too naïve to conceive of any elaborate plans. At all events, Stumpfegger had no intention of continuing to serve those whose usefulness was over; and once arrived at the

Fuehrer's headquarters, he became conspicuous for his unconditional and apparently genuine loyalty to Hitler. A faithful
giant (for he was of huge stature), he bowed in unfeigned
adoration before the god into whose presence he had at last
been admitted, and frequently spoke with contempt of the
sponsor who had shown him the way thither. It was on 31st
October that Stumpfegger first appeared at Hitler's headquarters. After that, his visits gradually became frequent. In
the diary there is recorded, almost daily, the word *Spazier-
gang*,—Hitler's single form of ventilation, his stroll round the
garden of his headquarters. Rarely is anyone recorded as accompanying him on these occasions; the only companions ever
mentioned are Himmler, Goering, Albert Bormann (an
adjutant of Hitler, brother of Martin Bormann), and Stumpfegger. In the last days Stumpfegger moved to Berlin with
Hitler. When others, including Morell, left or were dismissed,
he remained. Asked whether he really supposed that Germany
could still win the war, he answered, with the naïve conviction of the true believer, that though militarily ignorant, he
did not suppose,—he knew. The intense conviction in the
Fuehrer's eyes was his guarantee. Those walks in the garden
were not the walks of a patient with his doctor,—to the end
Hitler never needed a surgeon; they were the communion of
the Messiah with his disciple, of the divinity with his chosen
priest.

It goes without saying that Stumpfegger never fell into
the sin of Brandt. He never quarrelled with Morell. He kept
to his surgical duties, which entailed no disputes with the now
all-powerful physician. Morell's control over Hitler's person
for the last six months of his life was unchallenged. He even
succeeded in capping the dismissal of Brandt with the dismissal of Hitler's photographer Hoffmann, whose convenient
malady had been the beginning of his success, but whose
presence now only served to remind him of the humiliations
of patronage. With all the former doctors removed, his former

patron dismissed, and the new doctor obedient to his will, Morell could look forward comfortably, if only the war would allow it, to the last and most spectacular of his medical monopolies.

Thus, in his last days, though he suffered from no organic disease, Hitler had become, according to universal testimony, a physical wreck. Ceaseless work, the loss of all freedom, the frustration of all his hopes, Morell's drugs, and perhaps more than all these, the violence of his temperament when bitterness and disappointment had multiplied around him, had reduced that once powerful conqueror to a trembling spectre. All witnesses of the final days agree when they describe his emaciated face, his grey complexion, his stooping body, his shaking hands and foot, his hoarse and quavering voice, and the film of exhaustion that covered his eyes. They agree about certain less clearly physical symptoms too: his universal suspicion, his incessant rages, his alternation of optimism and despair. But two characteristics of his former temper he still possessed. The fascination of those eyes, which had bewitched so many seemingly sober men—which had exhausted Speer, and baffled Rauschning, and seduced Stumpfegger, and convinced an industrialist that he had direct telepathic communication with the Almighty [27]—had not deserted them. It was useless for his enemies to complain that they were really repellent. "They are neither deep nor blue," protested Rauschning; "his look is staring or dead, and lacks the brilliance and sparkle of genuine animation"; [28] nevertheless, in spite of his explanations and evasions, Rauschning had to admit, what Speer freely confesses and thousands of less critical

[27] The industrialist was Wilhelm Keppler, mentioned above, p. 21, n. 24. Keppler was sent by Hitler as one of his representatives to the World Economic Conference in London in 1933. Asked about Hitler by an English acquaintaince, he replied, "Der Fuehrer hat eine Antenne direkt an den lieben Gott."

[28] *The Voice of Destruction*, p. 13.

Germans (and not only Germans) too eloquently witness, that Hitler had the eyes of a hypnotist which seduced the wits and affections of all who yielded to their power. Even his doctors, and the most critical of them, admit the fascination of those dull, blue-grey eyes which compensated for all coarseness in his other features; "pictures," they say, "cannot reproduce the suggestive power of his face." This personal magnetism remained with him to the end; and only by reference to it can we explain the extraordinary obedience which he still commanded in the last week of his life, when all the machinery of force and persuasion had disappeared, the failure and cost of his disastrous rule was apparent, and only his personality remained.

Secondly, Hitler's lust for blood was unabated, perhaps even increased, by time and defeat. Though he was physically afraid of the sight of blood, the thought of it excited and intoxicated him, just as destruction in all its forms seems to have appealed to the inherent nihilism of his spirit. In his early conversations (we learn from Rauschning), when he spoke of the revolution by which the Nazis would attain power, "he lingered with special interest over the chances of a bloody destruction of Marxist resistance in the streets"; for he conceived that historical greatness was not to be achieved without the spilling of blood.[29] Nor did it matter to him whose blood was shed; for it was the spectacle, the imaginary contemplation of rivers of human blood that inspired him, not the thought of victory and its practical use. "Nature is cruel, therefore we too may be cruel," he said in 1934, when discussing the Jews and the Slavs; "if I can send the flower of the German nation into the hell of war, without the smallest pity for the spilling of precious German blood, then surely I have a right to remove millions of an inferior race that breeds like vermin!"[30] *Without the smallest pity* . . . As a logical

[29] *The Voice of Destruction*, p. 18.
[30] *Ibid.*, p. 137.

syllogism, the proposition is perhaps defective; but as a psychological illustration it needs no improvement.

Throughout the war Hitler continually gave evidence of this lust for blood, this physical delight in the intellectual contemplation of slaughter for its own sake. The generals, hardened automata, notorious as impersonal men of blood and iron, were shocked at such positive emotions, and have given numerous instances of it. During the Polish campaign, Halder maintained that the storming of Warsaw was unnecessary; it would fall of itself, since the Polish Army no longer existed; but Hitler insisted that Warsaw must be destroyed. His artist's temper aroused, he described the delicious scenes which he demanded,—the sky darkened, a million tons of shells raining down on the city, and the people drowned in blood; "then his eyes popped out of his head, and he became quite a different person. He was suddenly seized by a lust for blood." Another general has described how Hitler received the news that his personal S.S. division, the *Leibstandarte Adolf Hitler*, had been decimated in Russia. Apologetically General Reichenau sought to explain that German losses had unfortunately been high. Hitler cut him short. "Losses can never be too high!" he exclaimed triumphantly; "they sow the seeds of future greatness." We have seen how, after the Plot of 20th July, the mere mention of the great Blood Purge of 1934 set him off into one of his famous tantrums. Satisfaction never abated this terrible appetite for blood, which, like his appetite for material destruction, seemed rather to grow when the price was to be paid not in inferior currency but in good Aryan coin. In his last days, in the days of Radio Werewolf and suicidal strategy, Hitler seems like some cannibal god, rejoicing in the ruin of his own temples. Almost his last orders were for execution: prisoners were to be slaughtered, his old surgeon was to be murdered, his own brother-in-law was executed, all traitors, without further specification, were to die. Like an ancient hero, Hitler wished to be sent with human sacrifices to his grave; and the burning of his own body, which had never ceased to be the centre and totem of the Nazi state, was the logical and symbolical conclusion of the Revolution of Destruction.

Chapter Three

THE COURT IN DEFEAT

THE PROSPECT of universal destruction may be exhilarating to some aesthetic souls, especially to those who do not intend to survive it and are therefore free to admire, as a spectacle, the apocalyptic setting of their own funeral. But those who must live on in the charred remainder of the world have less time for such purely spiritual experiences. It is therefore not surprising that there were many in Germany who looked with dismay upon this orgy of deliberate destruction, and resolved, as far as they had any power to do so, to frustrate it. One such was Karl Kaufmann, Gauleiter of Hamburg. Having seen his city, the greatest port, and one of the most ancient and prosperous towns in Germany, shattered from the air, he was resolved not to see it still further ruined either by British shells or by Nazi dynamite. Another was Kaufmann's closest friend, perhaps the ablest and most interesting of all the Nazi Government, Albert Speer.

Speer has already been often mentioned, often quoted, in this narrative. He has not been quoted uncritically, or because it is easier to quote than to compete with him. Many other Nazi politicians have employed the aching leisure of their confinement to compile their personal autobiographies and apologias, and to enunciate those large cosmic propositions so dear to the German mind. Speer has been quoted because his observations do but give literary, and sometimes lapidary form to the conclusions already reached from the study of many less personal, and therefore, at first sight, less fallible records. It is not necessary, for instance, indeed it is inadvisable, to

74

quote the careful autobiography of Schellenberg; for the judgments and opinions of Himmler's expert on foreign affairs illustrate nothing except the jejunity of his intellect, the provincialism of his horizon. And the autobiography of Count Lutz Schwerin von Krosigk, though he had been a minister for thirteen years, will deserve quotation not for the sagacity, but for the imbecility of his observations. But Speer deserves quotation in his own right. His conclusions are never naïve, never parochial; they seem always honest; they are often profound. If he seems sometimes to have fallen too deeply under the spell of the tyrant whom he served, at least he is the only servant whose judgment was not corrupted by attendance on that dreadful master; at least he retained the capacity to examine himself, and the honesty to declare both his errors and his convictions. In the last days of Nazism he was not afraid to tell Hitler of his own acts of defiance; and in Allied captivity he was not afraid to admit, after his searching analysis of Hitler's character and history, the residue of loyalty which he could not altogether shed.

The whole political career of Speer is extraordinary, if "extraordinary" is not too obvious a word to use for any of the events of Nazi Germany. It is strange enough that such a man should have risen in the corrupted *entourage* of Hitler; and that having risen he should have survived, a single, solitary, disapproving figure in that ambuscade of vigilant and vindictive conspirators. That having never held any political or administrative position, he should suddenly, at the age of thirty-six, and in a time of crisis, be entrusted with the entire control of all armament production and co-ordination of production, of the building and maintenance of communications, and the direction and reformation of industry, is perhaps less surprising in the arbitrary world which we are contemplating; but that he should succeed, and succeed regularly, in this gigantic task, is indeed almost incredible; and that after such a triumph in such a world he should retain not merely an objective but an intellectual outlook on his experience, is a mystery past facile interpretation. For Speer began his career as an architect. In 1934, at the age of twenty-nine, he was building manager in the Reich Chancellery, a subordinate official working under Hitler's architect, Professor Troost. Himself an artist, Hitler took an interest in his architects, and after a few conversations he included Speer in his intimate circle, invited him to lunch, and took a close interest in him. From that moment Speer's future was assured. Hitler had "intuitively" chosen him, as he had chosen Ribbentrop, the champagne salesman, to be an ambassador and foreign minister, and Rosenberg, the Baltic mystagogue, to govern the conquered East. But Speer was a more felicitous choice than these. It is true he succumbed, like all others, to the mesmeric influence of his employer; like them, he could not withstand the mysterious intensity of those dull, glaucous eyes, the messianic egotism of that harsh, oracular voice. "They were all under his spell," he explains, "blindly obedient to him, and with no will of their own,—whatever the medical term for this phenomenon may be. I noticed, during my activities as architect, that to be in his presence for any length of time made me tired, exhausted, and *void*. Capacity for independent work was paralysed." It is true, too, that his architectural achievements were perhaps of questionable elegance,—the vast new Reich Chancellery, for instance, which he was ordered to complete in haste, in time for the reception of President Hacha of Czechoslovakia and Prince Paul of Yugoslavia, that these tributary kings might tremble before the geometric magnificence of the new Pharaoh. But at least, unlike the Third Reich, they were structurally sound. Even now, like the ruins of Memphis, the relics of that vainglorious edifice are the most substantial memorial in the great cemetery of central Berlin.

For in truth (and herein probably lies the secret of his survival) Speer was not an artist, nor a politician. He had no common interests or ambitions with the rest of the court. He observed their antics, but did not compete in their field; and since he was obviously a personal friend and immediate dependant of Hitler—perhaps the only personal friend he had—they found it safest to leave him alone in his unsympathetic isolation. Speer was a technocrat and nourished a technocrat's philosophy. To the technocrat, as to the Marxist, politics are irrelevant. To him the prosperity, the future of a people depends not upon the personalities who happen to hold political office, nor upon the institutions in which their relations are formalised—these are irrelevant phenomena of no ultimate significance—but upon the technical instruments whereby society is maintained, on the roads and the railways, the canals and bridges, the services and factories wherein a nation invests its labour, and whence it draws its wealth. This is a very convenient philosophy; and it is true that in certain times (so long, that is, as they can be taken for granted) politics can be ignored. For nearly two years after he had succeeded Todt as Armaments Minister, Speer found that he could take politics for granted, merely observing the antics of the politicians from his favoured seat in the royal box, while he concentrated his activities and interests upon the communications and factories which he so completely understood. Then he was disillusioned. When Hitler and Goebbels raised the slogan of "Scorched Earth," and called upon the German people to destroy their towns and factories, to blow up their dams and bridges, to sacrifice their railways and rolling-stock for the sake of a myth and a Wagnerian Twilight, then at last the fallacy of his philosophy became apparent to Speer. Politics do matter; politicians can affect the destiny of nations. The crisis of his life occurred.

The choice was not easy. For eleven years, supported by that convenient philosophy, Speer had enjoyed the sunshine of Hitler's favour. He had grown rich and powerful under the shadow of a tyrant whose tyranny (he had convinced himself), since it did not interfere with his own impersonal

ambitions, was irrelevant to him. He had been fascinated by
the personality and flattered by the attentions of his master;
but he remained (if we can forgive his initial error of yielding
to the totalitarian embrace) intellectually uncorrupted. His
impersonal ideals remained valid; and when Hitler declared
himself their enemy, Speer prepared to sacrifice not his ideals,
but Hitler, together with all the associations of patronage and
friendship and personal influence engendered by this long
relationship. Naturally he chose to deceive himself. Having
collaborated over so long a period, he could not admit (like
the exiled Rauschning) that this nihilism was always implicit,
and often explicit, in Nazi philosophy. He preferred to suppose a sudden change, the arbitrary reorientation of a despot
corrupted by the exorbitancy of unchallenged power. Hitler's
path, he said, had become suddenly random and erratic, and
was leading to terrible consequences. "He was deliberately
attempting to let the people perish with himself. He no longer
knew any moral boundaries; a man to whom the end of his
own life meant the end of everything." A more critical
observer would have realised that Hitler never knew any
moral boundaries; after all, he had often said so.

Between his public duty and his private relationship, Speer
did not hesitate. "From then on," he says, "—and not only
within my official jurisdiction—I had to plan, initiate, and
execute many acts which were directed against Hitler's policy,
or against himself." While Hitler, with increasing radicalism,
demanded the destruction of Europe, Speer, with increasing
zeal, sought to nullify his orders. He was himself responsible
for the destruction of industrial installations; he ordered their
preservation. To every order of industrial suicide which ema-
nated from the Fuehrer's headquarters, or the Party Chancery,
or Radio Berlin, Speer issued, through his own channels, a
countermanding order. By his great authority and his continual journeys throughout Germany, he everywhere stayed
the hand of the destroyer, and persuaded his agents, his sub-

ordinates, and his sympathisers that if communications and factories must be surrendered to the enemy, they should be surrendered intact. The mines and factories of Belgium and northern France, the canals of Holland, the nickel mines of Finland, the ore of the Balkans, the oilfields of Hungary, were all protected by his authority; and when the New Year came, and the Allied armies penetrated into Germany itself, Hitler and his single personal friend continued the same silent but bitter struggle over the body of Germany.

It was in February 1945 that Speer's intellectual dilemma became most acute. The situation was now clearly hopeless; but despair only intensified the nihilism of the Party. General Guderian, Chief of Army General Staff since the July Plot, himself told Ribbentrop that the war was lost. Ribbentrop reported the words to Hitler, and Hitler summoned both Guderian and Speer and told them that such words were treason; in future neither rank nor position would save such traitors from death, or their relatives from arrest. At the same time Goebbels, maddened by the great air raid on Dresden, demanded the repudiation of the Geneva Convention, the massacre of forty thousand Allied airmen, and the use of two new and terrible poison gases, *Tabun* and *Sarin*. On his side, Speer walked more openly in the way of treason. He decided at last to intervene even in politics, which he had so long thought it possible to ignore.

Speer's plan was nothing less than the removal by assassination of the entire political directorate of the Reich. Seven months ago such a project would have been inconceivable to him; he had neither known nor approved of the Generals' Plot; but since then his whole world had changed, and the chosen disciple had caught up with the most inveterate enemies of the Fuehrer. Hitler was now in Berlin, in the Reich Chancellery. There it was his custom to discuss policy with his immediate associates—Goebbels, Bormann, Burgdorf and Ley—in his underground Bunker, which no one, not even they, could now approach without being searched for hidden explosives. But Speer's plan did not entail the introduction of visible weapons. The Bunker was ventilated by means of an air-conditioning plant, of which the external funnel projected into the Chancellery garden. As an architect Speer was familiar with its construction, and he completed his knowledge by consultation with the chief engineer of the Chancellery. He discovered that if poison gas were introduced into the funnel at the time of one of Hitler's conferences, it would very quickly be distributed throughout the Bunker; and thus, in a few minutes, the whole disastrous coterie would be destroyed. Into this plan Speer initiated a few trusted collaborators, and the preparations for its execution went ahead; but it was never executed. When his preparations were complete, Speer visited the Chancellery garden, only to find that by a recent and personal order of the Fuehrer, a protective chimney, some twelve feet high, had been built round the funnel, and the plan was no longer feasible. Thus, for the second time in seven months, Hitler escaped assassination.

Nevertheless it was not merely a technical hitch which saved Hitler from the hand of Speer; for in one of the few reluctant statements which he has made on this evidently distasteful subject, he has described another incident which also contributed to his failure. About this time Speer visited the German Front on the Rhine, and there, one night, sat with a party of German miners in a dug-out. In the darkness, only occasionally relieved by a trench light, he was unrecognised; he listened silently to the conversation of the miners around him, and from it he drew a new political conclusion. These miners, he was convinced, represented the ordinary German soldier or worker; and they, it seemed clear to him, still believed in Hitler as they believed in no one else. They believed that he, and only he, both understood the working class from which he had risen, and the mystery of politics which had been concealed from the rest of the German race, and that he would therefore be able, as no one else, to work the miracle of their salvation from this forlorn predicament. Chastened by what he had heard and seen, Speer reconsidered his design. If he were to remove Hitler, he would remove the grand saboteur of German industry and communications; but he would also deprive the German people of the one political leader in whom, apparently, they still believed; in whom they reposed, by habitual abnegation, their common will; and whose orders they would still, in this penultimate moment, obey. Once again Speer realised the importance of politics, the alternative to his simple technocratic philosophy. His plan for destroying Hitler and his court was cancelled, and never revived; and Speer joined that great and discouraging company of Germans, the conspirators who have failed.

Which of these two factors, the technical fault or the political lesson, really determined Speer's failure as an assassin, is a question of little importance, to which he himself has given no clear answer; [1] but one fact emerges clearly from this curious history. No intellectual conversion can be entirely without an emotional backwash; and the apparent decisiveness of Speer's breach with Hitler, which at first sight contrasts so strongly with the infinite hesitations of Himmler, must not obscure the difficulty with which he made it, the psychological crisis which it entailed. How serious these were is clear from his subsequent history,—the history of a mind still divided between political antagonism and personal allegiance.

On 18th March, in spite of Hitler's explicit veto, Speer wrote to him declaring that militarily and economically the war was lost; if the nation was not to be lost also, it was essential that some material basis be preserved upon which the life of the people, however primitively, might be continued. It

[1] In his earlier statement, Speer ascribed his failure to his experience on the Western Front; at Nuremberg he referred only to the technical hitch. In general, he has given less emphasis to his personal dependence on Hitler in his statements at Nuremberg than in his earlier version; but this does not make them inconsistent, or suggest that one version is untrue.

was a manifesto against the declared policy of destruction; and
Hitler's answer was emphatic. Sending for Speer, he told him:
"If the war is to be lost, the nation also will perish. This fate
is inevitable. There is no need to consider the basis even of a
most primitive existence any longer. On the contrary it is
better to destroy even that, and to destroy it ourselves. The
nation has proved itself weak, and the future belongs solely
to the stronger Eastern nation. Besides, those who remain after
the battle are of little value; for the good have fallen." That
day new orders of destruction were issued by Hitler and Bormann: the fight was to be continued "without consideration
of the German people"; eight officers who had failed to destroy a bridge were shot by Hitler's order, and the fact was
published in the bulletin of the Armed Forces; and Speer's
authority over industry was suspended.

Nevertheless Speer continued his activity, which no longer
rested upon formal appointments. He ordered the conceal-
ment of high-explosive and reduced its manufacture, so that
existing stocks might be wasted; and he issued machine-pistols
to his works managers, to use against Gauleiters who might
insist upon destruction. He sent out orders in the name of the
Combined General Staff; and where his own channels failed,
he used those of the High Command or the Reich railways.
The suspension of his authority had made no difference, and
on 29th March he found himself summoned by Hitler once
again.

Hitler accused him of publicly stating that the war was lost
and ordered him publicly to assert the opposite. Speer replied,
"The war is lost." Hitler gave him twenty-four hours in
which to consider the matter; and at the end of this time
Speer returned with a letter defending his views.[2] Hitler re-

_____

[2] This letter, in which Speer describes to Hitler their conversation of
18th March, is extant and was used as evidence at Nuremberg. It is a remarkable document, showing the extraordinary freedom which Speer (and no
one else) could use in his relations with Hitler. The account of that meeting
printed above is taken from his letter.

fused to receive the letter and ordered Speer to go away on permanent leave. Speer refused; it was his duty, he said, to remain at his post. Thereupon a strange scene of reconciliation took place between the Angel of Destruction and his recalcitrant but unpunished disciple. "I declared to him," said Speer, "that even so he could rely upon me in the future"; and by that simple, lying formula Speer found himself restored to authority, which he used, as before, to circumvent the purpose of its bestowal. The duality of Speer's behaviour that is apparent in these episodes will be clear again in the course of this narrative. It will appear in his last visit to the Bunker and his frank confession to Hitler on 25th April. It is clear also from the words with which he concludes his own account of Hitler's personality. "Although inwardly I had broken with him by that time," he says, "it has been difficult for me even now to write this study. I feel it to be my duty to help in exploring his faults, which were the origin of his disastrous influence, as tragic for Germany as for the rest of the world. Even if sometimes I have had to speak in blunt terms, I should not like to be numbered among those who malign him in order to exonerate themselves."

Meanwhile it was not only Speer who had passed through an intellectual crisis in his attitude towards the Fuehrer, although "intellectual" is perhaps not quite the word to use in describing so incredibly simple a character as Himmler. For Himmler also had begun to notice the inconsequence, the eccentricity, the peevishness of Hitler's behaviour. He had not discovered it himself, of course; but once it had been pointed out to him (and eager conspirators were always willing to point it out), he had to admit that he no longer received those clear, explicit, and intelligible directives which had once enabled him to conceal, under the brisk efficiency of his executive action, the chronic indecision of his mind. The God had gone out of his world; what then was the high-priest to do? His litanies, his sacraments, his endless human sacrifices all seemed vain and meaningless now. He required another God. It is true he had found another God, in Heaven, thanks to the miracles of the past year; but that God was somewhat remote, and his advice somewhat too general to be of much practical assistance in the extraordinarily complicated political and military situation of contemporary Germany. He needed a more earthly god; and the personal tragedy of Himmler in these last months is that he could not find one; he could only find a missionary who was persuasive enough to dissolve his belief in the old revelation, but could never quite convince him of the validity of the new. This missionary was Walter Schellenberg.

In his first task of constructing a vast, efficient, totalitarian intelligence service, Schellenberg had already failed, and failed completely. It is not altogether fair to blame him for his failure; for the task was now quite impossible. In such a jungle of conflicting egoisms as "totalitarian" Germany, all planning, especially Schellenberg's planning, was an academic exercise. But in his second, more limited plan, the plan to build up Himmler into the rival, the successor, and if necessary the destroyer of Hitler, who would negotiate peace with the West and become the saviour of Germany, he was having, or at least he persuaded himself that he was having, more success. For nearly a year now he had not sought to conceal from Himmler the extent and exorbitancy of his plans; and convinced of his own subtlety, his brilliant perception of trends and nuances, on which the Chinese game of diplomacy, and the feminine game of seduction depend, he probably believed that Himmler both understood, and accepted, more of his ideas than could ever penetrate that slow, unagile mind. It is true Schellenberg had not dared to inform Himmler of the hopes which some of the wilder July conspirators had entertained of him; but he had dropped judicious references to Fraeulein Hanfstaengl of Munich, who had conceived a plan of evacuating Hitler by force to Obersalzberg, there to reign as nominal but impotent head of the state, while all the acts of government were carried out on the orders of Himmler. This suggestion had been ignored by Himmler, but Schellenberg was ready with another. In Hamburg he had discovered a promising astrologer called Wulf, a student of poisons, Sanskrit, and other interesting subjects. Wulf's prophecies, as seen by Schellenberg in retrospect, seemed remarkably accurate. He had prophesied that Hitler would survive a great danger on 20th July 1944; that he would be ill in November 1944; and that he would die a mysterious death before 7th May 1945. His prophecies concerning Himmler were equally remarkable, though discreetly enveloped in diplomatic silence. Schellenberg found that in politics Wulf was sound; he introduced him to Himmler as a counterweight to the unsound Kaltenbrunner; and this introduction was so successful that before the end of the Third Reich, according to Schellenberg, "Himmler seldom took any steps without first consulting his horoscope." No less valuable to Schellenberg was Himmler's Finnish masseur, Kersten. Himmler, in Schellenberg's opinion, suffered from cancer of the bowel; at any rate he suffered, and only Kersten could relieve the pain. Gradually Himmler became as dependent on Kersten's massage as Hitler upon Morell's drugs. Thus indispensable, Kersten soon found that he could say things to Himmler which even Schellenberg dared not; and Schellenberg, who also relied on Kersten's massage, found that his politics were sound too. From that time Kersten became another agent in Schellenberg's conspiracy; and Schellenberg congratulated himself on still further proof of his own subtlety.

Thus, little by little, by judicious hints and careful indiscretions, referring sometimes to minute particulars, sometimes to large generalities, and always stopping by the way to admire his own virtuosity, Schellenberg succeeded, or thought that he had succeeded, in fretting away that essential chain of unconditional loyalty upon which the whole of Himmler's personality hung, by which its whole balance was adjusted, its inherent instability concealed; and at the same time, in the niche of Himmler's private worship, from which the idol of Hitler was thus gradually crumbling away, Schellenberg substituted, slowly and tentatively and against stubborn and despairing resistance from the worshipper, a new and even more inappropriate image: the image of Himmler himself, crowned as the second Fuehrer, the second incarnation of the spirit of Aryan Germany. With what tenacity Schellenberg pressed, with what obstinacy Himmler resisted, is clear from the long, complacent, insensitive account which Schellenberg himself has given of his endless manœuvres. In February 1945, when Himmler, discredited as a general, broken in spirit, suffered a "physical and spiritual collapse" and retired to Professor Gebhardt's clinic at Hohenlychen, it was little rest he found there. How could Schellenberg leave him alone with the detested Gebhardt? At once he arrived at Hohenlychen with a fresh batch of prophecies from the astrologer Wulf, and the familiar theme was reopened. When Count Folke Bernadotte, representing the Swedish Red Cross, came to Berlin, with what self-admired diplomacy did Schellenberg arrange interviews with the reluctant Himmler so that not even Ribbentrop or Kaltenbrunner could complain! They were abortive interviews, it is true, for Bernadotte would not approach the Allies on his own initiative and Himmler could not bring himself to act independently of Hitler. "You may think it sentimental, even absurd," he protested, "but I have sworn loyalty to Adolf Hitler, and as a soldier and a German I cannot deny my oath"; [3] but Schellenberg did not despair

[3] Folke Bernadotte, *The Curtain Falls* (American translation, Copyright, 1945, by Alfred A. Knopf), p. 46. Count Bernadotte had altogether four interviews with Himmler, on 12th February, 2nd April, 21st April, and 23/24th April. The two last will be described later. It was at the interview of 2nd April that Himmler gave his interesting but overdrawn account of the Nazi leaders: Hitler almost entirely occupied in studying architectural plans for rebuilding German cities; Goering taking cocaine, dressing up in a toga, and painting his finger-nails red.

of altering that. There is an almost brutal relish in the words
with which he praises the pertinacity of his assaults upon
Himmler's agonised doubts. "I owe all I am to Hitler,"
Himmler would plead, "how can I betray him?"; "I have
built up the S.S. on the basis of loyalty; I cannot now abandon
that basic principle." But the subtle tempter was ready with a
hundred methods by which basic principles could be justifi-
ably abandoned. Himmler protested that his health was failing,
"and indeed," says Schellenberg, "he was the image of a torn
soul, the picture of unrest and discontent." But Schellenberg
was unaffected by the spectacle of mental torture in the man
he seems (incredible though we find it) to have genuinely
liked and admired. "I struggled with him," he says unfeelingly,
"like a devil struggling for a soul."

It was already the spring of 1945 when the decisive moment
came, and Schellenberg resolved to put aside prevarication, to
abandon infertile hints, and to admit to Himmler the full
implications of his project. He had hesitated for long, for
Himmler was still surrounded by other, more sinister advisers:
by Kaltenbrunner, the Austrian thug who controlled Himmler's central office, and therefore (in theory) Schellenberg
himself, and whose head was now swollen by the personal
favour of Hitler; by Skorzeny, the Viennese terrorist, who
had rescued Mussolini and kidnapped the son of the Regent
of Hungary, and who was now in charge, under Himmler, of
all the terrorist bands in the Reich; and by Fegelein, the ignorant horse-fancier who was now Himmler's representative
at the Fuehrer's headquarters and had become an intimate
member of Hitler's family circle, as close and regular in his
attendance as Bormann and Burgdorf. These were the "Southern" party, the diehards who advocated resistance, who hated
compromise and frothed in loud ignorance about a glorious
Goetterdaemmerung in the Alps, while the "Northerners"
like Speer and Schellenberg preferred to think in terms of
political compromise. Nevertheless Schellenberg now felt

strong enough to take the risk. "So you are demanding that I depose the Fuehrer?" asked Himmler. "Yes," replied Schellenberg. The issue was now clear, and the conversations continued on a new level.

"In the course of these conversations," says Schellenberg, "Himmler often spoke of Hitler's declining health. To my rejoinder, How then was he still able to exert such influence?, Himmler replied that his energy was undiminished, although the completely unnatural life he led, turning night into day and sleeping only a few hours, his continuous activity, and his constant outbursts of fury completely exhausted his *entourage* and created an unbearable atmosphere. I often suggested that perhaps the Plot of the 20th July had after all injured Hitler's health, in particular his head. Himmler thought this possible. He mentioned especially the constant stoop, the pale visage, the increased trembling of Hitler's left arm, and the operation on his ear, which took place in November, obviously a result of the concussion he had received."

These statements of Himmler, not strictly accurate, as can be seen, opened a new line of argument to the resourceful Schellenberg. At the beginning of April, he applied to his friend Professor de Crinis, director of the Psychological Department of the Charité, for information about Hitler's health. De Crinis was not one of the doctors who had actually attended Hitler, but in medical circles he had doubtless heard of the conjectures of those who had. "In my opinion," he replied, "Hitler's completely crippled movements, which I have observed in news films, are the visible signs of Parkinson's disease." At the mention of that exciting name Schellenberg's spirits rose. He arranged a meeting between Himmler and de Crinis, to which Himmler brought the Reich Health Leader, Conti,—perhaps the completest charlatan of all the Nazi doctors. De Crinis expounded again his notions of Hitler's condition and the symptoms of Parkinson's disease; and the Reichsfuehrer, he afterwards reported, "listened with great interest and considerable understanding."

Several days later, on 13th April, Himmler summoned Schellenberg to his headquarters in the old Ziethen castle in Wustrow, and there, for an hour and a half, they walked together in the flowering woods. "Schellenberg," said Himmler, "I believe nothing more can be done with Hitler. Do you think de Crinis is right?" Schellenberg replied that he had not seen Hitler for two years, "but from everything I have seen of his actions recently, I am inclined to think that the last moment for you to act has come." They digressed to matters of detail: the Jewish question; new contacts abroad; new negotiations in Schellenberg's ever more delicate diplomacy.

"Himmler was in great mental distress. Even openly he had been almost completely abandoned by the Fuehrer; for Hitler had ordered the *Leibstandarte Adolf Hitler* to remove their arm bands as a dishonouring punishment.[4] He said that except perhaps Standartenfuehrer Dr. Brandt,[5] I was the only man he could completely trust. What should he do? He could not kill Hitler, could not poison him or arrest him in the Chancellery, or the whole military machine would come to a stand-

[4] This refers to one of Hitler's most outrageous acts of spite towards his army. The *Leibstandarte Adolf Hitler* was a division of the *Waffen* S.S., and at this time was fighting on the upper Danube with the 6th S.S. Panzer Army, under the command of Hitler's gangster-favourite Sepp Dietrich. The *LAH* was ordered to attack according to Hitler's strategical plans, but owing to an error in the weather forecast, the attack was timed to take place on a day of torrential rain. Hitler's plan was nevertheless regarded as sacred; the attack was made; and a disastrous massacre was the consequence. When this failure was reported to Hitler, he was furious with the *LAH*, and ordered them to remove their armbands as a punishment. The indignant soldiers tore off their orders and decorations, and sent them to Hitler, through Himmler, in a tin chamber-pot. They also sent the arm, complete with armband, of one of their dead comrades. This order of Hitler was never rescinded, and the soldiers never forgave Himmler and Sepp Dietrich, who, though equally insulted by the gesture, had been unable to prevent it.

[5] *i.e.* Dr. Rudolf Brandt, Himmler's secretary, not to be confused with Dr. Karl Brandt, formerly Hitler's surgeon.

still. I explained that all this was of no importance. There were only two possibilities. Either he could go to Hitler, tell him openly of the events of the last two years, and persuade him to resign. . . . 'Quite impossible!' retorted Himmler, 'he would fall into one of his rages, and shoot me out of hand!' 'Then you must protect yourself against this,' I said. 'You have enough high S.S. leaders who can carry out a surprise arrest; or if there is no other way, the doctors must intervene.' "

To these suggestions Himmler made no answer. He was prepared to contemplate, in the abstract, such drastic measures, but Schellenberg had not yet so changed his attitude of mind that he would actually decide upon a course of action, far less embark on one. When the walk was over, all that Himmler would say was that he would like to bring together, with one of his own representatives, Professor de Crinis, Professor Morell, Dr. Stumpfegger, and Bormann. Nothing could better illustrate the unreality of Himmler's ideas, or the essential naïvete of Schellenberg in thinking that Himmler could ever be a conspirator. Morell and Bormann lived entirely by Hitler. Their power rested on no political independence, no private armies, no personal indispensability. As for Stumpfegger, though Himmler may have thought that he was still loyal to his old patrons at Hohenlychen, in fact he was already burning incense at the new shrine in the Reich Chancellery. These men were not going to declare Hitler incapable and enable Himmler to put him quietly aside. In fact de Crinis did do as he was told. He consulted Stumpfegger about Hitler's health. But Stumpfegger could not agree that the Fuehrer was suffering from Parkinson's disease; and although de Crinis offered to make up some medicines which, Stumpfegger agreed, might do the Fuehrer some good, Stumpfegger unfortunately never sent round to collect them. Indeed, why should he? He was a surgeon, not a physician; and after the experience of Brandt he was much too wise to interfere in the business of Morell.

Frustrated once again, Schellenberg now remembered an-

other collaborator who might come to his help and persuade
Himmler to act. He arranged for Himmler to meet, on 19th
April, Count Lutz Schwerin von Krosigk, Hitler's minister of
finance. But before descending down the scale of ineptitude
to Count Schwerin von Krosigk, the narrative must return to
Berlin.

For Hitler was now back in Berlin, facing the last desperate
battle of the war. From Bad Nauheim, in December, he had
directed his last counter-attack in the west, the Ardennes
offensive; it had failed, and the Western Allies were now
across the Rhine. He had turned east and massed divisions for
a counter-attack against the Russians on the Danube; it had
failed, and the Russians were now over the Oder and on the
upper Elbe. Now, in his underground bunker beneath the
Reich Chancellery, he was directing the final operations.
All his staff, all his court knew inwardly that the war
was lost; some of them had known it for years; but he continued to believe in his star, in Providence, and in his own
indispensability. He was more indispensable than ever now,
for there was now no successor. The decree appointing
Goering as his successor was still valid, but Goering was completely out of favour and almost forgotten.[6] Bormann's monopoly of the internal affairs of the Reich and Himmler's control
of the S.S. suggested their claims, but no formal announcement consecrated their aspirations. The military leaders were
of course out of the question since 20th July; only compliant
toadies had survived the suspicion that now attached to their
whole order. In a discussion with his secretaries in March
1945 Hitler admitted that in the matter of the succession he

---

[6] In January 1945, Lammers (head of the Reich Chancery) asked Bormann
whether Hitler might be willing to reconsider the question of the succession,
since Goering had fallen into disrepute. Bormann replied, "If the question
had not already been settled, I do not think the Fuehrer would now nomi-
nate the Reich Marshal; but I do not think he will change the appointment
he has once made. Let us drop the matter." (Statement by Lammers.)

had failed utterly. Hess, he said, had gone mad; Goering, thanks to his style of life and the failure of the Luftwaffe, had been rejected by the German people; as for Himmler, who seemed the obvious third choice, whose very title of Reichs-fuehrer was supposed by many to denote the predestined successor to the crown,—he, said Hitler, would never do: he was on bad terms with the Party (that is, with Bormann), "and anyway useless, since he is so completely inartistic." He did not know whom he could choose, and in consequence he chose no one. At this time Hitler of course did not know that Himmler was preparing to deny him, and that Speer had already denied him; but he felt the atmosphere of treachery everywhere. Fortunately he also had the company of those two creatures whom he believed to be exempt from that spreading infection—Blondi and Eva Braun.

"For all writers of history," says Speer, "Eva Braun is going to be a disappointment"; and for readers of history too. She had none of the colourful qualities of the conventional tyrant's mistress. She was neither a Theodora, nor a Pompadour, nor a Lola Montez. But then neither was Hitler a typical tyrant. Behind his impassioned rages, his enormous ambitions, his gigantic self-confidence, there lay not the indulgent ease of a voluptuary, but the trivial tastes, the conventional domesticity, of the petty-bourgeois. One cannot forget the cream buns. It was to this permanent, if submerged element in his character that Eva Braun appealed; and because she appealed to the triviality not the extravagancy of his nature, she is herself uninteresting. Indeed, the most interesting fact about her is probably the well-kept secrecy of her existence; for their friendship had lasted at least twelve years, and both parties were dead before the knowledge of it was extended beyond their immediate circle. A conspiracy of silence surrounded her life; the servants were forbidden to speak to her; and her picture was expurgated from photographs of the Fuehrer before they could be published or circulated.

Eva Braun's introduction to Hitler had been effected, like Morell's, through the photographer Hoffmann, in whose business she worked. Pretty rather than beautiful, with a fresh colour and slightly high cheekbones, unobtrusive, uninterfering, anxious to please, she soon achieved an ascendancy over Hitler, supplying that ideal of restfulness which was so lacking to his political life, but for which his bourgeois soul so hankered. In her company Hitler found the rest which elsewhere he never sought; and she in turn, by providing a domestic retreat, and never seeking to influence him in external, political matters, lubricated the routine of his harsh, distempered life. Good at ski-ing and mountain-climbing, fond of dancing (which she had studied professionally), passing for erudite among that ignorant clique, eager to discuss books and pictures, and to help Hitler in his purchase of *objets d'art*, she fitted well into the Alpine, "artistic" world of Berchtesgaden to which, for the most part, she was confined; for it was only in the last two years of his life that Hitler allowed her to come to Berlin. In his affection for her Hitler never wavered; she had no rival; [7] the blowsy Nordic actresses whom Goebbels introduced to the Chancellery for the sake of publicity never interested him. In general indeed, Hitler seems to have been frightened of women; he was afraid they would interfere in politics, and he dreaded "petticoat politics,"—although the politics of an absolute court are not very different. In this matter Eva Braun was safe. She confined her attentions to the intervals of politics, presiding over the tea-cups and keeping the politicians away during the few hours of relaxation. All praised her moderation. In spite of all her temptations and

[7] Not even the mysterious Olga, whose name was discovered on the door of the room "next to Hitler's private apartment" in the temporary headquarters of the OKW at Ohrdruf in Thuringia. When Ohrdruf was captured, imaginative journalists speculated eloquently about Olga, her style of beauty, her influence on Hitler, and the nature of her meditations on the balcony of her room. Unfortunately she never existed. "Olga" was simply the code-name for the signals office at Ohrdruf; nor was Ohrdruf ever visited by Hitler.

opportunities, she exploited none of them, which makes her even duller. Though she disliked Bormann, she never sought to influence Hitler against him; and Hitler would not have tolerated it if she had. In his turn Hitler fussed over her, over her health and her habits and her safety. She was not allowed to fly, or to drive a car faster than forty miles an hour.

Of their more intimate relations nothing is known. "They slept in different beds," says the odious Dr. Morell, "nevertheless, I believe . . ." But the mere beliefs of Dr. Morell are irrelevant. Hitler enjoyed in their relationship what he considered its idealism; "many years of true friendship" was how he described it in his will; and in order not to mar it by conversation on such base but necessary subjects as cash, he established her independence by granting her, with Hoffmann, a monopoly of the sale of his photographs. Nevertheless there were undoubtedly inhibitions about her status. The servants, who referred to her always as "E.B.," dropped their voices when they mentioned her; and even now, when the whole affair is of merely historical interest, continue to do so. For over twelve years she had no admitted status: she was neither wife nor acknowledged mistress; and this ambiguity of her position induced, or increased, in her the symptoms of an inferiority complex, showing itself in the appearance of haughtiness and conceit. It was probably from this cause, too, that other unattractive features derived; for her letters and diaries show signs of mental and psychological immaturity, of schoolgirl melodrama. When Hitler was absent, or when she did not see him often enough, she would strike rhetorical attitudes and threaten suicide. But these are matters of taste, in which, perhaps, he himself did not set a perfect example.

Since Hitler undoubtedly loved her, one cannot avoid asking why he kept her for so long in this undefined and evidently embarrassing position. Though the details of their relationship will probably always remain an enigma the easiest answer may perhaps be correct. If their relations were, or

were meant to be understood as platonic, then the position of
either wife or mistress would have been meaningless and compromising. Certainly a platonic relationship would have been
most appropriate to the German Messiah, the revolutionary
spirit who seemed, and must seem, to transcend all human
limitations. If this answer is correct, the marriage which ultimately took place on the eve of their death is of purely symbolic significance; without some definition of her status, Eva
Braun had no better right to share in the ritual death of the
Fuehrer than his secretaries, or Fraeulein Manzialy, the vegetarian cook, who shared Hitler's meals with him in her absence.
But that final act Eva Braun was determined not to miss. As
the battle approached Berlin, Hitler had sent her away to
Munich; but she would not stay there. On 15th April, when
the capital was already preparing for a siege, she arrived un-
bidden at the Reich Chancellery. Hitler ordered her to leave,
but she would not go. She had come for her wedding, and
her ceremonial death.

Of the political atmosphere in Berlin in these last days we
happen to possess a document of unusual and ironical interest.
It is the diary of Count Lutz Schwerin von Krosigk, the friend
in whom the indefatigable Schellenberg now misplaced his
hopes. Schwerin von Krosigk, like Schellenberg, was one of
those conscientiously cultured Germans who, by their efforts
to identify themselves with western civilisation, only show
how completely they misunderstand it. Schwerin von Krosigk
had used every opportunity of understanding the West; he
had even been a Rhodes scholar at Oxford. But he had acquired none of its values. Though he spoke its language, he
neither thought its thoughts nor acted its actions. Just as
Schellenberg deplored the Nordic nonsense and gaseous metaphysics in which the true German felt at home, and carefully
warned Himmler, when talking to educated Swedes, "not to
speak of the *Karma* between the two peoples, nor of *Weltan-
schauung*, etc.," but would himself solemnly vaporise about

"what I like to call the cosmic outcome of the event"; so Schwerin von Krosigk, for all his careful education, was continually striking operatic attitudes, and losing himself in cloudy German rhetoric. Like Schellenberg, he was also completely unrealistic. Indeed, the two form a perfect pair, the Tweedledum and Tweedledee of pretentious German silliness. The truth is that, as some sage philosopher has observed, one cannot touch pitch and be undefiled; and both Schellenberg and Schwerin von Krosigk were long-standing members of the Nazi administration. Their belief that they could preserve their independence within it, could influence it for good, and could be accepted as themselves anti-Nazi or at least non-Nazi, only showed the extent of their blindness. All Nazis misunderstood foreign politics; it was left to the Schellenbergs and Schwerin von Krosigks to misunderstand Nazi politics as well. It was perhaps because he misunderstood them so thoroughly that Schwerin von Krosigk was able to survive among them for so long. Certainly he showed a genius for survival. He had been a minister before the Nazis came to power in 1933; he was a minister throughout the Nazi era; the new government recommended to Doenitz in Hitler's political testament still includes his name; a place was reserved for him in the shadow government projected by Himmler; and though this project never materialised, Schwerin von Krosigk had his consolation. When Doenitz set up his administration, though he refused to be bound by Hitler's will, and rejected every other name contained in it, he appointed as his foreign minister (it was his only appointment) Count Schwerin von Krosigk.

Schwerin von Krosigk kept his diary for two periods in this long but inconspicuous political career: in the winter of 1932-3, when the Nazis were climbing to power, and in April 1945, when they were collapsing in ruin. He kept it (he has stated) not, as might have been expected, to acquaint posterity with the events of those historic times, but "so that my descendants may know what kind of a man it was who was a member of the Reich cabinet during the years of Germany's greatest rise and deepest decline." If posterity concludes that Schwerin von Krosigk was a ninny, he has only himself to blame for that deliberate revelation.

The second part of the diary begins on the 15th April 1945, but goes back a few days to describe an important incident. Goebbels told Schwerin von Krosigk how he had recently been reading aloud to the Fuehrer, to solace him in his universal discomfiture. He was reading from his favourite book, Carlyle's *History of Frederick the Great*; and the chapter he was reading described "how the great king himself no longer saw any way out of his difficulties, no longer had any plan; how all his generals and ministers were convinced that his downfall was at hand; how the enemy was already counting Prussia as destroyed; how the future hung dark before him, and in his last letter to his minister, Count Finckenstein,[8] he gave himself one last respite: if there was no change by February 15th, he would give it up and take poison. 'Brave king!' says Carlyle, 'wait yet a little while, and the days of your suffering will be over. Already the sun of your good fortune stands behind the clouds, and soon will rise upon you.' On February 12th the Czarina died; the Miracle of the House of Brandenburg had come to pass." At this touching tale, said Goebbels, "tears stood in the Fuehrer's eyes." They discussed the matter to and fro, and in the course of the discussion sent for two horoscopes that were carefully kept in one of Himmler's research departments: the horoscope of the Fuehrer, drawn up on 30th January 1933, and the horoscope of the Republic, dated 9th September 1918. These sacred documents were fetched and examined, and "an astonishing fact" was discovered, which might well have repaid an earlier scrutiny.

[8] Schwerin von Krosigk has not quoted either Carlyle or the facts correctly. The minister to whom Frederick wrote was in fact Count d'Argenson.

"Both horoscopes had unanimously predicted the outbreak of war in 1939, the victories till 1941, and then the series of defeats culminating in the worst disasters in the early months of 1945, especially the first half of April. Then there was to be an overwhelming victory for us in the second half of April, stagnation till August, and in August peace. After the peace there would be a difficult time for Germany for three years; but from April 1948 she would rise to greatness again. Next day Goebbels sent me the horoscopes. I could not fathom everything in them; but in the subjoined interpretation, newly drawn up, I found it all; and now I am eagerly awaiting the second half of April."

Such were the incidents which enlivened the dreary hours of waiting in the underground Bunker of the Reich Chancellery. The horoscopes, which had so accurately prophesied the past, were less reliable for the future, and Schwerin von Krosigk waited in vain for the resounding victory which was to brighten the second half of April; but the reading from Carlyle had a sequel which deserves to be recorded.

A few days later, after a long and heavy air raid on Berlin, Schwerin von Krosigk was sitting up after midnight, drinking wine with some friends, when he learned that the last powder factory in Germany had been evacuated by order of the General Staff. The end must now be near, his friends agreed; "without ammunition even the bravest soldiers cannot fight." "Would this really be the end," asks the rhetorical diarist, "which my reason had so long seen as inevitable, but which my spirit had striven so hard not to see? At that moment the telephone rang; the state-secretary wished to speak to me. What could he want at so late an hour? He only uttered one short sentence: 'Roosevelt is dead.' We felt the wings of the Angel of History rustle through the room. Could this be the long-desired change of fortune?" Next morning Schwerin von Krosigk called Goebbels on the telephone to congratulate him on this signal event,—and not only to congratulate, but to advise. For Schwerin von Krosigk, like Schellenberg, was a very subtle man; he always saw the fine shades, the slight nuances, imperceptible to less sensitive observers; and he was afraid that, unadvised by him, the somewhat crude German Press might miss its golden opportunity. He suggested to Goebbels that the new President should not be abused, nor yet too obviously praised, but that the differences between him and Roosevelt should be judiciously emphasised. Goebbels indicated politely that the Ministry had already considered these points, and that the necessary instructions had been given. Then Goebbels described how yesterday he had been at General Busse's headquarters at Kuestrin, and how in the evening he had sat with the officers of Busse's staff and "had developed his thesis that, for reasons of Historical Necessity and Justice, a change of fortune was inevitable, like the Miracle of the House of Brandenburg in the Seven Years War. One of the staff officers had somewhat sceptically and ironically asked, What Czarina will die this time? That, Goebbels had replied, he could not say; but Fate still held many possibilities in her hand. Then he had driven home, and had heard the news of Roosevelt's death. Immediately, he had telephoned to Busse, and said, 'The Czarina is dead.' Busse had told him that this made a great impression on his soldiers; now they saw another chance. Goebbels believed that this news would awaken a new spirit of hope in the whole German people; they would surely see in it the power of Historical Necessity and Justice. . . . I [says the sententious Count] interrupted, 'Say rather, of God'. . . ."

Schwerin von Krosigk is so fond of rhetoric and apostrophe, so free with abstract nouns, and so prone to hear the wings of the Angel of History rustling about him, that his account may seem overdrawn; but we happen to have indirect confirmation from another quite independent source: from one of the secretaries in the Propaganda Ministry.[9] "I well remember Friday April 13th," she says. "Every week Goebbels paid a visit to the Eastern Front to address the troops, taking them supplies of cigarettes, cognac, and books. On this day he had been to Kuestrin. . . . While he was on his way back to Berlin by motor-car, we received the news of the death of President Roosevelt. Goebbels, as usual, returned very late at night. A very heavy bombardment was going on and the Chancellery and the Adlon Hotel were burning. We met Goebbels on the steps of the Propaganda Ministry. A reporter said to him, 'Herr Reich Minister, Roosevelt is dead.' Goebbels jumped up out of his car and stood for a moment as if transfixed. I shall never forget the look on his face, which we could see in the light of Berlin blazing. 'Now,' he said, 'bring out our best champagne and let us have a telephone talk with the Fuehrer.' We went into his study, and champagne was served. Goebbels spoke to Hitler on his private line, and said, 'My Fuehrer, I congratulate you! Roosevelt is dead. It is written in the stars that the second half of April will be the turning-point for us. This is Friday, April the 13th. It is the turning-point!' Hitler said something to him, and then Goebbels put down the receiver. He was in an ecstasy." [10]

To us it seems incredible that in these last days of the Third Reich its leaders should have thought that the stars, or a stroke of subtlety, could save them; nevertheless all the evidence is clear that they never understood the real certainty of their ruin. Isolated for twelve years behind a Chinese wall of political and intellectual self-sufficiency, they had long ceased to understand, if they had ever understood, the politics, the ideas, the habits of mind of other nations. Not one of the German

[9] Frau Inge Haberzettel, who worked in the same room with Goebbels' secretary, Fraeulein Hildebrandt. I am indebted to Mr. Leslie Randall, correspondent of the *Evening Standard*, for this report.
[10] Both Steengracht, an official in the German Foreign Office, who gave evidence for Ribbentrop at Nuremberg, and Speer have also mentioned Goebbels' exhilaration on hearing of the death of Roosevelt.

leaders could appreciate that whatever political or diplomatic differences might be concealed beneath the surface of the Grand Alliance, all the members of it were determined that these should not interfere with the defeat of Germany, and that no diplomatic or other arrangement was conceivable until the Nazi Government was destroyed. We read with incredulity of the elaborate unreality of Schellenberg, of the naïve consolations of Schwerin von Krosigk, of the astrological assurances of Goebbels and Himmler. At this time, when the armies of East and West had almost cut Germany in two, Goebbels was still saying that the inevitable breach between the Russians and the Anglo-Americans was so near (presumably for reasons of Historical Necessity and Justice) that the German Government need only wait in Berlin and let it mature. But the most striking, most conclusive proof of the fools' paradise in which these men were living is the eagerness with which these doomed marionettes were still competing for the dwindling fragments of power. The succession to Hitler was still undetermined, still legally vested in Goering. By now, one would have thought, it was an uncoveted heritage. Not at all. Himmler still took it for granted that it would be his, though he still flinched from Schellenberg's suggestion that he should hasten its devolution. Bormann still schemed at the centre of affairs, distilling his subtle poison in his master's ear and ruining, whenever he could, his rivals. Goebbels was now intriguing for the post of Foreign Minister in the place of Ribbentrop.[11] Only Ribbentrop was unconcerned in these feverish intrigues; for Ribbentrop had now no party, no supporters, with whom to combine in the incalculable politics of the court. All the others, bitter rivals in all else, were agreed upon one thing: Ribbentrop must go. It was the cry alike of Goering and Himmler, of Goebbels and Bormann, of Speer and Schellenberg and Schwerin von Krosigk. Not long ago they had sung it in harmonious chorus to Hitler himself; but

[11] Schwerin von Krosigk.

Hitler had replied that they misjudged Ribbentrop's ability: he was a "a second Bismarck" and could not be spared; and Ribbentrop's dearest wish, at this important juncture, was at last gratified: a picture was published in the Press showing the Foreign Minister at the Front.[12]

Throughout these days of intrigue and conspiracy, Schellenberg and Schwerin von Krosigk, having once met,[13] were cementing their alliance. Each was favourably impressed with the other. Schellenberg found the Count well-informed about foreign and especially English affairs; the Count found Schellenberg "young, very able, and sympathetic." They had several conversations together. They agreed that some attempt must be made to open negotiations with the West. Together they deplored Ribbentrop. On a theoretical level only one difficulty obstructed their aspirations. Schwerin von Krosigk insisted that any foreign powers with which they might negotiate must of course understand that although the other Nazi leaders would at once be jettisoned, Hitler and Himmler were indispensable and must stay; they were the only guarantees against chaos. Unfortunately, foreigners seemed to regard Hitler and Himmler as the most objectionable of all. . . . Gently Schellenberg prepared his ground. It was true, he admitted, that Himmler's name had unfortunate associations abroad. He was blamed for many things which were done under his name but not under his orders (this gentle phrase referred doubtless to Belsen and Buchenwald). But Schellenberg was doing his best to remedy this misunderstanding. For a long time he had seen seeking, by subtle means, to influence the Foreign Press in his favour. . . . Would Schwerin von Krosigk agree to meet Himmler? There was a difficulty of

[12] Speer; Schwerin von Krosigk; and cf. Bernadotte, *The Curtain Falls*, p. 39, who also indicates that in the spring of 1945 Ribbentrop apparently "still had Hitler's ear and enjoyed his support."

[13] Through the intermediacy of Schellenberg's subordinate, Ottfried Dewitz.

course,—the two had quarrelled earlier in the year; but Schellenberg could smoothe that over. Of Hitler Schellenberg said nothing. He had no interest in sweetening that reputation.

On 19th April the formalities had been arranged and Himmler and Schwerin von Krosigk had a long conversation together at the Count's house. The Count had been well briefed by Schellenberg. He urged upon Himmler the necessity of negotiation with the West; for the German people could only be asked to continue its heroic resistance if the respite thus gained were used to find a solution. But how could such negotiations be carried on? asked Himmler. Schwerin von Krosigk was full of resource. There were numerous possibilities, he explained. First there was the Pope. The Roman Catholics in America were a large, compact bloc, while the Protestants were divided into multiple, ineffective sects. If the Pope were to be got at . . . Then there was Dr. Burckhardt, head of the European Red Cross, and Dr. Salazar in Portugal, and all kinds of useful business men and travelling professors. And then there was always the impending breach between East and West. But what of Hitler? objected Himmler. That was indeed a difficult problem, Schwerin von Krosigk admitted, a psychological riddle. "However high-flying his plans may be, the Fuehrer is after all a man, standing with both feet on the ground; he can see the position in black and white; surely he has no illusions? What then, I ask myself, is he waiting for?" Himmler fidgeted uneasily. The Fuehrer had some plan, he said vaguely, and was doubtless right; he himself was also convinced that all would be well in the end. It was not a rational belief, he agreed; it was an instinctive conviction. Did Schwerin von Krosigk realise that Himmler was no longer an uninstructed heathen, but believed in God and Providence? So he told him the story of the miracles that had converted him—of the Fuehrer's escape of 20th July 1944, and of the thaw on the Oder. Thus Schwerin von Krosigk had fared no better than Schellenberg in his conversations with Himmler.

He had no sooner drawn towards the crux of the problem than Himmler had slid away under vague, irrelevant generalities, and the conversation ended leaving everything exactly as before.

When Himmler and Schwerin von Krosigk had finished, they joined Schellenberg and the Count's friend Seldte [14] outside. These two had also been discussing the same problem, but, as usual, had travelled a little further than their superiors. They had decided that Himmler should take over the power of the state and force Hitler, on his birthday (that was, tomorrow), to broadcast a manifesto to the German people, announcing the end of the single party and the People's Courts, and promising elections. When Himmler emerged, Seldte appealed to him to use his influence with the Fuehrer and to negotiate for peace. It was no longer a personal matter, he protested; "the biological substance of the German people" was at stake. There could be no doubt of the origin of those words; it was one of Schellenberg's favourite phrases. In the car, as they returned from Schwerin von Krosigk's house, Schellenberg again took up his familiar theme. He also urged upon Himmler the virtues of Schwerin von Krosigk,—the only man, he assured him, fit to be Foreign Minister in Himmler's government.

Thus through Schwerin von Krosigk and Seldte, as through Kersten and Wulf, Schellenberg ceaselessly urged Himmler to detach himself from Hitler, to depose Hitler, if necessary to murder Hitler, and to open negotiations with the West. Naturally a sanguine man, confident of his skill and ignorant of reality, with each new effort he believed that he was nearing his goal. But the evidence is clear against him. Himmler was as obstinately undecided as ever, suspended between loyalty and doubt. That night, at midnight, he sent for cham-

[14] Seldte was formerly leader of the *Stahlhelm*. Like Schwerin von Krosigk, he was a skilful survivor, having been *Reichsarbeitminister* since 1933.

pagne to toast the Fuehrer; for it was now the Fuehrer's birthday. When Schellenberg heard the order, he left the house. He could not participate in such a ceremony. He set out on his way to Harzwalde, the estate of his ally Kersten, there to continue his desperate, incessant machinations.

Chapter Four

CRISIS AND DECISION
(20TH-24TH APRIL)

APRIL the 20th was Hitler's birthday; and Germans were reminded of the fact by a broadcast speech from Goebbels, calling upon them to trust blindly in the Fuehrer and the stars, who together would lead them out of their present difficulties. On that day Hitler had planned to leave Berlin for Obersalzberg, thence, from the fabulous mountain cave of Barbarossa, to direct the battles for the south. Ten days ago, he had sent his servants before him to prepare the house for his reception.[1] But in those ten days disaster had followed disaster. "All through the week," says Schwerin von Krosigk, "there was nothing but a succession of Job's messengers." Germany was now almost cut in two; only a narrow corridor of land divided the Americans, already over the Elbe, from the Russians, already over the Oder and Neisse and threatening both Dresden and Berlin. In the north, the British were in the outskirts of Bremen and Hamburg; in the south, the French were on the upper Danube, the Russians in Vienna. In Italy, the armies of Field-Marshal Alexander had captured Bologna and were pouring into the valley of the Po. And in the heart of the Reich, General Patton was thrusting south through Bavaria, the cradle of the Nazi movement, towards the Alps, its intended grave.

Hitler's headquarters were in the Reich Chancellery, the vast mausoleum which he had built to house his pride and awe his tributary kings. The huge rooms, with their vast slabs of

[1] Statement by Artur Kannenberg.

106

porphyry and marble, their ponderous doors and multiple candelabra, were now disused. Bombed out and burnt, they had been abandoned as offices and were only manned as a command post. But underneath the old Chancellery and the garden, fifty feet below the ground, a bunker had been built during the war. It could be reached from within the Chancellery, by stairs leading down through the butler's pantry. At the foot of these stairs was a narrow space enclosed by three air-tight, water-tight bulkheads. One of these bulkheads closed the passage to the butler's pantry, or "Kannenberg-alley" [2] as it was called (Artur Kannenberg was Hitler's butler); the second led to an outer stair with access to the garden of the Foreign Office; the third led into the Bunker.[3] The Bunker was in two parts. The first part consisted of twelve rooms, none larger than a large cupboard, six on each side of a central passage. These were lumber rooms and servants' quarters, and included the *Diaetkueche* or vegetarian kitchen where Hitler's meals were prepared. At the end of the central passage, which was now used as a general dining-place for the shelterers, a curved stair led downwards to a still deeper and slightly larger bunker. This was the *Fuehrerbunker*, Hitler's own bunker, the stage on which the last act of the Nazi melodrama was played out. Contracted within these narrow limits, it could at least preserve the essential dramatic unities of Boileau.

The Fuehrerbunker consisted of eighteen rooms, all of them small, cramped, and uncomfortable, and a central passage. There could be no greater contrast than that between the Egyptian vastity of the rooms of the new Chancellery, which trembling ambassadors had taken, as it seemed, a fragment of eternity to cross, and these miserable underground hutches in which the diminished court now paid its less elaborate but still servile homage. The central passage was divided in two by a

[2] *Kannenberggang.*
[3] For a plan of the Bunker see p. 108.

KEY TO PLAN OF HITLER'S BUNKER

1-4   *Diaetkueche* (Kitchen, scullery, etc.).
5-6   Lumber rooms.
7-8   Servants' quarters.
9-12 Frau Goebbels' and children's rooms.
13   Electric light switchboard.
14   W.C.s.
15   Private bathroom.
16   Eva Braun's dressing-room.
17   Eva Braun's bed-sitting room.
18   Hitler's study.
19   Anteroom to Hitler's suite.
20   Hitler's bedroom.
21   "Map room" or small conference room.
22   "Dog bunker" or guards' rest room.
23   Power house (Diesel engine).
24   Telephone and guard room (also used by secretaries).
25   Emergency telephone exchange
26   Drawing room.
27   Goebbels' bedroom (previously used by Morell).
28-29 Stumpfegger's rooms.
30   Anteroom and cloakroom.

partition. On the near side of the partition, it was used as a general sitting-room, and the rooms to which it gave access were utilitarian offices, the lavatories and guard-room, the emergency telephone exchange and the power-house. Beyond the partition was the holy of holies. There the central passage became the conference room in which Hitler presided over the daily staff conferences. A door on the left led into a suite of six rooms, the private apartments of Hitler and Eva Braun. Eva Braun had a bed-sitting-room, a bathroom, and a dressing-room; Hitler a bedroom and a study. The sixth was an ante-room. Two other doors on the left led into a small "map-room," used for small conferences, and a narrow cupboard known as the "Dog-bunker," [4] and now used as a rest-room for the personal detectives who guarded the Fuehrer. At the end of this Dog-bunker a ladder gave access to an unfinished concrete observation tower above the ground. On the right of the passage were the rooms occupied by Hitler's two doctors, Morell and Stumpfegger, and Stumpfegger's first-aid room. At the beginning of April Hitler had ordered Stumpfegger to set up a dressing station in the Chancellery, for the casualties of the fighting, and Stumpfegger had fetched his surgical equipment from his old hospital at Hohenlychen. This dressing station was not in the Bunker, but under the new Chancellery; the surgery in the Fuehrerbunker was his personal store.

At the end of the passage, a door led into a small ante-room, used as a cloakroom; and thence four flights of concrete steps led up again into the Chancellery garden. This was the emergency exit.

Apart from the Fuehrerbunker, there were other underground bunkers within the complex of the government buildings. There was the bunker of the Party Chancellery, where Bormann and his staff lived, with the service officers and S.S. guards, and a third bunker which housed S.S. Brigadefuehrer Mohnke, the commandant of the Chancellery, and his staff; while Goebbels and his staff sheltered in the cellars of the Propaganda Ministry. From all these bunkers, officers and officials came daily to the Fuehrerbunker for the continuous conferences that took place in the narrow central passage.

[4] *Hundebunker.*

Jodl and Keitel also came thither from their headquarters at
Zossen or Potsdam; but the new chief of the Army General
Staff remained with Hitler in Berlin. He was General Hans
Krebs, who had recently succeeded Guderian; and he is de-
scribed as "a smooth, surviving type." [5]

To this subterranean bunker, then, on 20th April, came
some usual and some unusual visitors, bringing their formal
and for the most part insincere congratulations on the
Fuehrer's birthday. From noon onwards they came and went,
and the day was taken up by receptions, speeches, and conferences. In spite of the catastrophic situation, they found the
Fuehrer still confident; the Russians, he still believed, were
going to suffer their bloodiest defeat of all before Berlin. In
the Chancellery garden he received a delegation of boys from
the Hitler Youth, under their leader Artur Axmann, and in
the presence of Himmler, Goering, and Goebbels (but no
soldiers were there to overshadow these young warriors) he
thanked and decorated them for their efforts in this now decisive battle. Then he withdrew to his small conference room
and received, singly, and in turn, Doenitz, Keitel, Jodl. The
rest were then lined up in his presence, and he shook hands
and spoke with all. To Keitel he was particularly affable. "I
will never forget you," he said; "I will never forget that you
saved me on the occasion of the Plot, and that you got me out
of Rastenburg.[6] Those were the right decisions, and the right
actions, for the times." Among others present on this last
ceremonial occasion were Bormann, Ribbentrop, and Speer.

After the receptions came the conference. The great question before the conference concerned the imminent threat to
the geographical unity of the Reich. In a few days, perhaps

[5] By Speer. Captured German generals are agreed in describing Krebs as
able but time-serving, a complete toady to Hitler. He had served for a long
time in Moscow before the war,—which may account for his last mission to
Marshal Zhukov (see below p. 209).

[6] On 20th July 1944 Hitler had fallen into Keitel's arm (see above p. 29;
and cf. p. 65.) Hitler's words on this occasion are reported by Keitel.

hours, the last land route to the south would have been cut. Would Hitler, or would he not, move his headquarters to the south, whither all the service headquarters and ministries had gone or were going? His advisers were unanimous that the Russian ring around the city would ultimately close; that once caught in it, there would be no escape; that the only alternative was to withdraw to the south, to Obersalzberg; and that such a withdrawal must be made now, while the road remained open, or perhaps never. Goering and Keitel, Himmler and Bormann, Goebbels, Krebs, and Burgdorf all entreated Hitler to leave the doomed city; but Hitler would neither agree nor disagree. The most he would do was to implement the decision reached ten days earlier against such a situation as had now arisen. Then it had been decided that if the Allied armies should cut the Reich in half, two separate commands should be set up in the two disconnected areas. In the north, Grand Admiral Doenitz, in the south Field-Marshal Kesselring should command all the German forces, unless Hitler himself chose to move his headquarters to one or other of the two theatres. Now Hitler decided to confer upon Doenitz full military powers in the north; but in regard to the south he still made no appointment. It was not that he distrusted Kesselring, or knew the truth,—that even this favourite field-marshal had now abandoned hope, and was meditating unconditional surrender.[7] Hitler simply had not yet made up his mind. Sooner or later he would decide,—or rather, as he put it, he would leave it to Providence to decide. For Hitler's indecisions were not, like Himmler's, a permanent state of mind; they were a preliminary to decision; and once he had declared his decision, it was as impossible for any other man to alter it, as it would have been futile to have sought to hasten

[7] The unconditional surrender of all German armies in Italy was actually negotiated by Kesselring's successor in Italy, General Vietinghoff, and SS General Wolff; but the first steps had been taken by Kesselring before his transfer. Kesselring and Schoerner were generally regarded as "Hitler's field marshals."

it. How he would decide, no one as yet could tell. When the conference was over, Bormann assured his secretary that in a day, or at most two days, Hitler and the rest of his staff would leave Berlin. Others were less certain. Colonel Nicolaus von Below, Hitler's air-force adjutant, who had worked with him for eight years, was convinced that now he would never leave.

After the conference the visitors left the Bunker, and a long convoy of lorries and airplanes led the general exodus from Berlin to Obersalzberg. Among those to leave were the high commanders of the Luftwaffe. They left with relief. In Obersalzberg at least they would be free from the endless insults, the impossible orders, the violent recriminations with which Hitler had recently received their every failure. "One or two Luftwaffe officers should be shot!" he would shout at some self-exculpating general; "then we would have a change!" "The entire Luftwaffe should be hanged!" he would scream down the telephone at the trembling General Koller, and bang the receiver on the hook. For the Luftwaffe had failed, failed utterly; and nothing now could reverse the consequences of its failure. With it, there left Berlin the author both of the Luftwaffe and of its failure, Hermann Goering. He took his leave of the Fuehrer on the evening of the 20th April. It was an icy farewell. They never met again. Behind him Goering left two of his senior officers, to maintain contact with the Fuehrer's headquarters: General Koller, his chief of staff, and General Christian, his chief of operations.[8] General Christian, a young and successful officer, had risen rapidly in the new and once favourite service; as his second wife, he had married Hitler's secretary, Fraeulein Gerda Daranowski; and he was now one of the domestic circle at court. General Koller was less young, less effective, and less

---

[8] Christian's correct title was *Chef Luftwaffenfeuhrungsstab*. Both Koller and Christian have supplied information on the events in which they participated.

favoured. On him would fall the accumulated insults, the continuous threats of the Fuehrer, which he, being a conscientious, nervous, and rather fussy old gentleman, would ceaselessly but fruitlessly deplore. Nevertheless he is of value in the reconstruction of this complicated story: for he was keeping a diary.

Another who left the Bunker on the night following Hitler's birthday conference was Albert Speer. For many weeks now Speer had been developing his plans for saving German industry, German plant, and German communications from the destructive policy of the Party. Everywhere his most trusted technicians, his industrialists and works managers, had been ordered to let the front roll over them; to stay at their post and then, when the tide was past, to preserve and reconstruct what they could under Allied control.[9] When Speer came to Berlin on 20th April, it was not solely to congratulate Hitler on his birthday. It was to argue his cause, the sole cause that now preoccupied him, the cause of saving not the German Government, or the German Army, or the Nazi Party, but the material inheritance of the German people. A week ago he had written a speech, which he intended to broadcast, on a suitable occasion, to the German nation. Now that the war was clearly drawing to its end, he dreaded the wilful holocaust with which the Party might signalise its downfall. In this speech, therefore, he announced that the war was lost and ordered the German people to hand over intact to the Allies all plants and factories, all concentration camps and prison camps, with their inmates. All demolition, all activity by the Werewolves, was to cease. A few days later, his speech still undelivered, Speer had visited the armies east of Berlin and had proposed to the generals that, when the time came for their retreat, they should by-pass Berlin on the north and south, without fighting for the city, thus reducing the destruc-

---

[9] Speer's account of his policy is confirmed by Koller and by Karl Kaufmann, Gauleiter of Hamburg.

tion and leaving Hitler to his fate; for he was now convinced
that his only public loyalty was to the German people, and
the sooner Hitler died the better. At the same time Speer suggested that, in course of their retreat, they should seize Radio
Werewolf at Koenigswusterhausen. From that station, appropriately, Speer would broadcast his speech. The generals
had agreed to these proposals. Now, on 20th April, he had
come to Berlin to dissuade Goebbels from his declared intention of destroying some hundred bridges in the Berlin area;
an act of destruction which would have paralysed the delivery of food to the city for a long time to come. Goebbels
ultimately yielded to his argument, and agreed that the *Volkssturm* should fight outside, not inside the city. The decision
was reported by Krebs to Hitler, and confirmed by him.

Successful in this, Speer now left for Hamburg. His plan
for broadcasting from Radio Werewolf now seemed less
feasible, and he was preparing an alternative scheme. At Hamburg he met his friend Kaufmann, the Gauleiter. Together
they made arrangements for the preservation of the plant and
bridges of Hamburg. Then Speer told Kaufmann about the
speech, the text of which was still in his pocket. Kaufmann
approved of both the plan and the text; and together they
agreed that Speer should have the speech recorded at Hamburg radio station. In the underground studio of the radio
station Speer uneasily delivered this treasonable oration before
two unknown officials. Before beginning, he told them to consider it as they listened, and at the end to decide whether the
record should be kept or destroyed. They listened impassively,
and at the end, since they made no objection, Speer took the
record and deposited it with Kaufmann. It was to be broadcast, he explained, if anything happened to him,—if the
Werewolves, whom he feared, should murder him, or if
Hitler, hearing of it, should order his death. In any case, it
was to be broadcast on Hitler's death. For even now, Speer
was inhibited by some shreds of personal loyalty to the tyrant

whose disastrous policy he was resisting, but whose long
patronage he could not forget. Even now, he could not bring
himself to oppose, in politics, the one man in whom, as he
believed, the German people still put its trust.[10] Speer's speech
was directed not against Hitler personally, but against the still
unknown Nazi who would attempt to carry on Hitler's policy
of destruction after Hitler had fallen in Berlin. Nor was this
the full extent of Speer's inhibition. Soon it will be time to
describe an even more curious episode in this history of
divided loyalties.

After the conference of 20th April, Himmler also left the
Fuehrerbunker. Late in the evening he reached his headquarters at Ziethen castle, and there, awaiting him, found the
persistent Schellenberg. Schellenberg had a message for him.
While Himmler had been in Berlin, he had been at Harzwalde,
negotiating with his friends of the International Red Cross
about the Jewish question. There he had been telephoned
from the Swedish Embassy. Count Bernadotte was leaving
Germany at half-past six tomorrow morning. Schellenberg
had acted at once. Count Bernadotte was now at Hohenlychen, spending the night, and Himmler was to meet him for
breakfast there at six o'clock.

Promptly at six o'clock, Himmler and Schellenberg arrived
at Hohenlychen and breakfasted with Count Bernadotte.
Schellenberg was full of hope. Now at last, he thought,
Himmler would admit the logical consequence of his behaviour; would break the invisible chain of loyalty that still
bound him to Hitler and interfered with his freedom to follow
the advice of Schellenberg; would accept the opportunity,
the last opportunity, that had thus spontaneously presented
itself; and would speak to Bernadotte not, as in his two previ-

[10] I have taken this account from Speer's earliest statement on the subject.
At Nuremberg, a year later, Speer's version was slightly different: he then
ascribed the provision that the speech should only be broadcast after Hitler's
death to the demand of the recording officials, who were constrained by their
oath of loyalty to Hitler.

ous interviews, as a subordinate official, limited by his instructions, but as *de facto* Fuehrer of Germany, prepared to offer terms to the West. But Himmler did none of these things. He merely discussed certain technical details,—the release of certain Polish women from Ravensbrueck concentration camp; and even to this he had insisted on securing Hitler's approval by representing it as an anti-Russian gesture. After half an hour Bernadotte took his leave, and the opportunity had been missed for the third and perhaps last time. Schellenberg accompanied Bernadotte for part of the way. He piqued himself on reading the secret thoughts of others, and always found that they coincided with his own wishes. "Himmler secretly hoped," he says, "that I would again request the Count to fly to General Eisenhower on his own initiative and thus prepare the way for direct negotiations between Eisenhower and Himmler." But Bernadotte saw the facts and possibilities more clearly than Schellenberg. Nothing but a direct and explicit mandate from Himmler would cause him to interfere in these high matters. "The Reichsfuehrer is no longer in touch with reality," he said, as they motored together on the road to Waren. "I can help him no more. He should have taken the affairs of the Reich into his own hands after my first visit." When Schellenberg returned to Hohenlychen, he found Himmler paralysed with indecision, tormented by doubt. "Schellenberg," he said, "I dread the future"; and the irrepressible Schellenberg at once retorted that that should encourage him to act. Himmler made no reply. He was "a torn soul."

It was not in this cloud-cuckoo-land that the affairs of Germany were being, or would be, decided. All this time the evacuation of ministries from Berlin was continuing; but Hitler remained in his bunker, undecided, at least until he had made one further effort to throw the Russians back from the city. On 21st April, Hitler, who in all these days personally directed the movements of every battalion, ordered a final, all-out attack by the troops in Berlin. It was the Steiner attack, under the command of an S.S. general, Obergruppen-fuehrer Steiner; it was to be launched in the southern suburbs of the city; and every man, every tank, every airplane was to be diverted to take part in it. "Any commanding officer who keeps men back," Hitler shouted, "will forfeit his life within five hours." "You will guarantee with your head," he told Koller, "that absolutely every man is employed."

So Hitler ordered; but his orders bore no relation now to any reality. He was moving imaginary battalions, making academic plans, disposing non-existent formations. The Steiner attack was the last, most symbolic instance of Hitler's personal strategy; it never took place.

The facts emerged at the staff conference of 22nd April. All through the morning, a series of telephone calls from the Fuehrerbunker had never ceased to demand whether the attack had been launched. At one time a telephone message from Himmler reported that it had; at another a report from the Luftwaffe stated that it had not. At three o'clock in the afternoon, there was still no news. Then the conference began. Bormann, Burgdorf, Keitel, Jodl, and Krebs were there, and Herrgesell and Hagen, the two stenographers. Doenitz was not; during the night he had moved, with his staff, to his new headquarters at Ploen in Schleswig-Holstein, leaving only a liaison officer, Admiral Voss, in the Bunker. Voss, with the other liaison officers, Hewel and Fegelein, and adjutants and others, remained on the profane side of the partition, ready to join the conference on demand. General Koller, Goering's chief of staff, was not there. He was pre-occupied with com-mand work; "and anyway," he records plaintively, "I should never have been able to tolerate being insulted all day long." He had therefore arranged for General Christian to deputise for him.

The conference opened with the usual expositions of the

military situation by Krebs and Jodl. As usual they were un-
favourable, but not hopeless. Then came the news of the
Steiner attack. It had not materialised. Nothing had happened.
In spite of elaborate plans, in spite of ferocious threats, the
Luftwaffe had not gone into action. No orders had been received from Steiner. And then, following on these negative
tidings came reports of positive calamities. While troops had
been withdrawn to support Steiner in the south, the Russians
had broken into the suburbs in the north, and their armoured
spearheads were now within the city of Berlin.

Then came the storm, which made the conference of 22nd
April famous and decisive in the history of Hitler's last days.
It has been variously described, both by the principals who
witnessed it, and by the trembling adjutants and secretaries
who waited on the far side of the partition and pumped the
participants when they emerged, exhausted, after a three-
hour session. Their narratives are confused and fragmentary,
for emotion, on this notable occasion, interfered with the
memories of all; but on the main points there is agreement.[11]
Hitler flew into a rage. He shrieked that he had been deserted;
he railed at the Army; he denounced all traitors; he spoke of
universal treason, failure, corruption, and lies; and then, exhausted, he declared that the end had come. At last, and for
the first time, he despaired of his mission. All was over; the
Third Reich was a failure, and its author had nothing left to
do but to die. His doubts were now resolved. He would not
go to the south. Anyone else who wished might go, but he
would stay in Berlin and there meet the end when it
came.

The generals, the politicians, everyone protested. They reminded him of the sacrifices of the past, which had not been

[11] The principal sources for the conference of 22nd April are: Keitel,
Jodl (reported by Koller), Christian, Freytag von Loringhoven, Lorenz,
Herrgesell, von Below, and Fraeulein Krueger. Their opportunities of
knowledge vary, and their accounts are not always consistent; but I am satisfied that the relevant points, as given in the above account, are correct.

in vain. They pointed out that the Army Groups of Schoerner and Kesselring were still intact. They assured him that there was no reason for despair; and again they urged him to leave for Obersalzberg now, before it was too late. Fegelein telephoned Himmler, Voss telephoned Doenitz; and Himmler and Doenitz entreated him to think again, promising to send all naval and S.S. troops at their disposal to the relief of Berlin. Ribbentrop called the Bunker and sent a message to the Fuehrer; he had great hopes, he said, of a diplomatic coup which would set all right; but Hitler refused to hear him. Even the second Bismarck was now, at last, failing to convince. Hitler repeated that he would stay in Berlin; he would personally take over the defence of the city; and he ordered an announcement to be made to the people of Berlin, telling them that the Fuehrer was in Berlin, that the Fuehrer would not leave Berlin, and that the Fuehrer would defend Berlin to the very last. Next day the news was relayed to the world. Berlin and Prague, said the German radio, were the invincible twin citadels of the Reich, and in Berlin Hitler and Goebbels, the Fuehrer and the Gauleiter, would remain to the end.

With that the full conference ended, and the astonished participants withdrew to the outer bunker, where the adjutants and secretaries were waiting. They could not conceal their emotions of indignation and gloom. Everyone seemed to have lost his bearings. "When they came from the conference-room," says one of the secretaries,[12] "they were all distraught, saying that the end had come." "So much has broken up within me," exclaimed General Christian, who had witnessed the scene, "that I still cannot grasp it. The atmosphere in the Bunker has made a deep impression on me,—an impression I cannot begin to explain."[13] Even Krebs admitted cautiously to his adjutant that the Fuehrer had become violently excited

[12] Fraeulein Krueger.
[13] Christian, quoted by Koller. Christian's account, given under interrogation some months later, was still confused.

and had thrown unworthy reproaches at the high command.[14]

Meanwhile the drama was not over; in the Fuehrer's private quarters it was continuing before a narrower group of witnesses. Hitler sent for Goebbels, and then for Frau Goebbels and the children. Hitherto Goebbels and his family had lived in their own house, or in the Propaganda Ministry; henceforth their home was to be in the Fuehrerbunker. Frau Goebbels and the six children would live in the further of the two bunkers, Goebbels himself would have a room in the private part of the Fuehrerbunker. They all sat together and discussed the future. Goebbels said that he too would stay in Berlin and commit suicide there; his wife, resisting the remonstrances of Hitler, declared that she would do the same; and they would give poison to the children. After this, Hitler sent for his papers and sorted them out, personally selecting the documents which must be destroyed. The selected papers were then taken out into the garden by one of his adjutants, Julius Schaub, and burned.

After this scene, as if he had not sufficiently emphasised his decision, Hitler called Keitel and Bormann back to him and said, simply, "I will never leave Berlin—*never!*" Again there were protestations, again expressions of astonishment; but Hitler was unmoved. He sent for someone from the Press Division and asked whether his announcement had yet been made in the streets of Berlin. Then he pointed his finger at Keitel and said, "You are ordered by me to leave tomorrow for Berchtesgaden." Keitel protested that he would not go except in the Fuehrer's company. Hitler sent for Jodl and told him that he too must go to the south; and he told Bormann to leave the room.

The scene which followed was the climax among the extraordinary events of that day; for it was a scene which entailed dramatic consequences. Only Jodl and Keitel witnessed

[14] Freytag von Loringhoven.

it; but though the words in which they describe it differ, the sense, in all important particulars, is the same, and there is no reason to doubt their circumstantial versions. Hitler repeated his resolve to take over the defence of Berlin which others had failed to secure; when it fell, he said, he would shoot himself at the last moment. He could not fight, he explained; for physically he was a broken man; and neither alive nor dead would he fall into enemy hands. Jodl and Keitel sought vainly to dissuade him; they offered to divert troops from the west, to abandon western Germany to the British and Americans, and thus at least to save Berlin from the Russians. They protested that three-quarters of the armed forces were in the south, and if the Combined General Staff, with its operational command, were to go south too, how could he possibly direct it from Berlin? If negotiations were necessary,[15] it was thence that they must be made. Still Hitler would not listen. "I have taken up a fixed position," he said; "I cannot change it." There was no need of further orders, for the whole Reich was falling apart. There was nothing further to be done. It was the end. They begged him for orders; at least if he had himself abandoned hope, let him remember that he was Supreme Commander of the armed forces. His generals awaited his commands; what were they to do? "It is simply impossible, after you have been directing and leading us for so long, that you should suddenly send your staff away and expect them to lead themselves!" Hitler repeated that he had no orders to give; and then, in the words which had such far-reaching consequences, he added that if they wished for orders, let them apply to the Reich Marshal. "There isn't a single German soldier," they protested, "who

[15] There seems no doubt that at this time Hitler spoke of the possibility of negotiation. The versions of Jodl (given verbatim to Koller within a few hours of the incident) and of Keitel (given under interrogation several months later) both explicitly refer to the possible necessity of negotiation, and Goering's qualifications for such a task; and cf. Hitler's remarks to Speer on 23rd April (quoted below, p. 139).

would fight under the Reich Marshal!" "There is no question
of fighting now," Hitler replied; "there's nothing left to fight
with. If it's a question of negotiating, Goering can do that
better than I." [16]

After these pregnant words, Hitler discussed with Keitel
the manner in which Berlin might yet be relieved. The
Twelfth Army, commanded by General Wenck, Hitler's
personal creation, was now on the Elbe, southwest of Berlin;
it must disengage itself and fight its way in the direction of
Potsdam to rescue Berlin, the Chancellery, and the Fuehrer.
Keitel offered to go at once to Wenck with this message, but
Hitler insisted that he must stay and take a meal first; for it
was now eight o'clock in the evening. He sent for his servants
and ordered food to be brought, and himself sat by and
watched while Keitel ate. He was now perfectly quiet again;
his nervous fit seemed completely past, and he became once
more the kindly, simple host of Obersalzberg, taking personal
care to see that sandwiches were put up for the Field-Marshal's
journey, and half a bottle of cognac, and chocolate, and all
the accessories of a picnic. Then, while Krebs had orders to
remain in the Bunker as the Fuehrer's military adviser, Keitel
and Jodl left together, Keitel to visit Wenck, Jodl to the new
headquarters of the Combined General Staff at Krampnitz.[17]
Keitel was the compliant puppet, Jodl the overdriven brain,
through which Hitler had exercised his control over the armed

[16] These words are quoted from Jodl's account. Keitel's version contains
the same explicit statement that orders should be sought from Goering,
adding later: "I think he also said, 'Well, Goering is much better at these
things: he can deal much better with the other side'—or words to that
effect."

[17] Although the main service departments had been and were being
evacuated to Bavaria, and all departments would have gone thither had Hitler
himself agreed to go, Hitler's refusal compelled Keitel and Jodl to keep a
skeleton-staff of the OKW in the north, where it could be in touch with
him. The headquarters of this staff were first at Krampnitz, in the western
suburbs of Berlin, then at Fuerstenburg, near Mecklenburg. Ultimately it
joined Doenitz's staff in Ploen, and moved with it to his final capital in
Flensburg.

forces. Now apparently he had abandoned it. They went for part of the way together. "There is only one thing I can say to Wenck," said Keitel, as they sat in the car, "and that is, the fight for Berlin is on, and the fate of the Fuehrer is at stake." What Jodl replied to this loyal phrase, if he replied at all, we do not know; but his views at least were different. He at least shared the opinion of the more orthodox, more independent generals, who had been less affected by the melodrama than by the military irregularity of Hitler's behaviour. Toadies though they were, the mere servile rump of a thrice-purged institution, there were still some of them who remembered that Hitler was supposed to be a soldier; that a soldier's duty is to give orders and to take responsibilities; and that in this their Supreme Commander had failed, preferring to act like an overwrought *prima donna*. The threatened suicide, the gestures of despair, seemed to them a cowardly dereliction; it made no favourable impression on those cold, practical hearts; and they withdrew to their new headquarters filled with secret contempt to plan the strategy which their self-appointed war-lord had thus rhetorically resigned.

Meanwhile the news of this dramatic conference was having other repercussions elsewhere. At Hohenlychen, whither he had moved his headquarters at midday, Himmler had received the astonishing news from Fegelein. With him at the time were two of his subordinates: Professor Gebhardt, his "evil genius," whom yesterday he had proposed as head of the German Red Cross,[18] and Obergruppenfuehrer Gottlob Berger, head of the S.S. Head Office [19] and Himmler's Prisoner of War Administration,[20] already about to leave for Bavaria (it was one of Schellenberg's schemes) to counteract the influence of the sinister Kaltenbrunner.

[18] In place of Professor Grawitz, who had committed suicide in Berlin.
[19] *S.S. Hauptamt.* The office was in the Douglasstrasse.
[20] *Kriegsgefangenenwesen.*

"Everyone is mad in Berlin!" Himmler exclaimed to Berger when he had heard Fegelein's news. "The Fuehrer is raging, saying that the armed forces have deceived him all along and that now the S.S. is leaving him in the lurch.[21] I still have my Escort Battalion here, six hundred men, mostly wounded or convalescent; what am I to do?"

Berger was a Swabian, a simple, elementary character, full of honest good-nature, indefinite garrulity, and unsophisticated emotion. The political subtleties, the psychological refinements of Schellenberg meant nothing to him. He had no sympathy with a soul in doubt, no understanding of the conflicting pressures, the divergent loyalties, to which Himmler had so long been subjected. To him it was an uncomplicated moral matter, and he spoke with the clear, unhesitant voice of the undivided man. "You go straight to Berlin, Herr Reichsfuehrer, and your Escort Battalion with you, of course. You have no right to an Escort Battalion here, at a time when the Fuehrer intends to stay in the Reich Chancellery. . . ." "The words failed me," he says, "to voice my disgust; I was at the end of my tether. I said, 'I am going to Berlin, and it is your duty to go too'." [22]

Himmler was in a quandary. On the one hand he remembered Schellenberg. What would Schellenberg say if he went to Berlin now? Of all things Schellenberg most dreaded Himmler's visits to Hitler, and the reawakening, in that devoted character, of the never wholly exorcised spirit of loyalty. He had tried to dissuade Himmler from visiting Berlin even on Hitler's birthday. This time he was not there to dissuade. After lunch he had stayed behind, alone with

[21] A reference to the failure of Steiner and Sepp Dietrich, both S.S. generals.
[22] Berger's accounts of his activities in these days are all characterised by indistinct and sometimes inconsistent loquacity. They have been carefully checked against statements of Gebhardt and Grothmann; but the accounts of his conversations with Himmler and Hitler, which rest on his testimony alone, are given with some reservations.

Himmler, and had heard words which gave delight to his optimistic spirit. "I almost think, Schellenberg, that you are right," Himmler had said; "I must act in one way or another." It was not a very definite pronouncement, but it was enough for Schellenberg. He had obtained leave to pay one more visit to Count Bernadotte, now on the Danish frontier, and to inform him of Himmler's readiness to begin negotiations; and full of confidence, he had stepped into his car and driven to the north-east. Within a few hours Fegelein was telephoning from the Bunker urging Himmler to come and persuade the Fuehrer to leave, and Berger was assuring him, in unhesitant, imperative tones, that it was his duty to go. Himmler could not make up his mind. He was once more a torn soul.

Himmler telephoned again to the Bunker. He spoke to Hitler himself and urged him to leave; but in vain. He spoke to Fegelein again, and listened to his entreaties. In the end they reached a compromise. Himmler would drive halfway to Berlin, to Nauen, and Fegelein would drive out to Nauen, and there they would discuss the matter. At dusk he left Hohenlychen by car, accompanied by his adjutant Grothmann. Gebhardt followed in another car; for he had reasons of his own for visiting Berlin. He wished to be confirmed by Hitler as head of the Red Cross; and that afternoon he had had a telephone conversation with his former pupil, Dr. Stumpfegger.

The party drove to the cross-roads at Nauen, and there Himmler waited for Fegelein. He waited for an hour, nearly two hours, and still Fegelein had not come. Then Gebhardt asked if he might go on alone to the Bunker. Himmler agreed, and since Fegelein had not arrived to take it, and he himself was afraid to go on to Berlin, he entrusted to Gebhardt the message which he wished to send to the Fuehrer: the offer of his Escort Battalion to fight in defence of the Chancellery.

It was about eleven o'clock at night when Gebhardt arrived in the Bunker. He learned from Stumpfegger the details of

the momentous conference, and then was admitted to the
Fuehrer's presence and delivered his messages. First, as agreed
with Stumpfegger, he offered to evacuate the women and
children from the Chancellery,—Eva Braun, the secretaries,
Frau Goebbels and her children. Hitler replied that all these
had decided, of their own free will, to stay with him. Then
Gebhardt delivered Himmler's offer of his Escort Battalion.
Hitler accepted it, and showed on the map the position which
he wished it to hold in the Tiergarten. Finally Hitler confirmed Gebhardt's appointment as head of the German Red
Cross. The interview lasted twenty minutes; then Gebhardt
turned to go. Before leaving, he asked whether Hitler wished
to send any message to Himmler. "Give him my love," said
Hitler; and Gebhardt withdrew.

Scarcely had Gebhardt left Hitler's presence when another
visitor arrived. It was Berger, who had been summoned by
telephone to report to Hitler before leaving for the south. He
had immediately motored to Berlin. When he arrived, Russian shells were falling near the Chancellery. Berger reported
to the Bunker, but Hitler was in conference and he had to
wait. Now he was admitted. He found a few Army officers
still there. Hitler, he says, was finished, a broken man. They
spoke about Berger's mission, about the disloyalty that was
universally springing up in the south, and which would have
to be investigated and suppressed. Then they spoke of Hitler's
decision to remain in Berlin. Hitler explained that Himmler
had made a long speech to him on the telephone, seeking to
dissuade him; it was senseless, he had said, to remain; why
would he not go to the south to the still defensible Alpine
Redoubt? But Berger, if his own account is to be believed,
encouraged Hitler to stay. To the simple all things are simple;
and to his elementary, boy-scout nature the duty of the
Fuehrer was as clear as the duty of the Reichsfuehrer had
been. "I told him," he says, "that it was out of the question;
he couldn't betray the German people. It was quite simple

to put a bullet through one's head, or to take one of those pills or tubes that are issued, which work instantaneously. One couldn't desert the people, after they had held out so loyally and so long. . . ." *Loyally and long* . . . that was not what Hitler thought of the German people in this hour. "All this time," says Berger, "the Fuehrer had never uttered a word; then suddenly he shrieked, 'Everyone has deceived me! no one has told me the truth! the armed forces have lied to me!'—all in that vein. He went on and on in a loud voice. Then his face went bluish-purple. I thought he was going to have a stroke any minute. I had the impression that he had had a stroke already, on his left side,—but of course they kept one in the dark. His arm, which a fortnight before used to jerk, was suddenly still, and he never put his left foot to the ground properly. He didn't rest his left hand properly, either, as he used to do; he only rested his right hand on the table."

At the end of the interview they discused the *Prominente*, the well-connected British and American prisoners of war who were being held as hostages. These prisoners had been in camp in western Germany; but as the Allied armies moved forward, they had been separated from their fellow prisoners and removed to Bavaria, where they would come under Berger's control. They also discussed the outbreak of separatism in Austria and Bavaria. When Berger left, Hitler, who had been sitting at the table, rose to his feet. His whole body was trembling. "His hand was shaking, his leg was shaking and his head was shaking; and all that he kept saying was, 'Shoot them all! shoot them all!' or something like that." But whether it was the prisoners or the separatists that were to be shot does not transpire from the incoherent narrative of Berger.

It was one o'clock in the morning when Berger left Berlin, under the fire of the Russian batteries, to fly to Bavaria in Himmler's four-engined plane. Others were leaving too. "Any man who wants may go!" Hitler had said; "I stay here." All that night, parties were leaving Berlin for Obersalzberg; it was the last stage of the great exodus. Hitler's adjutant Schaub, his naval adjutant Admiral von Puttkamer, his two stenographers Herrgesell and Hagen, two of his four secretaries, Fraeulein Schroeder and Fraeulein Wolf, and many others. Among them was the odious physician, Professor Morell. "I don't need drugs to see me through," were Hitler's last words to him, and he too went out to the aerodrome. From the Party Chancellery too, three omnibuses had taken, or were taking, the fugitives. Only Martin Bormann stayed, with his assistant S.S. Standartenfuehrer Zander, and his secretary Fraeulein Krueger. He had not wished to stay; he still had political ambitions; to his undramatic spirit the prospect of a glorious *Goetterdaemmerung* made no appeal, and he had joined his voice to those of the generals who had urged Hitler to leave. But since Hitler had decided otherwise, he would not even now leave the sole source and centre of his authority; and he stayed.

Another who left the Chancellery that night was General Koller. Koller had been sitting at his command post when the telephone had rung, and General Christian, in an excited voice, had told him that "events of historical importance" were taking place in the Bunker; but when Christian had arrived himself to amplify this bald summary, his account had been emotional and confused, and Koller went at once in search of Jodl for a more explicit version of this important episode. He found him at Krampnitz. Jodl told him all, and Koller wrung his hands in dismay over the deplorable details. "When the Mayor of Leipzig shot himself and his family, the Fuehrer said it was 'senseless, a cowardly evasion of responsibility'; now he's doing exactly the same himself." Jodl agreed. "Was there any chance that the Fuehrer might change his mind?" asked Koller. "None at all," replied Jodl. But the incident most significant to Koller, as Jodl told him the story, was

Hitler's phrase about leaving everything to the Reich Marshal. The Reich Marshal was now in Obersalzberg, and Koller was his representative in Berlin. It was plainly his duty to fly at once to Obersalzberg and inform Goering of these tremendous developments; "he would be justified in reprimanding me severely if I failed to do this, and it cannot be explained in a radiogram at all." Jodl agreed. At half-past three on the morning of 23rd April, Koller flew from Gatow to Munich, and a new sub-plot in the drama began.

At noon on 23rd April, Koller reported to Goering at Obersalzberg. Word for word, he repeated his conversation with Jodl. Goering's eyes popped as the astonishing details were recounted to him. He collected a group of adjutants and advisers around him, and sent for Reich Minister Lammers, head of the Reich Chancery and official expert in Nazi legalities. Lammers had once possessed a power equal to that of Bormann, and the two had co-operated closely in the quest of further authority; but Bormann had gradually elbowed his partner out, and now Lammers was a comparatively insignificant figure. Goering felt himself in a very delicate position. By decree, he was Hitler's successor; now, according to Koller's account, Hitler had resigned and devolved his powers upon him. The legal position was quite clear. Goering sent for a tin box, and from it extracted the text of Hitler's decree of June 1941. All agreed that the meaning was unmistakable. But what of Bormann? All knew that it was Bormann's dearest wish to eliminate Goering from the succession to that post which, it now seemed, would soon be vacant. At present, since there was no other suitable candidate, Goering's right had not been altered; but any indiscretion might be fatal. He picked his way carefully among the possible traps. Might not the Fuehrer have issued other orders since 1941, he asked, which would have invalidated this decree? "No," replied Lammers. "If the Fuehrer had ever issued any other orders, they would certainly have come to my notice." Senatspraesident Mueller,

Bormann's personal assistant, was present at the conference, but apparently raised no difficulties. Goering asked all in turn for their opinion. They were unanimous. Supposing Koller's statement to be correct, Goering was by law obliged to take over the inheritance. Goering then proposed that he should send a telegram to Hitler, and supplementary telegrams to Keitel, Ribbentrop, and von Below,[23] seeking approval for such an interpretation. All agreed; or at least, if Lammers, Mueller, and S.S. Obersturmbannfuehrer Dr. Frank, leader of the S.S. in Obersalzberg, did not agree, it was by reservation, not expression of their opinion.

There was now no communication with the north except by wireless. Goering himself began to draft the telegrams, but his style was too voluble for that parsimonious medium and alternative versions were supplied by Koller and Goering's adjutant, Colonel von Brauchitsch. Goering demanded the inclusion of the phrase "of all powers at home and abroad"; for he was determined, once in power, to open immediate negotiations with the west, and even declared himself ready to fly personally to General Eisenhower. After all, that was precisely why Hitler had handed over to him: "if it is a question of negotiating, Goering can do that better than I." He also demanded a deadline for reply; otherwise, if communications were cut off, he might have to wait indefinitely; and events would not wait. Perhaps Hitler was already dead. The final version seemed admirably phrased:

My Fuehrer!—In view of your decision to remain at your post in the fortress of Berlin, do you agree that I take over, at once, the total leadership of the Reich, with full freedom of action at home and abroad, as your deputy, in accordance with your decree of 29 June 1941? If no reply is received by ten o'clock tonight, I shall take it for granted that you have lost your freedom of action, and shall consider the conditions of your decree as fulfilled, and shall

[23] As Hitler's Luftwaffe adjutant, von Below would naturally handle service relations between Hitler and Goering.

act for the best interests of our country and our people. You know what I feel for you in this gravest hour of my life. Words fail me to express myself. May God protect you, and speed you quickly here in spite of all. Your loyal,—HERMANN GOERING.

Suitable telegrams, explanatory, supplementary, and conciliatory, were sent to Keitel, Ribbentrop, and von Below.

The same evening, another meeting was taking place at Luebeck between Himmler, Schellenberg, and Count Bernadotte. The important events which had taken place in the Bunker were unknown to both Schellenberg and Bernadotte; but Himmler knew of them, and they had had a great effect on his hitherto divided mind. They had solved, or seemed to have solved, his problem. For years Himmler had had no problem, and his cumbrous mind had never needed to think. The principle of loyalty, on which his whole life, his whole success, his whole system was based, had spared him from any introspective or intellectual difficulty. To that principle he remained, in spite of many ambiguities and vacillations and inadvertencies, ultimately true; and thanks to that principle, his life had been as simple and uncomplicated as his naïve faith in the metaphysical Nordic balderdash of the Nazi religion. Protected by that magic armour, he had known neither thought nor doubt; he had believed and acted. He had worshipped the Aryan deities, contemplated the Aryan truth, and partaken of the Aryan sacraments. He had extirpated heresy, and in the name of orthodoxy had sent millions, unthinkingly, even benignly, to the torture-chamber and the gas-van. Imagination cannot comprehend the sum-total of the human suffering, or even of the mere deaths, which had proceeded from the authority of that single true believer, whose wife remembers him only as a somewhat insignificant person but a good breadwinner, and whom his subordinates, hating each other with a bitter detestation, united to admire as a paternal governor; and who himself never seems to have considered, far less examined or relished or regretted, the consequences of his authority. Then Schellenberg had come, and little by little, by suggestion and insinuation, by persistence and persuasion, by flattery and protestation, he had sapped the strength of that fundamental principle; and Himmler, lacking it, from a terrible, impersonal priest of Moloch, had become a weak, vacillating, purposeless human being, incapable of thought or action, always looking nostalgically back to the lost rule from which his life had drawn its significance.

Such was Himmler's condition in the middle of April, when Schellenberg was urging him to assume the Fuehrerdom of Germany and make peace with the West. If Himmler were Fuehrer, he would indeed act as Schellenberg bade him; but he was not; Hitler was still alive; and the shreds of loyalty which Himmler still cherished made all Schellenberg's earnest and persuasive counsels vain. It was psychologically impossible for Himmler to eliminate, or even to ignore Hitler. Even if it had been possible, there were further difficulties. If Himmler deposed or ignored Hitler, how could he be sure that he would be obeyed? From the German people, as Speer had realised, Hitler, so long as he lived, was the one man who could command unconditional obedience. It was a spell wherewith the whole German people had been bewitched, and Himmler and Speer among them. Indeed, their problem was essentially the same. Both had come to believe, by different processes, that Hitler's continued rule was disastrous; both had, or thought they had, alternative policies; but neither was prepared fully to implement his policy as long as Hitler was alive, the sole source of inspiration, the sole focus of devotion, the sole centre of power and authority. Neither Speer nor Himmler could act against Hitler, or independently of him. To carry out their policy they had only one course,— to wait until God, or chance, or time should remove the terrible figure whom they themselves could not touch; and while they waited, events were moving and their policies were becoming daily less possible of fulfilment.

Then came the conference of 22nd April. For Himmler it was of decisive importance. He had heard all the details from Gebhardt and Fegelein when all three met for breakfast at Hohenlychen next morning; and when he set out for Luebeck in the afternoon, his mind and conscience were clear as they had never been since the day when he had walked through the woods of Wustrow with Schellenberg. Hitler had declared his intention of staying in Berlin and dying in its ruins. Himmler knew enough of Hitler to be sure that he would not change his mind. In a day or two Berlin would fall, and Hitler would be dead without the interposition of any sacrilegious hand. For two days Himmler could indulge his loyalty, —he had already sent half of his Escort Battalion to fight in defence of the Fuehrer and the Chancellery.[24] Then, when all was over, he would be free to become, as Schellenberg persuaded him, the negotiator of peace, the saviour of Germany.

The meeting took place in the Swedish consulate in Luebeck. It has been described independently by both Schellenberg and Bernadotte. The electric light had been cut and they sat in candlelight. They had scarcely taken their seats when an air raid sent them to the cellars. After midnight they returned. For the first time in all these days of negotiation and vacillation, Himmler spoke clearly. "The Fuehrer's great life," he said, "is drawing to its close." Possibly he was already dead; if not, he would certainly be dead within the next few days. He had gone to Berlin to perish with its inhabitants, and it would be only a matter of days before Berlin would fall. Hitherto, he went on, he had agreed with Bernadotte in his heart but had been unable to break his oath to the Fuehrer. Now it was different. He empowered

[24] It had been sent under the command of S.S. Ostubaf Persch, Fegelein having arrived too late to lead it.

Bernadotte to communicate to the Western Allies, through the Swedish Government, his offer of surrender. In the East he would not surrender; there the Germans would continue to fight until the Western Allies had advanced to relieve them. Thus the entire northern sector would escape senseless destruction. Himmler also promised that Danish and Norwegian internees should be transferred to Sweden; and he wrote a personal letter for Bernadotte to take to the Swedish Government as proof of his offer. The interview was over in an hour, and Bernadotte left to return at once to Stockholm. His greatest problem solved, Himmler now began once more to turn his mind to the details of procedure; what name he should choose for the new political party which his government should represent, and whether he should bow or shake hands when introduced to General Eisenhower.[25]

Thus Hitler's staff-conference of 22nd April, which created a problem for Goering, brought a solution to the long doubts of Himmler; but Schellenberg—for the faith of the optimist feeds on trifles—could not deny himself the comfort of one additional theory. To him, knowing nothing of the conference, Himmler's words were capable of another meaning. When Himmler said that Hitler would be dead in a matter of days, Schellenberg at once remembered his own suggestions; how he had urged Himmler to make use of physicians and poisoned drugs; how he had elaborated the astrological predictions of Wulf in that direction, and discussed with de Crinis the symptoms of Parkinson's disease. He convinced himself, and remained long convinced, that Himmler had made secret arrangements for the murder of Hitler and was waiting daily for news of their success; and to help himself

[25] Count Bernadotte (*The Curtain Falls*, p. 114) ascribes the statement that Hitler could only last a few days and that Himmler was prepared to offer surrender, both to Himmler and (before Himmler's arrival) to Schellenberg. This must be a slip of memory. Schellenberg had no means of knowing, and says himself that he first heard the words from Himmler in Bernadotte's presence.

in that conviction, he conveniently forgot to record in his account of the interview, what Bernadotte has explicitly given in his,—Himmler's own clear explanation:—that Hitler was staying in Berlin deliberately to share its imminent fate.

On the very same night, while Goering was awaiting a reply to his telegram in Obersalzberg and Himmler was offering his capitulation to Bernadotte in Luebeck, yet a third significant meeting was taking place in Berlin. Albert Speer was paying his last visit to the Fuehrer whom, like Goering and Himmler, he was seeking both to supersede and to obey. On 23rd April, in Hamburg, having heard that Hitler had decided to remain in the capital, he decided that personal loyalty required him to go to Berlin and take his leave. His political acts of disobedience were done, and could not be undone. His speech, though undelivered, was recorded, and in safe hands in Hamburg; Hitler would soon be dead, and the occasion for its delivery was imminent; since it could be delivered whether Speer was alive or dead, he had now no further political function to perform. He therefore decided to go to Berlin and explain to Hitler the decision which he had made in his "conflict between personal loyalty and public duty." What would happen to him in consequence of such a confession, Speer did not know. He assumed that he would be arrested, probably shot; but it was immaterial to him, for his work was finished and he was ready to accept the consequences of the breach which it had entailed in his otherwise undiminished personal loyalty.

It was now no longer possible to reach Berlin by road. Speer motored as far as Rechlin, and then flew in a training plane to Gatow, the western aerodrome of Berlin. At Gatow he met General Christian, who had just left the Fuehrerbunker for the last time. Then he flew on into the city in a Fieseler Storch, and landed on the East-West Axis—the great boulevard which leads up to the centre of Berlin—close to the

Brandenburger Tor. He went straight to the Bunker. Hitler was there, with the remainder of his court: Bormann, Goebbels, Ribbentrop, Krebs, von Below, his personal adjutants, and Eva Braun. Speer gave Hitler a full account of his recent activities; Hitler listened, and seemed to Speer to be "deeply moved" by his candour. At the end he did nothing. Speer was not arrested, not shot. The incident was closed.

Why Hitler, who, in these days of universal suspicion, was shrieking for blood—the blood of hostages and prisoners, of German officers and his own servants—was thus unexpectedly lenient to the transgressing Speer is a question which may admit of many answers. Dr. von Hasselbach has observed, in his professional examination of Hitler, that he "could hate fiercely in some fields, while forgiving almost anything to those he loved"; and perhaps this is an illustration of this general characteristic. Certainly Hitler entertained a strong affection for Speer, who came from his favoured "artistic" world, and whom he had himself chosen, intuitively, for one of the most difficult and testing tasks in Germany. That Speer had succeeded, and always succeeded, in this gigantic task was an additional reason for satisfaction; it showed that Hitler's intuition was sometimes justified by results—he did not always choose Rosenbergs and Ribbentrops. Hitler referred to Speer, with his customary indifference to the subtler distinctions of language, as "the greatest genius of all time." But there is perhaps another explanation also. On 23rd April, when Speer visited him, Hitler was in a state of unnatural calm: the calm after the storm. All who saw him on that day have borne witness to this relaxation, this inner peace, which had followed the tempestuous scenes of the day before.[26] It was a long time, says Speer, since he had seen him so composed, so human. For more than a year his behaviour had been harsh and strained, the result (Speer believed) of his obstinate belief, against all advice and all evidence, that Germany would

[26] Christian and Keitel confirm Speer's observations in this respect.

win the war. Now that he had at last abandoned that impossible conviction, the tension of his spirit was relaxed, and he looked upon the world with more dispassionate, philosophical eyes, awaiting death (he said) as a release from a hard life full of difficulties. In this serene mood, he was perhaps uninterested in a disobedience which, since Speer had come voluntarily to confess it, seemed formal only and implied no fundamental disloyalty; and Speer escaped from the lion's den unexpectedly free. Nevertheless, in a few days Hitler would recover from this unnatural calm. Bormann had long been seeking to persuade him that Speer was betraying him; Speer's own confession had confirmed, in part, these suggestions. In his last days Hitler complained that Speer, like all the rest, was deserting him; [27] and in his political testament the name of Speer was silently dropped from the new Nazi Government. Even now, Hitler's calm was not such as to extend beyond Speer, who was soon to witness the very different treatment of a less voluntary disobedience.

Speer remained in the Bunker for eight hours, while Allied planes bombed the city of Berlin, and the Propaganda Ministry went up in flames. He spoke with Eva Braun, who told him of Hitler's collapse on the day before and of Bormann's intrigues against his rivals. He also took part in two other conversations with Hitler.

The first concerned Hitler's decision to stay in Berlin. Though he had declared his fixed intention to stay, and it had been announced to Berlin and to the world, Bormann and Ribbentrop still sought to dissuade him. Perhaps they thought that a decision taken in a period of mental storm might be altered in the calm which had followed it. If so, they were wrong. Goebbels and Eva Braun supported him in his decision to stay; Goebbels even urged him, as he had so often urged the German people, not to be so "defeatist" about the outcome of the battle. Bormann appealed to Speer for his sup-

[27] Axmann.

port; but Speer would not give it. Instead he opposed the
policy of flight. If the defence of Berlin should fail, he told
Hitler, then the end would clearly have come; and it would
be more dignified to meet it here, in the Reich capital, than
in his "week-end bungalow" at Obersalzberg. His advice was
perhaps as irrelevant as the protestations of Bormann. Hitler
had already made up his mind; and no occasion has ever been
recorded when he changed it. Firmly and quietly he reasserted
his decision; and he repeated to Speer, what he had already
described to Keitel and Jodl, the manner in which he intended
to die. He would not go out of the Bunker, he said, to die fighting among the barricades, lest he should be wounded and captured by the Russians. He would shoot himself in the Bunker.
Nor would even his dead body fall into the hands of the
enemy, who would use it for propaganda. He had made all
arrangements for it to be burned away.

The second conversation concerned the telegram from
Goering which had arrived in the course of the afternoon.

For four years Bormann had waited for an opportunity
to ruin Goering; but none had arisen. Now the time was short.
Any day now Hitler might be dead, and then, by law, unless
the law was altered, Goering would be his successor, and Bormann's day of power would be past. For in the universal
unreality of German politics, Bormann, like Himmler and
Schellenberg and Goering and Schwerin von Krosigk, still
believed that there would be power to inherit and to exercise
after Hitler's death. Now, at the last moment, such an opportunity had come; and it had come at the most favourable
time, when no personal explanations were any longer possible,
no rival views could be heard. By his telegram, Goering had
played into Bormann's hands at a time when Bormann, as
never before, monopolised the ear of Hitler. It is true that
Goering had sought to provide against such an event by sending parallel telegrams to Keitel, Ribbentrop, and von Below;
but Keitel and Jodl had by now left the Bunker for the last

time and were at their new headquarters, and Ribbentrop would not intervene to save Goering. The telegram to von Below asked him to see that the telegram to the Fuehrer was properly delivered, and to use his influence to persuade Hitler, if possible, to fly to the south. This telegram was taken from von Below by Bormann, and never returned.[28] Bormann was determined to play this hand alone.

How Bormann had handled the incident can be deduced from the explanation later given by Hitler to Goering's successor, Ritter von Greim.[29] Unerringly, Bormann had directed Hitler's attention to the passage in which Goering had demanded a reply by ten o'clock. It was an ultimatum, he had said; and he had also reminded Hitler that six months ago Goering had been suspected of seeking to open negotiations with the Allies. Clearly he now wished to usurp power in order to resume them. Hitler's suspicions, never more than half asleep, had been easily awakened. A telegram had therefore been sent to Goering assuring him that Hitler still possessed full freedom of action, and forbidding any independent move. Now, in Speer's presence, the next stage was considered: the fate of Goering. "Hitler was highly enraged," says Speer, "and expressed himself very strongly about Goering. He said that he had known for some time that Goering had failed, that he was corrupt, and a drug-addict . . ."; "and yet," he commented, "he can negotiate the capitulation," adding as an afterthought, "not that it matters who does that." "His contempt for the German people," says Speer, "was expressed in the manner of this remark." In the end Hitler would not agree that Goering should be shot; but he agreed that he should be dismissed from all his offices and from his right of succession. He told Bormann to draft a telegram accordingly. Bormann withdrew, and returned with the proposed text.

---

[28] Von Below.
[29] Quoted by Koller, *s.d.* 8th May 1945, and confirmed by Hanna Reitsch (cf. below, p. 151).

Hitler authorised it, and it was sent. It informed Goering that his action represented high treason to National Socialism and to the Fuehrer; that the penalty for this was death; but that Goering would be excused this extreme penalty, in view of his earlier services to the Party, provided he resigned at once from all his offices. He was to answer yes or no. At the same time, a telegram was sent by Bormann to the S.S. leaders in Obersalzberg, Obersturmbannfuehrer Frank and Obersturmfuehrer Bredow, ordering them to arrest Goering for high treason. His staff and advisers, including Koller and Lammers, were to be arrested or confined to their houses. "You will answer for this with your lives." [30] The orders were obeyed. Shortly after midnight the entire party at Obersalzberg was arrested. Next day it was announced from Berlin that Goering had resigned from all his offices for reasons of health. Bormann had triumphed. The question of the succession was now open again.

But why, we ask, did Bormann succeed so easily? Why did Hitler yield so readily to his obvious designs? Had not Hitler himself authorised Goering to assume authority, and to use it for negotiation? At first we wonder whether perhaps Hitler's words on that momentous occasion have not been wrongly reported. But the evidence is too strong for such a method of escape. The crucial words, as taken down verbatim by Koller from Jodl that very night, were reasserted by Jodl five days later,[31] and after six months were independently confirmed in all substantial points by Keitel. Had Hitler then forgotten them, or did he refuse to remember them? Or did he attach a different meaning to the words which the hearers had too literally interpreted? The truth may lie anywhere among these alternatives.

Words at all times have two possible functions: sometimes

[30] This telegram was seen and quoted by Karnau; the text, as given by him, has been recognised and pronounced authentic by Zander.

[31] Koller, s.d. 27th April 1945. "Jodl again confirms the accuracy of everything he told me that night" (i.e. 22nd–23rd April).

they convey ideas, and sometimes they merely express moods. When a man says, in a moment of desperation, that he wishes he were dead, he does not always mean to be literally understood; and it is possible that in that sudden outburst of despair Hitler's words, which were interpreted as a statement of his intentions, were in fact merely a liberation of his feelings,—or at least were afterwards so regarded by him, if he remembered them; for it is immaterial, in such circumstances, whether he failed to remember or refused to admit what he had said. Nor is this the only instance in which he afterwards disregarded the utterances of that night. For during that stormy afternoon he had also renounced control of the armed forces. In spite of all the protests of Keitel and Jodl, he had insisted that they should direct the strategy of the war themselves, and it was in answer to their protests at such a suggestion that he had referred them to the Reich Marshal. And yet, four days later, without ever explicitly announcing that he had resumed control, Hitler was issuing orders as if he had never abandoned it. When Goering, at Nuremberg, sought to rehabilitate himself in Nazi eyes as the loyal paladin of the movement, it was clearly not without some justification that he represented his dismissal as the unfortunate consequence of a technical error. What he did not explain was why that technical error was knowingly exploited, universally welcomed, and never corrected. The occasion of Goering's fall was supplied by his incautious telegram; but the reason was more fundamental than that. It was the ruin of the Luftwaffe.[32]

At four o'clock next morning, 24th April, Speer left Hitler's Bunker for the last time. Ribbentrop had already left and did not return. Jodl and Keitel had visited it for the last time on 23rd April; and Field-Marshal Schoerner had also been and gone. For two days Hitler had steadfastly resisted all those who had sought to dissuade him from his fixed purpose of staying in Berlin; now the time was running short, for the

[32] Almost every Luftwaffe officer has agreed that Goering was personally responsible for the failure of the Luftwaffe.

Russian armies were closing around the city and soon it would
be impossible to leave, at least by land. Nevertheless, a few
last efforts of dissuasion were still made. On 24th April a
telegram from Schoerner urged him to leave Berlin and join
the Army Group, as yet undefeated, in the mountains of
Bohemia; but Hitler replied once more that he would defend
Berlin, or die there.[33] That evening Gauleiter Wegener, whom
Doenitz had made responsible for civil affairs in the northern
area, aghast at the magnitude of his problems, sought allevia-
tion in a change of policy in Berlin. He telephoned to the
Bunker: would not the Fuehrer sanction a surrender in the
West to reinforce the East and avoid a double devastation? He
was crying for the moon. Hitler did not want to avoid
devastation; devastation was just what he wanted,—the more
the better,—to illuminate his Viking funeral. "It was terrible
to hear," records Schwerin von Krosigk, now with Doenitz
in the north, "that no counsel, no reasoned arguments, no
reference to the fearful sufferings of our poor people, can
break through those walls which the Fuehrer has erected
around his convictions, and behind which he allows nobody to
see. Can it be that there is really nothing there,—only the
gigantic obstinacy of a deluded spirit, sacrificing all to its
self-worshipping Ego?" The former Rhodes scholar did not
attempt to answer this question; no doubt he was satisfied that
the posing of it alone would impress posterity with his
philosophical profundity.

Thus by 24th April Hitler had in turn rejected every attempt to alter the decision which, after his customary vacillation, he had firmly reached. Thereafter there was no purpose
in further attempts; for next day the Russians had completely
encircled Berlin and only a dangerous communication by air
was possible. The period of crisis and decision was over; the
siege of the Bunker had begun.

[33] Lorenz.

Chapter Five

THE SIEGE OF THE BUNKER
(25TH-28TH APRIL)

WITH THE departure of Speer on 24th April, the last of the casual visitors to the Bunker had gone, and from that time on, apart from two interesting pilgrims from the outer world, the *dramatis personae* of the tragi-comedy remained constant. They were also few. In the Fuehrerbunker were Hitler and Eva Braun; Goebbels (who occupied the rooms abandoned by Dr. Morell) with his wife and children and his adjutant, Hauptsturmfuehrer Schwaegermann; Dr. Stumpfegger; Sturmbannfuehrer Heinz Linge, Hitler's personal attendant; Sturmbannfuehrer Otto Guensche, his S.S. adjutant and faithful shadow; his two remaining secretaries, Frau Christian and Frau Junge; and Fraeulein Manzialy, his vegetarian-cook. Apart from these, there were others who lived in the other bunkers, and came as occasion drew them to the Fuehrerbunker. Most regular in their attendance were of course Martin Bormann, with his assistant S.S. Standartenfuehrer Zander and his secretary Fraeulein Krueger; General Krebs, with his adjutant Major Freytag von Loringhoven and his aide-de-camp Rittmeister Boldt; General Burgdorf, with his assistant Colonel von Below, Lieut.-Colonel Weiss, and Major Johannmeier; General Weidling, the commandant of the city; Hitler's two pilots, Gruppenfuehrer Baur and Standartenfuehrer Beetz; Brigadefuehrer Mohnke, the commandant of the Chancellery; Artur Axmann, leader of the Hitler Youth, who were defending positions in the city;[1]

[1] There were about 1000 *Hitler Jugend* fighting in Berlin. Their main task was to hold the Wannsee bridges against the arrival of Wenck's reliev-

Werner Naumann, Goebbels' assistant in the Propaganda Ministry; Heinz Lorenz, of the Press Service, who delivered news to the Bunker; Brigadefuehrer Rattenhuber, head of the detective force which watched the Fuehrer's safety, and Standartenfuehrer Hoegl, his deputy; the officers of the S.S. Bodyguard; and the liaison-officers Admiral Voss, Gruppenfuehrer Fegelein, and Ambassador Walter Hewel, who represented Doenitz, Himmler, and Ribbentrop. Eleven of these have been captured and interrogated by British or American authorities; [2] and their statements, supplemented by the evidence of less prominent persons, of guards and drivers, clerks and batmen, a casual visitor and a tailor, and checked against documents, diaries, and captured telegrams, have shed what light now illuminates the dark period of Hitler's last week of life.

It is an unsteady light. It could not be otherwise. Though some of the documents are contemporary, the full investigation was not begun till five months had passed, when memories were already beginning to fade, and imagination and conjecture to fill the gaps. On some matters they had never been strong—particularly dates and times. This can hardly surprise us as we envisage the life that was led in those doomed, subterranean bunkers, amid perpetual shelling and bombing, often in total darkness, in which all count of the hours was lost; when meals took place at wayward hours, and the boundaries of night and day had been forgotten. Nevertheless, there are a few certain incidents, a few established

---

ing army. Axmann's command post was at 86 Kaiserdamm until 26th April, and from then until 30th April in the cellar of the Party Chancellery at 64 Wilhelmstrasse.

[2] Viz. Schwaegermann, Frau Christian, Frau Junge, Zander, Fraeulein Krueger, Freytag von Loringhoven, Boldt, Below, Johannmeier, Axmann, Lorenz. Subordinate witnesses are the chauffeur Erich Kempka, the guards Karnau, Mansfeld, and Poppen, the batman Matthiesing, the casual visitor Baroness von Varo, and the tailor Mueller. For full list of sources see *Note on Sources*, pp. 245–246.

facts and dated documents upon which, with careful analysis, the otherwise uncertain sequence of events can be confidently suspended. The coming and going of Ritter von Greim, the telegrams to Doenitz, the news of Himmler's treachery, the signing of Hitler's will, the suicide of Hitler and Eva Braun, the mass escape from the Bunker,—these are events which can be ascribed with certainty to days and hours; and the other events whose occasions rest on the fallible testimony of bewildered men, though they cannot be minutely dated or firmly guaranteed, can at least be related to each other, and to those fixed moments, in a probable sequence and interdependency.

Apart from these eleven resident witnesses who have fallen into our hands, we must refer to the two outsiders, whose three-day sojourn in the Bunker was perhaps the most interesting episode in those dull days of siege. On 24th April, a telegram from the Fuehrerbunker arrived in Munich ordering Colonel-General Ritter von Greim [3] to report to the Reich Chancellery. A second telegram required the presence of General Koller, whose message to Goering had precipitated the crisis, and who had now been released from his imprisonment in Obersalzberg, under S.S. supervision. Koller refused to go. It was meaningless, he said, suicidal. Wireless communication with the north had been cut, and no one could learn which aerodromes were fit for landing; he did not intend to fly straight into Russian hands. He had a good excuse, for he had an appointment next day; his health was broken; his morale was low; everything he had heard of life in the Bunker suggested that they were all mad anyway; and he replied that for reasons of health he was unable to come. No such considerations occurred to Ritter von Greim. Greim was a Luftwaffe

[3] Ritter von Greim was in command of Luftflotte 6, with headquarters in Munich, Oberfoehring-Friemann. Greim committed suicide after capture on 24th June 1945; but contemporary evidence from him is included in the diaries of Koller and Schwerin von Krosigk, the interrogation of General Christian, and the statement of Hanna Reitsch.

officer with a distinguished record; he was also a Nazi, whose
acceptance of the Nazi system, even at this hour, is attested by
his shrill, insensitive utterances. That night he planned to fly
immediately to Rechlin, but his plane was damaged on the
ground in an air raid. Next day he turned up at Obersalzberg
to visit Koller. The Allies had just raided Obersalzberg from
the air, and the place, according to those who saw it in the
morning, looked like a landscape on the moon. Hitler's
Berghof was half destroyed, Bormann's house destroyed,
Goering's house almost entirely gone. General Koller, as
usual, was wringing his hands, writing exculpatory reports to
the Fuehrer, to the Reich Marshal, to everyone, seeking to
explain that the whole incident arose from some misunderstanding and that Goering was guiltless. His explanations were
in vain. "Greim was more angry with the Reich Marshal than
ever before. He condemned him sharply for not staying with
the Fuehrer in the Bunker, and was just as savage about his
behaviour on 23rd April, which he calls treason. He told me,"
says Koller, "that I ought not to defend the Reich Marshal."
But Koller defended him: "I can understand why he didn't
stay in the Bunker. He hadn't a single friend there. He was
surrounded by enemies who, instead of helping him, had
fought against him and the Luftwaffe in the most malevolent
and insidious way for many months,—one might say, for the
last two years. Moreover, what would happen to Germany if
all those who were responsible for the conduct of affairs were
to lock themselves up in bunkers? It isn't for me to defend the
Reich Marshal,—he has too many faults for that. He has made
my life almost impossible—has treated me abominably, has
threatened me with court-martial and death for no reason at
all, and has threatened to shoot General Staff officers in front
of the assembled General Staff. In spite of all this, I cannot
change the facts which happened on 22nd and 23rd April. The
Reich Marshal has done nothing that can be called treason."

Koller's protestations were futile; but they have their interest. To Greim, to Christian, to von Below, to the leaders of the Combined General Staff, to Hitler himself,[4] Koller continued to explain the real cause of the incidents which had precipitated the fall of Goering; but neither the condemnation nor the punishment was reversed. Rather, both were accentuated; for in the last days, Bormann ordered Goering's execution, and Hitler, in his will, formally denounced him and expelled him from the Party. Clearly the truth was of no interest to those who had condemned him. What they wanted was not justice in this particular incident, but judgment on his whole career; and having secured that judgment, they were no longer interested in the technical details by which it had been secured.

On the night of 25th/26th April, Ritter von Greim flew to Rechlin. He was piloted by another exotic character, who accompanied him throughout his last adventures—the celebrated test pilot, Hanna Reitsch. Since Hanna Reitsch's account of her three days in Berlin has already been published,[4a] some account both of her personality and her reliability is necessary.

There is a somewhat incomplete type of woman whose personal affections are (as the psychologists say) sublimated into abstract terms. When such a woman loves or hates, the object of her love or hatred appears to her not as a human being, but as the visible embodiment of some abstract quality. But since an abstraction is of necessity an inhuman, intellectual, and invariable thing, it can be the object only of narrow, concentrated, and uncompromising emotions: sympathy becomes religious adoration, detachment becomes theological hate. To this tiresome category of persons Hanna Reitsch belongs. Shrill, vain, and voluble, her character was well suited

---

[4] Koller sent a full written report to Hitler by hand of Greim, and Greim reported its delivery. Nevertheless Hitler continued to rail at Goering to the end, and when Greim and Reitsch met Koller at Zell-am-See on 8th May 1945, they "attacked the Reich Marshal with coarse insults." Greim threatened to have Goering shot, and Reitsch begged Koller not to defend him.

[4a] News Chronicle, 28th, 29th, and 31st December 1945.

to the atmosphere in that last subterranean madhouse in Berlin. An ardent Nazi, she had long worshipped at the shrine of Adolf Hitler; in him, she says, she recognised the true quintessence of German honour, whatever that may mean. But later she discovered that she had made an error: Adolf Hitler's nature was rather more complex than she had supposed; it contained a certain quantity of impure and disastrous alloy; the true quintessence was represented by Ritter von Greim. Hanna Reitsch is too vain to suppose that her error in respect of Hitler was more than an error of interpretation; her emotions in respect of him are not reversed, they are divided. Half of him remains the incarnation of German honour, only half is the corrupting leaven; and under interrogation she is careful, before committing herself to an answer, to consider which part of his character is involved, and then to answer accordingly.

If half of Hitler and the whole of Ritter von Greim fall within the field of devotion, most of the other characters whom Hanna Reitsch mentions fall within the icy regions of her absolute hatred; they are abstractions of evil—of treachery, "dishonour," incompetence, and all vices. Goering, Goebbels, and Eva Braun fall within this category; and in her detestation of them, Hanna Reitsch is often misled by rhetoric into inaccuracy. Thus it is difficult to conceive of Goebbels "striding about in his small luxurious quarters," when those quarters contained no room for either strides or luxury; and some of her statements on Goering are refuted by the very witnesses to whom she appeals for confirmation. It is noticeable that Hanna Reitsch, like many vain people, most resents in others the qualities which are most characteristic of herself. She attacks Eva Braun in particular for feminine vanity, schoolgirl rhetoric, exclusive devotion to the man she loved, and denunciation of those whom she believed to have betrayed him. Her description of Eva Braun is no doubt substantially true; but it does not apply only to Eva Braun.

Such is the bias which runs throughout Hanna Reitsch's account of life in Hitler's Bunker; and where this bias may affect her presentation of facts, it must be read with caution.[5] Those who habitually deal in rhetoric sometimes find more matter for it than the subject affords. One significant error of fact must also be mentioned. Hanna Reitsch states that she and Greim left the Bunker in the early morning of 30th April. If that were so, they would have been witnesses of facts about which they are silent, and on which their silence would have been significant;[6] but it is not so. They left, as can be established with absolute certainty from several sources,[7] exactly twenty-four hours earlier.

Nevertheless, whatever tiresome qualities or historical inaccuracies Hanna Reitsch's account may reveal, it must be regarded as a document of unusual importance. The shortness of her stay in Berlin concentrated and sharpened her observation. For her, it was an exceptional experience, while the more regular inmates looked with duller eyes upon what had become a meaningless routine. Her bias, such as it is, is an involuntary bias; and although her character may be unattractive, her courage commands respect. The journeys which she made with Greim to and from Berlin were more hazardous and exciting than any she can have made as a test pilot.

Arriving at Rechlin in the early morning of 25th/26th April, Greim and Reitsch had intended to fly on into Berlin in a helicopter which could land in the gardens of the Reich Chancellery or the streets of the city. They found that only one helicopter was available, and it had been damaged that day. But the sergeant-pilot was there who had piloted Speer

[5] In this account Reitsch's narrative has been checked carefully against other sources, and no material statement is based on her account alone without explicit indication.

[6] E.g. both Greim and Reitsch insisted that no marriage had taken place when they left, and it could not have taken place without their knowledge.

[7] E.g. telegram from Christian's staff to Koller, quoted by Koller, s.d. 29th April; interrogation of Christian; Schwerin von Krosigk; etc.

on his last visit to the Bunker, and since he had had that experience once, he was ordered to repeat it, and to take Greim into Berlin by the same route. The plane was a Focke Wulf 190; it had room for one passenger only, behind the pilot's seat; but Hanna Reitsch was determined not to miss this last stage of the journey; and since Greim agreed to take her, and she was small, she was stuffed into the tail of the plane through a small emergency opening. Forty fighter planes accompanied them as they hedge-hopped through continuous Russian air attacks towards Gatow, the only Berlin aerodrome still in German hands. They reached Gatow with only a few shots in the wings; but many of the escorting fighter planes had been lost.

From Gatow Greim tried to telephone to the Chancellery, but it was impossible. Finding a training plane on the aerodrome, he therefore decided to fly into the city, and land on the street within walking distance of the Chancellery. The remainder of the German fighter planes engaged the Russians while Greim took off from the airfield. He was now himself at the controls, and Reitsch was with him as a passenger. They flew at treetop-level towards the Brandenburger Tor.

Below them, in the city, street fighting was in progress; above them, Russian planes were in the air. Within a few minutes heavy Russian fire tore the bottom out of the plane and shattered Greim's right foot. Reitsch leaned over his shoulder to take the controls, and by dodging and squirming close to the ground, brought the plane to rest on the East-West Axis. A passing car was commandeered and Greim was taken to the Chancellery, receiving first-aid on the way. In the Bunker he was taken to Stumpfegger's surgery, and Stumpfegger dressed his injured foot. It was now between six and seven o'clock in the evening of 26th April.

Hitler came into the surgery and welcomed Greim. His face, says Reitsch, showed gratitude for his coming. Even a soldier, he said, had a right to disobey orders which seemed

futile and hopeless. He asked Greim if he knew why he had
been summoned. Greim did not know.

"Because Hermann Goering has betrayed both me and his
Fatherland," Hitler explained. "Behind my back he has established connexions with the enemy. His action was a mark of
cowardice! And against my orders he has sent me a disrespect-
ful telegram, saying that I once named him as my successor,
and that now, since I can no longer rule from Berlin, he is
ready to rule from Berchtesgaden in my place. He closes the
telegram by saying that if he had no answer from me by 9.30
that night,[8] he would take my assent for granted!"

As Hitler spoke, there were tears in his eyes. His head
sagged; his face was white; and when he handed Goering's
fatal telegram to Greim to read, it fluttered with the trembling
of his hands. While Greim read, Hitler watched, breathing
hard in short, convulsive puffs. The muscles in his face
twitched. Suddenly he screamed:

"An ultimatum! a crass ultimatum! Nothing now remains!
nothing is spared me! no loyalty is kept, no honour observed;
there is no bitterness, no betrayal that has not been heaped
upon me; and now this! It is the end. No injury has been left
undone!"

After a pause, Hitler recovered his composure, and told
Greim that he had summoned him to declare him Commander-
in-Chief of the Luftwaffe, with the rank of Field-Marshal, in
succession to Goering. It was for this formality alone that the
lives of German airmen, and badly needed machines, had been
sacrificed to bring Greim into the Bunker. A telegram would
have been sufficient; but Hitler preferred this dramatic, if
expensive method, which incidentally imprisoned Greim for
three days, bedridden and useless, in the Bunker. Day after
day planes were sent from Rechlin to bring him out to his new
headquarters, now that he had received his commission,—for
although Greim and Reitsch begged to be allowed to stay in

[8] Actually 10 P.M.

Berlin and atone with their lives for the honour of the Luftwaffe (whatever that may mean), Hitler insisted that they
must return; but every plane in turn was shot down by the
Russians before it reached Berlin.[9]

That night, Hitler summoned Hanna Reitsch to his own
room. His face was lined, and his eyes were glazed by a constant film of moisture. He told her that the cause now seemed
hopeless, unless, as he still hoped (and his confidence grew as
he mentioned the hope), Wenck's army could advance to
relieve the city from the southwest. But if not,—if the Russians took the city,—then he and Eva Braun had made all
plans to commit suicide and to have their bodies consumed by
fire; and he gave Hanna Reitsch phials of poison for herself
and Greim, to be used in that emergency. There was a melodramatic scene, such as seems to have happened so regularly
in the life, or at least in the diary, of Hanna Reitsch.

That night Russian shells began to fall on the Chancellery
itself, and the inhabitants of the Bunker sat up in various postures of fear and bravado while the vast and solid-seeming
superstructure cracked and crashed above their heads. Hanna
Reitsch spent most of the night watching at the bedside of
Ritter von Greim, and in preparing for their common suicide
if the Russians should break in in the morning. They had
agreed that they would swallow the poison which Hitler had
given them, and then quickly, before it had taken effect, pull
the pins from heavy hand-grenades close to their bodies. Thus
in one movement they would die of poison and their corpses
be blown to pieces. It was not only Hitler and Eva Braun who
would go out of the world with a bang.

[9] The fact that every plane was shot down emerges from a careful reading of Reitsch's narrative, and is explicitly stated by General Christian.
Reitsch's statement that a plane which succeeded in landing in Berlin on 27th
April was sent back empty since Greim and Reitsch wished to stay in Berlin
is inconsistent with the statements of both Christian and Koller, who were
responsible for sending such planes. Koller quotes a telephone conversation
with Greim on 27th April in which Greim asked for planes to be sent to
fetch him away.

Meanwhile the unfortunate General Koller was not being allowed to stay in sense and safety at Obersalzberg. His excellent excuses of health, reason, and duty were ignored. In the afternoon of 26th April he was informed, by Bormann's representative in Berchtesgaden, that whatever the state of his health, he must fly to Berlin and report to the Fuehrer; it was the Fuehrer's personal order. Even a soldier, it seemed, had not the right to disobey orders which seemed futile and hopeless. Koller wrung his hands, telephoned hither and thither, and soliloquised eloquently but indecisively in his diary. How was he to know that the order came from the Fuehrer? How could anyone tell who had signed a telegram? And why had an order from the Fuehrer come through Bormann's office, and not through the Luftwaffe's own representative with the Fuehrer? It was very curious. He thought of the unfortunate Goering, the malevolence of Bormann, and the inadequate protection of mere innocence. But then the whole situation in the Bunker was somewhat curious; in that looking-glass world the Fuehrer's actions were bound to be a little queer; and it certainly seemed, from an order which had arrived in Munich for General Winter, that Hitler had resumed that full authority over the armed forces which, on 22nd April, he had seemed to renounce. Koller decided after all to fly to Berlin. He had caused one muddle by too original an interpretation, and now he would risk his life rather than his judgment. He said goodbye to his family, resisted the dissuasions of his orderly officers, and prepared to go. "The officers of the staff pulled long faces," he records; "they said afterwards that they wouldn't have given a brass farthing for my life, and had believed that Bormann would get rid of me. That would have been easy to do in encircled Berlin. No one need know of it." In the early hours of the morning Koller landed at Rechlin, prepared to fly on into the city and land, like Speer and Greim, on the East-West Axis. The accounts he received at Rechlin were discouraging. Since last night, he was told, it was impossible to fly to Berlin. Columns of smoke were rising from the doomed city; all airfields were closed, even Gatow; and a chain of defensive fires blazed along all approaches to the East-West Axis. All agreed that the last plane had visited Berlin; Ritter von Greim and Hanna Reitsch were there for good.

At the headquarters of the Combined General Staff at Fuerstenburg, Koller alternately listened to such gloomy tales, and sought consolation in the distressing matter of the Reich Marshal. He consulted Jodl; Jodl was sympathetic but inconclusive. He consulted Keitel, but Keitel pleaded pressure of work and slid away. He found Himmler, and applied to him for enlightenment. "A bad business," said Himmler ambiguously, and disappeared, expressing a polite hope of conversation at some later time. Then Doenitz arrived for the briefing, and Koller turned to him. "The Grand Admiral said that he was convinced the Reich Marshal's motives had been of the best; but then he cut the conversation short, saying that he must go to lunch. He also said that he wanted to speak to me later, but he left very suddenly." It was all very queer, thought Koller. He had expected these important events to be the main topic of discourse and speculation; "but I got the impression that no one wanted to talk about the affair of the Reich Marshal or about the seriousness of the situation. It had always seemed to me that these people were living on a different planet, and were afraid to open their mouths."

In perplexity of spirit, Koller went to the telephone and spoke to the Fuehrerbunker to report his arrival at Fuerstenburg. The Fuehrer himself had retired and could not be disturbed. He spoke to Ritter von Greim. Greim told him not to attempt to fly to Berlin. The Fuehrer had not ordered it; it was quite unnecessary; and it was probably impossible. Even if it were possible to get in, it would be quite impossible to get out. Greim himself was doomed, lying in bed in the Bunker, with the Fuehrer talking at his bedside. . . .

Koller condoled. He condoled with Greim's plight, his wounds, his unprofitable appointment. He lamented the frustration of their efforts, and philosophised mournfully on the impending fate of Germany. "We shall not be able to work together for long, Herr Feldmarschall," he intoned lugubriously into the telephone; "we cannot make much out of the Luftwaffe now, and the end is approaching." Then he awaited a mournful echo from the Bunker. But the world was full of surprises for General Koller. Life in the Bunker seemed even madder than life in Fuerstenburg. Ritter von Greim, like everyone who had been drawn into the magic circle around Hitler, had been seduced away from his wits by that extraordinary personality. It had happened to them all,—it had happened to Stumpfegger, who had forgotten Himmler and Gebhardt and all their interests and was now bowing before a new shrine; it had happened to Burgdorf, the regular officer who had deserted his caste and now, when overcome by wine, danced with Bormann and denounced treacherous fieldmarshals; [10] it had happened to Hewel, Ribbentrop's liaison officer; it had happened to Himmler; even the sagacious Speer had not been able to resist that compelling enchantment; and now it had happened to Ritter von Greim. Instead of lugubrious admissions of defeat, Koller was astonished to hear hilarious promises of inevitable victory. "Just you wait," replied the voice of the stricken Field-Marshal. "Don't despair! Everything will be well! The presence of the Fuehrer and his confidence have completely inspired me. This place is as good as a fountain of youth for me!" Koller could not believe his ears. "The whole place is a lunatic-asylum!" he protested to himself. "I simply don't understand it. I often ask myself whether I am really too stupid to follow the spiritual soarings of these people and to recognise the way of salvation.

[10] Burgdorf's dance with Bormann took place at a party at Rastenburg at which he committed many indiscretions. There is general agreement about his drinking habits.

Or perhaps they have a sixth sense and can see things to which we ordinary mortals are blind. One begins to doubt one's own sanity."

Shortly afterwards another telephone call gave Koller another breath from the Bunker. It was the voice of Hanna Reitsch. She wished Koller to give her last message to her family in Salzburg, explaining that she could not refuse Greim's appeal.[11] Then she gave a detailed description of her flight, omitting nothing and repeating everything. In vain Koller sought to stem the flood; nothing would stop her. After twenty minutes he hung up the receiver and left her rhapsodising into the void. "That was the only line to the Bunker, and it was required for more urgent business."

Nevertheless not everyone in the Bunker was equally mad, or equally inspired by the fountain of youth. On this same day, 27th April, one man at least showed signs of sanity. Unfortunately for him, it is as inadvisable to be sane in a madhouse as mad in a sane world; and such was the experience of Fegelein.

Fegelein was Himmler's personal representative at the Fuehrer's headquarters. Like Himmler, and all the more detestable of the Nazis, he was a Bavarian. He had begun his career as a gentleman of the turf. There the elegancy of his horsemanship had excited the admiration of Christian Weber,[12] "the uncrowned king of Bavaria," who had himself been a groom in a fashionable stable before the favour of the Nazis had raised him to magnificence and the vast increase of his girth had incapacitated him for the saddle. Through the good graces of

[11] In fact Greim had not appealed at all; Reitsch had insisted on accompanying him.

[12] Weber, one of the most corrupt and fraudulent of the Nazi bosses, was President of the municipal council of Munich. He amassed a colossal fortune by various forms of privileged speculation. The stables which he built for his ten race-horses (some of them looted from French racing-stables) have been described as "a horses' paradise." He was murdered during the Bavarian rising of April–May 1945.

Weber, Fegelein's promotion had been rapid. He had joined
the Waffen S.S., and soon had the command of a cavalry division. Lucky in all his enterprises except the last, he attracted
Hitler's notice by fortunate successes on the Eastern Front;
and in 1944 he succeeded Wolff as Himmler's liaison officer
with Hitler. In the same year he achieved what seemed to
many his most brilliant success. Observing, with the keen eye
of the opportunist, that the centre of power in the Nazi hierarchy had left the cabinet and the ministries for the court and
the levée, he married Gretl, the sister of Eva Braun. Thus, at
what seemed the most favourable moment, he detached himself from sole dependence on the fortunes of Himmler, now
beginning to wane, and secured his position in the family circle
of the Fuehrer. At the same time he did not omit to protect
his rear by a judicious alliance with Bormann. From that time
onwards, in the words of one who was well qualified to
judge,[13] "he thoroughly betrayed Himmler to the Fuehrer,"
whose side he rarely left.[14] It was he, says Schellenberg, who
advised Hitler publicly to dishonour the S.S. regiment which
had been massacred in a hopeless effort to conform to the
Fuehrer's strategy,—an insult which the soldiers never forgave to Himmler, who had been powerless to prevent it.[15] He
was, says Speer, "a very unpleasant type," and exercised "a
pernicious and radical influence" at court; and the loyal subordinates of Himmler—men not unfamiliar with the infinite
varieties of human depravity—are unanimous in their delinea-
tions of the vices of Fegelein.

Nevertheless, if Fegelein was a cad, he was not a fool; or at
least not such a fool as Ritter von Greim. His actions, his
loyalties, his betrayals, had always been inspired by a calcu-
lated, almost intellectual self-interest, quite unencumbered by

[13] Ohlendorf.
[14] According to Berger, "Bormann, Fegelein, and Burgdorf formed a very
close circle round Hitler, and it was hardly possible for an outsider to
penetrate it, especially after the attempt on his life." Speer has said the same.
[15] See above, p. 89, n. 4.

principles or scruples. If he had deserted Himmler for Hitler, that was not because he, like so many less critical spirits, had been bewitched by that hypnotic influence; it was because Himmler was losing his value and the personal court of Hitler promised more advantages to a resourceful climber. His allegiance, his alliances, his marriage,—all these had been based upon expediency: they were the methods by which he hoped to share the privileges of the family circle. But on 25th April, when Fegelein returned to the Bunker from his last visit to the outside world,[16] it was clear to that lucid mind that the privileges of the family circle were becoming daily less enviable; for the declarations of Hitler and Eva Braun on that subject had been painfully explicit. Fegelein did not hesitate. He had not secured his adoption into the family circle merely in order to burn on the family pyre. Leaving the other inhabitants of the Bunker to cluster hysterically round the Fuehrer and beg participation in the sacrament of his death,[17] Fegelein seized a favourable opportunity, slipped unnoticed out of the Bunker, and disappeared.

From the timeless records of the Bunker, and the dark, lugubrious secrecy in which the whole episode was enclosed, it is impossible now to extract with certainty the dates and stages of this last, uncharacteristic episode in the life of Fegelein: his failure. His ordinary residence in the Chancellery was not in the Fuehrerbunker, but in one of the other two bunkers, and his disappearance was for some time unnoticed by Hitler's immediate *entourage*. Occasional telephone calls, in which he asked for the latest news, were at any rate evidence that he was still in Berlin; and they enquired no further. It was appar-

[16] Fegelein had left Berlin by car, with S.S. Hstuf. Bornholdt of the S.S. Begleitkommando, to visit Ogruf. Juettner, head of the S.S. Fuehrungshauptamt, at Fuerstenburg. On 25th April return by car was impossible, and Fegelein had flown back, leaving Bornholdt at Fuerstenburg. (Statement by Bornholdt.) Fegelein's last words to Juettner had been, "I certainly don't intend to die in Berlin" (Juettner).

[17] At least this is the picture given by Hanna Reitsch, although less rhetorical witnesses have not recorded the same details.

ently on 27th April, late in the afternoon, that Hitler demanded his presence and learnt that Fegelein was no longer
in the Chancellery. Enquiries were made. None knew whither
he had gone. In that unnatural atmosphere suspicion was
quickly aroused, and once aroused, became certainty. Suspicion was anyway part of Hitler's nature now. It had become
chronic after the Generals' Plot, and every recent experience
had confirmed it. At once he sent for the head of his personal
police-guard, the trained detectives who shadowed him and
every other high Nazi leader. This officer, S.S. Standartenfuehrer Hoegl, was ordered to go out into the city, taking
with him a party of armed guards from the S.S. Escort.[18] He
was to find Fegelein, and to bring him back into the Bunker.
Hoegl went out into the Charlottenburg area of Berlin, where
Fegelein lived, and there, in his own house, found him quietly
resting on his bed, in civilian clothes. Free at last, as he
thought, from the safe but stormy atmosphere of the Bunker,
Fegelein was able, in this more civilised *milieu*, quietly and
dispassionately to survey the world; to compare, in philosophical detachment, the relative advantages of life and death, and
to choose, freely, the alternative which seemed more attractive
to his opportunist mind. He explained to Hoegl that he had
chosen survival, and suggested that, with his assistance, an
airplane might be found to take him away from the doomed
city to his wife and pleasant family life in Bavaria. This sug-

[18] Hitler had two distinct guards: (1) *Reichssicherheitsdienst* (RSD), an
organization under the command of Brigf. Rattenhuber (who remained in
the Bunker), which consisted of separate units (*Dienststellen*) allocated to
the personal protection of high Nazi leaders. *Dienststelle 1* of this organisation, under the command of S.S. Staf. Hoegl, was Hitler's personal guard,
and was at this time partly at Obersalzberg, partly in the Bunker. The RSD
guard was composed of trained detectives from the Criminal Police (*Kripo*),
who also (since the whole German police was under Himmler) held S.S.
ranks. The guards who witnessed the burning of Hitler's body came from
this force. (2) The *S.S. Begleitkommando*, or Escort, under the command
of S.S. Ostuf. Franz Schedle. This was a purely military guard, consisting of
smart and loyal, but unintelligent soldiers, who kept watch over official
buildings, and were regarded with some disdain by the more observant but
less obtrusive RSD.

gestion aroused no response from the obedient Hoegl. No
such arrangement was thinkable, he replied, without the explicit authority of the Fuehrer. Fegelein was not dismayed.
Picking up the telephone, he put through another call to the
Bunker and spoke to his sister-in-law, Eva Braun. There had
been a misunderstanding, he explained; would she smooth the
matter over, use her influence with the Fuehrer, and obtain
the necessary sanction? Alas, the cool exercise of the intelligence, which could so easily be indulged in the free, if somewhat sulphurous atmosphere of Charlottenburg, was quite
impossible in the cramped, subterranean Bunker of the Chancellery, where threats and promises, preachings and protestations, high-pitched oratory and meaningless generalities (if we
are to believe Hanna Reitsch) excluded all rational noises. Eva
Braun replied curtly that such a proposal could not be considered; Fegelein must return to the Bunker; and while Fegelein
was marched back to the Chancellery under armed guard, she
wrung her hands at yet another betrayal. "Poor, poor Adolf!"
she would declare, "deserted by everyone, betrayed by all!
Better that ten thousand others die than that he be lost to
Germany!" The Fuehrer was spared nothing, she said sadly;
Goering had wickedly betrayed him; and now, at the end of
his life, he had been deserted even by his old and trusted friend
Fegelein. On his return, Fegelein was degraded from his rank
of Grupenfuehrer and kept, for the time being, under armed
guard in the second bunker.[19]

That night, the night of 27th/28th April, the Russian bombardment of the Chancellery reached its highest pitch. To
those who cowered in the Bunker and heard the shells falling
above them, the accuracy seemed deadly; every shell, it
seemed, fell exactly in the centre of the Chancellery buildings.
At any moment they now expected the Russian ground troops

[19] The details of Fegelein's arrest are given by Fraeulein Krueger, who
had them from Beetz. Other details in this paragraph are taken from Reitsch
and von Below.

to arrive and overrun the ruins. During the night, according to Hanna Reitsch, Hitler called his court around him, and in this macabre conclave all rehearsed their plans for suicide and considered, in maudlin detail, the various methods in which their corpses might be destroyed. The first appearance of Russian solders, they agreed, would be the signal for the execution of this ritual self-sacrifice. Then everyone made a short speech, swearing perpetual allegiance to the Fuehrer and Germany. If such was really the climate of the Bunker, few sensible people will blame the prudent decision of Fegelein.

In fact, of course, it was mostly humbug: the artificial emotion and corresponding verbiage so easily generated, and once generated so easily accepted as both true and moving, by the immature Teutonic mind. The competitive servility of a court is always odious; combined with eloquent humbug, it is nauseating. In fact, as will appear, very few of those who thus professed a desire for communal death gave effect to their heroic resolutions. Ritter von Greim, it is true, when a month had passed and his untended wound made further movement impossible, swallowed his poison in captivity; and one or two others may possibly have done the same in Russian hands. But it is interesting to reflect how many whose resolve to die has been recorded have since been found in continued health and restored sanity, eagerly explaining to their British and American captors that they never really owed any allegiance to Nazi Germany.

Of Hitler at least it can be said that his emotions were genuine. He at least intended to die if Berlin fell. And yet,— such was the extraordinary confidence which still alternated with his despair,—even now he still believed that the city might be saved. Though he was prepared to die if it fell, nevertheless it seemed impossible that the capital of the Reich really could fall with the Fuehrer inside it. He regarded himself, it seems, as a kind of palladium, a totem whose presence rendered any citadel impregnable, so long as he stayed. "If I leave East Prussia," he had told Keitel at Rastenburg, "then East Prussia will fall; if I stay, it will be held." Keitel had persuaded him to leave East Prussia, and East Prussia had duly fallen; but he did not intend to leave Berlin, and Berlin therefore could not fall. So he deluded himself as he held out, in an ever-contracting pocket of the city, awaiting the arrival of Wenck's army, for which the Hitler Youth were desperately holding the bridgeheads on the Havel. Wenck's army was in fact already a defeated force; but Hitler had long been accustomed, from underground bunkers, to direct the operations of non-existent armies, to dictate their strategy and tactics, dispose their forces, calculate their gains, and then to denounce the treachery of their generals when the actual results failed to correspond with his private conclusions. So in these days he would expound the tactics whereby Wenck would relieve the city. Pacing up and down in the Bunker (according to the dramatic Hanna Reitsch), he would wave a road-map, fast decomposing with the sweat of his hands, and explain to any casual visitor the complicated military operations whereby they would all be saved. Sometimes he would shout orders, as if himself directing the defenders; sometimes he would spread the map on the table, and stooping over it, with trembling hands he would arrange and rearrange a set of buttons, as consolatory symbols of relieving armies. In the tropical climate of a court, emotions and beliefs quickly change their direction. No one except Hitler still believed in Wenck's army, but no one disagreed with his assurances; and in a moment of time the chorus which had been chanting *lamentoso*, the dirge of despair and suicide, would suddenly break out *allegro vivace*, with a triumphant welcome for the army of Wenck.[20]

[20] Hans Fritzsche, head of the radio department of the Propaganda Ministry, described at Nuremberg (27th June 1946) how "in the days when Berlin was surrounded by the Russian Army, the people of Berlin was told that a relief army, the Wenck Army, was marching on Berlin . . . and leaflets were printed in Berlin containing approximately this text: 'Soldiers of the

The most obstinate illusions are ultimately broken by facts. On 28th April the Russians were already fighting near the centre of Berlin, and still there were no signs of Wenck. Hysterical telegrams began to flow outward from the Bunker. "I expect the relief of Berlin," Hitler wired to Keitel. "What is Heinrici's army doing? Where is Wenck? What is happening to the Ninth Army? When will Wenck and the Ninth Army join?" [21] All day the inhabitants of the Bunker waited for news, and since none came, repeated rumours instead. What could be the explanation of Wenck's failure? One explanation, the obvious, the true explanation, was that Wenck's army, as a fighting force, no longer existed; but obvious truth was unlikely to be heard among the conflicting noises of the Bunker. There only one explanation could be entertained. Whatever the problem, the answer was always the same: it was treachery. As the day proceeded, this explanation seemed more obvious. Communication with the outer world was diminishing; only the radio-telephone to the Combined General Staff still served as a channel of information, but could even Keitel now be trusted? At eight o'clock that night Bormann sent a telegram which vividly illustrates the temper now prevailing in the beleaguered Bunker. It was sent to Admiral von Puttkamer in Munich, to be relayed to Doenitz. "Instead of urging the troops forward to our rescue with orders and appeals," it ran, "the men in authority are silent. Treachery seems to have replaced loyalty! We remain here. The Chancellery is already in ruins." An hour later authentic news at last reached the Bunker from the outside world. It

---

Wenck Army, we Berliners know that you have reached Potsdam. Hurry! Help us!'" These leaflets were scattered in Berlin, as if by mistake, to raise the morale of the citizens.

[21] Keitel has given the text of this telegram from memory, saying that he received it at Waren on 28th April. (It is possible that he has mistaken the date, as his dates are sometimes incorrect; but I have given him the benefit of the doubt.) Generaloberst Gotthard Heinrici had succeeded Himmler in command of the Army Group Vistula, now fighting west of Berlin.

was brought over from the Propaganda Ministry by the official of the Press Service whose duty it was to translate and deliver to the Fuehrerbunker such items of foreign news as seemed important. This official was Heinz Lorenz, and the news which he brought was the news of Himmler's negotiations with Count Bernadotte. There had been a leakage to the Press.

Chapter Six

ET TU BRUTE
(28TH-29TH APRIL)

SINCE he had left Luebeck after his last meeting with Bernadotte, Himmler had thought no more of his, or rather Schellenberg's complicated conspiracies; those he had left to Schellenberg, who, for the next three days, waited eagerly in Flensburg and Denmark, his delicate antennae quivering in the direction of Stockholm, ever ready to catch the first faint message of success. Thence, on 27th April, Bernadotte had returned, bringing with him the news which the head of any but a Nazi intelligence service might have expected: that neither Himmler nor a limited surrender was acceptable to the Western Powers. With a sinking heart Schellenberg had heard the news of this, to him, quite unexpected failure. For so long now he had admired his own subtlety, his diplomatic virtuosity and Swedish connexions, that it had never occurred to him that he would fail utterly. He had staked his reputation, and Himmler's, on success. How could he now face Himmler, whom he had so pertinaciously and (as it now appeared) so indefensibly forced into this false and vulnerable position? He was relieved when Bernadotte offered to accompany him into Himmler's presence and give him countenance; but when he telephoned to Himmler's office and explained to Dr. Brandt, Himmler's secretary, that the result had been negative, and that Count Bernadotte was anxious to come and see Himmler, the answer was an absolute refusal. Himmler had seen quite enough of Count Bernadotte, and never wished to see him again.

Trembling with apprehension, Schellenberg made diplomatic excuses to Bernadotte, and then set out alone to face his master. On the way, he reflected on the reception he was likely to have. His thoughts were gloomy; but once again his ever-resourceful diplomacy came to his aid. "As I knew," he writes, "that my position with Himmler was now very difficult, and that in certain circumstances I must expect to be liquidated, I hit on the idea of sending for an astrologer from Hamburg, personally known to Himmler, whom I took with me, in order that an astrological session might absorb some of the bitterness of disappointment; for I knew that Himmler had a great opinion of this particular gentleman." [1] By such ingenious expedients did the high politicians of the Third Reich lubricate their personal diplomacy. It is agreeable to record that when Schellenberg faced Himmler, in the early hours of 29th April, he was not liquidated, although his situation had now become even worse, since the news of the negotiations had by this time become public. Himmler was not unnaturally irritated, and expressed bitter disappointment. He saw that nothing but ill could come of the whole business; he feared that his letter to the Swedish Foreign Minister would now be published; he pointed to the consequences which this affair would have in his relations with Hitler; and he blamed Schellenberg as the moving spirit in the whole matter. "Nevertheless," records the complacent Schellenberg, "I managed, with the help of the aforementioned astrologer, to put forward the proposals for a more limited solution so convincingly that he withdrew for an hour to think it over." Ultimately Himmler agreed to pursue this more limited solution, which entailed a cessation of hostilities in Norway and Denmark, and instructed Schellenberg accordingly. He did this the more confidently because he still felt sure of the future. Hitler was taking a long time to die, but the end must come soon; and then, as the new Fuehrer, Himmler would have power to make all necessary decisions.

[1] The astrologer was of course Wulf. Cf. above, pp. 22, 85.

For all this time it had never occurred to Himmler to doubt that he was the heir-apparent to Hitler's throne. He was Reichsfuehrer; he had his private army; his numerous offices, his long record, his hitherto undisputed loyalty all emphasised his claims; and one reason why he would never conspire to seize power lay in his confidence that it would automatically devolve upon him. He even had a programme prepared for the occasion,—though not of course by himself; such originality was not within his narrow faculties. He contemplated a new party, for which Schellenberg had obligingly supplied a name,—the Party of National Union; [2] and he had a shadow government composed of high police leaders and others who, like Schellenberg, believed that a government headed by Himmler could both survive and enable them to survive under the favour of the Western Allies.[3] Among these optimists we must include the murderous Ohlendorf and the asinine Schwerin von Krosigk; neither the record of the one, nor the intellect of the other, was considered incompatible with political office under the rule of the supreme crank and prime criminal of the Nazi system.

Such illusions may seem to us desperate; but it was not only Himmler's subordinates who entertained them. Almost every Nazi recognised in Himmler the natural successor to Hitler, once Goering had fallen. On the very day when his relations with Bernadotte were published, Himmler described to one of his followers how he intended to exercise his new authority, adding that he had spoken to Doenitz, and that Doenitz, who equally regarded Himmler as Fuehrer-designate, had volunteered to work under his command.[4] On the same day, Schwerin von Krosigk discussed the same question with two of Doenitz' supporters. Since both Goering and Hess were out of the question, they agreed, there were three possibilities.

[2] *Nationale Sammlungspartei.*
[3] This shadow government is mentioned by Ohlendorf and Speer as well as by Schellenberg.
[4] Ohlendorf.

Either Hitler would make no alteration in his so-called "will," [5] in which case only Himmler would fulfil the conditions of inheritance; or Hitler would alter his will,—and then, they agreed, he could name only Himmler as his successor; or the decision would be left to the emergency provision of the constitution,—but when they considered what that would entail, they found that it only led to Himmler again. Even two days later, when Himmler's negotiations were known throughout the world, Speer and others were solemnly discussing the same problem, and agreeing that there was no conceivable alternative to Himmler.[6]

Like so many in those last days, they forgot that Hitler was not yet dead. Besieged in the shattered capital, cooped up fifty feet below the ground, cut off from ordinary communication, a physical and mental wreck, without power to enforce, or reason to persuade, or machinery to execute, Hitler still remained, in the universal chaos he had caused, the sole master whose orders were implicitly obeyed. Goering, imprisoned under an S.S. guard at Mautendorf, now had leisure to reflect on the dangers of anticipating that fatal inheritance. Soon Himmler was to learn the same lesson. The power of the Fuehrer was a magic power, and no profane hand might reach out to touch it until the reigning priest was really dead.

We turn our attention therefore back to the underground Bunker whither Lorenz had brought from the Propaganda Ministry the British Reuter report of Himmler's negotiations with Count Bernadotte. In the Bunker, Lorenz found Bormann, Goebbels, and Hewel sitting together, and to them he gave one copy of the text. They told him that Hitler was in conference with Ritter von Greim. He therefore gave a second copy to Heinz Linge, Hitler's personal servant, to be handed to the Fuehrer.

[5] This does not of course refer to the testament of 29th April, which was not known in Ploen, but to Hitler's pre-war declaration.
[6] Schwerin von Krosigk.

The scene which followed the delivery of that note has been variously described, according to the opportunities of knowledge, and the resources of vocabulary, possessed by the various witnesses of it. All agree that it was a terrible scene. Hitler stormed with indignation. "He raged like a madman," says Hanna Reitsch; "his colour rose to a heated red, and his face was almost unrecognisable." This was the last, the unkindest cut of all: *der treue Heinrich*—faithful Heinrich—had betrayed him; the one Nazi leader whose loyalty had always been above suspicion had now stabbed him in the back. As the news spread round the Bunker, the obedient chorus again echoed the voice of its leader, and men and women competed to denounce the traitor. Then Hitler withdrew with Bormann and Goebbels behind locked doors and a conference began.

What occurred, or was decided, at that conference we shall probably never know in detail. The participants are all dead or missing; and although Krebs and Burgdorf may afterwards have been called in, they are missing too. But from that moment the events in the Bunker acquired a new momentum; the period of waiting for Wenck was followed by a period of decision and action comparable with the crisis of 22nd April; the last phase of the comedy had begun.

There can be no doubt that to Hitler the treachery of Himmler, as he conceived it to be, was the signal for the end. Always he had hesitated before his decisions; he had wavered and waited, and by his wavering had perplexed his impatient followers; then he had made his decision, and it had been final. He had wavered for two days before deciding whether to stay in Berlin or not, and then he had decided to stay, and had stayed, and no pressure, no persuasion had shaken that decision. After that he had waited for a week before deciding how to make an end of it; now he faced that decision. During the night of 28th/29th April he disposed finally of Himmler's claim to the succession; he wrote his last will and testament; and he married Eva Braun.

First he sent for Fegelein. Since the incredible news of Himmler's defection had been brought to him, old problems had suddenly assumed a new complexion. Now he realised why the Steiner attack had failed on 21st April; Himmler had never meant that it should succeed and had ordered Steiner not to move. Now he knew why Fegelein had deserted from the Bunker; it was part of an elaborate S.S. plot. Fegelein was closely questioned, apparently by Gruppenfuehrer Mueller, head of the Gestapo.[7] It is said that he admitted to a knowledge that Himmler had had meetings with Count Bernadotte. That may easily be true, for Himmler's meetings with Bernadotte were no more secret than those of Kaltenbrunner or Ribbentrop. Whatever he may have known or admitted, he can hardly have confessed (as overheated minds afterwards imagined) to a plot by Himmler to murder Hitler, for no such plot existed. Though some high members of the S.S. had envisaged such a plot,[8] Himmler, as we have seen, had never countenanced it; only the wishful thinking of Schellenberg had made him so imagine. And though Steiner himself desired negotiation with the West, the failure of his attack needs no political explanation and certainly was not intended by Himmler, who believed in its necessity.[9] Nevertheless it was not

---

[7] Mueller is mentioned by Frau Junge, Kempka and Axmann as having conducted the examination of Fegelein, and others have referred to his appearance in the Bunker during the last days; but the whole Fegelein incident is somewhat obscure. As a high S.S. officer, Mueller might have been suspect after Himmler's treachery; but his position was by now almost independent of Himmler, and he was never trusted by Himmler's other subordinates.

[8] Apart from Schellenberg, such a coup was certainly contemplated by certain other police and S.S. leaders (including Steiner, Ohlendorf, Gottberg, and Hildebrandt); but it seems never to have developed beyond the stage of loose talk.

[9] Steiner's political views are given by Ohlendorf, but it is clear from Schellenberg's complaints that Himmler believed in the necessity of the Steiner attack, and intended it to succeed. "Himmler was still," he says (on 22nd April), "convinced of the necessity of this order of the Fuehrer [i.e. for the attack], while I agreed with his military adjutant Grothmann that it was an unnecessary spilling of blood. My protests were ignored, as I was supposed to understand nothing of military matters."

justice that Hitler required, but revenge. Himmler's defection, he declared,[10] was the worst act of treachery he had ever known; Fegelein's attempted escape was in itself sufficiently criminal; and he wanted blood. Dr. Brandt had escaped his clutches at the last minute: Fegelein should not. After a brief formality, Fegelein was taken out of the Bunker by guards of the Escort, led into the Chancellery garden, and shot.[11]

Relieved by this incident of blood-letting, Hitler turned aside to consider the military situation. Russian tanks had now been reported in the Potsdamer Platz, and Greim was ordered to ensure that every available plane was sent forward to attack them. Greim gave his orders to General Christian by telephone; but more personal supervision would soon be possible. For on 28th April, after nearly three days of imprisonment in the Bunker and against all expectation, a plane had at last made its way into Berlin to take the new commander-in-chief of the Luftwaffe back to his operational headquarters. It was an Arado 96 training plane, and the sergeant-pilot who had brought it in from Rechlin had circled down from a height of 13,000 feet to land it upon the East-West Axis.

Shortly after midnight, Hitler came into Greim's room to convey to him his last orders. His face was white, and sitting on the edge of the bed he explained to Greim the twofold nature of his mission. Firstly, he was to mount an attack by the Luftwaffe against those Russian positions from which the assault on the Chancellery would be made. With the help of the Luftwaffe, Wenck might yet force his way to Berlin. Secondly, he must order the arrest of the treacherous Himmler. As he mentioned that name, Hitler's voice became more unsteady, and his lips and hands trembled. "A traitor must never succeed me as Fuehrer," he shouted; "you must go out to ensure that he does not!"

[10] To Axmann.
[11] See note on *The Execution of Fegelein*, p. 247.

Both Greim and Reitsch protested; they wished to stay; the attempt, they said, would be futile; they would never reach Rechlin. . . . But Hitler insisted that they must go. It was the only chance of success. To this Greim yielded. The insufferable Hanna Reitsch continued her rodomontade, and left the Bunker, as she had entered it, in a profusion of tears, rhetoric, and abstract nouns. With her she carried hastily-written letters from the inhabitants of the Bunker—official letters from Hewel to the headquarters of the Foreign Office at Schloss Fuschl, near Salzburg, and from Bormann to the Party Chancery at Obersalzberg, and private letters from Goebbels and his wife to her son, and from Eva Braun to her sister Frau Fegelein. Goebbels' letter contained some fine phrases about his exemplary devotion to the Fuehrer's pure and holy cause. The letter from Eva Braun does not survive. It was, says Hanna Reitsch, "so vulgar, so theatrical, and in such poor, adolescent taste" that its survival could only do harm; and she tore it up. In these qualities Hanna Reitsch preferred to remain without a rival. In this eloquent, egotistical letter it is to be observed (if Hanna Reitsch has remembered the text aright) that no reference was made to the health of Frau Fegelein's husband, whose body, at the time of writing, was being buried in the Chancellery garden.

When Greim left the Bunker, he carried with him one consolation for his wounded spirit. For many months Hitler had stormed at the incompetence and cowardice of the high command of the Luftwaffe, had insulted its officers, demanded the impossible, and threatened savage revenge. Now that Goering had gone, his resentment seemed to have evaporated too. To Greim he praised the Luftwaffe with particular and redeeming emphasis; it had fought best of all the Armed Forces, he said, from the beginning to the end. Even the enemy had allowed that everybody, even the ground personnel, had fought with exceptional bravery. For its technical inferiority others, he said pointedly, were to blame. He even, in the course of this *amende honorable*, threw a dewdrop to poor old General Koller, who had so often wrung his hands unavailingly under the torrent of inspired abuse that had formerly been discharged upon that universal scapegoat, the Chief of Staff of the Luftwaffe.[12]

The later history of Greim and Reitsch can be shortly described. They flew out of Berlin, as they had entered it, amid scenes of destruction and experiences of danger which lose nothing of dramatic property in the narrative of Hanna Reitsch. Explosions tossed the plane to and fro like a feather, till they had climbed to a height of 20,000 feet, and, looking down, could see Berlin like a sea of flame beneath them. From Rechlin Greim gave his orders for all available aircraft to support the relief of Berlin. Thence they flew on to Ploen, to Doenitz' headquarters; and we are favoured with a graphic, but perhaps inaccurate, account of an interview between Hanna Reitsch and Himmler, in which the loyal denunciations of the stage heroine glanced ineffectually away from the hard, cold skin of the stage villain, until a dramatic air raid terminated the argument. After a few days at Ploen, Greim and Reitsch, the wounded hero and the devoted heroine, set out on their travels again, flying to Koeniggraetz, to Graz, to Zell am See, with patriotic messages for Schoerner and Kesselring. At Zell am See they met the plodding General Koller; and from his more pedestrian pen we have a last glimpse of this curious couple,—Greim, now a total wreck, his skin yellow, hobbling on two crutches; Reitsch weeping and posturing; and both singing their tedious duet, now a ferocious denunciation of Goering, now a devout litany about the Fuehrer and the Fatherland. "In these circumstances," complained Koller, "it is very difficult to discuss practical matters."

---

[12] Greim, quoted by Koller (8th May 1945). Part of the foregoing account, which is based largely on the statements of Greim (to Koller) and Reitsch, is also confirmed by von Below.

After the dismissal of Ritter von Greim,[13] Hitler turned to the next item of business. He married Eva Braun. For this symbolic ceremony, Goebbels had introduced into the Bunker a certain Walter Wagner, a Gau Inspector who worked under him in his capacity of Gauleiter of Berlin, and who, having an honorary position as an official of the city administration, was therefore considered a proper person to officiate at this civil ceremony. He appeared in the Bunker, where he was completely unknown except to Goebbels, in the uniform of the Nazi Party and the arm-band of the Volkssturm. The ceremony took place in the small conference room or "map-room" in the private part of the Bunker.[14] Besides Hitler, Eva Braun, and Walter Wagner, Goebbels and Bormann were present as witnesses. The formalities were brief. The two parties declared that they were of pure Aryan descent and were free from hereditary disease. In consequence of the military situation and other extraordinary circumstances, they proposed a war-time wedding, by simple word of mouth, and without any delay. In a few minutes the parties had given assent, the register had been signed, and the ceremony was over. When the bride came to sign her name she began to write "Eva Braun," but was checked before completing it. Striking out the initial letter B, she corrected it to "Eva Hitler, *née* Braun." The ceremony over, the bride and bridegroom walked out into the conference passage. There a few generals and secretaries were waiting. They shook hands with all in turn, and then withdrew into their private apartments for a wedding breakfast. Shortly afterwards, Bormann, Goebbels,

[13] Both Greim and Reitsch disowned any knowledge of the marriage, which I have therefore placed after their departure. Since they were actually in the Fuehrerbunker, it is inconceivable that it could have taken place without their knowledge; and it seems certain from several sources that they left soon after midnight. Zander and Lorenz both say that the marriage took place between 0100 and 0300 in the morning; and the marriage certificate itself is clearly dated 29th April (*i.e.* after midnight). In these circumstances I have rejected the statements of von Below, Fraeulein Krueger, and Frau Christian that the ceremony took place before midnight.

[14] Room 21 in the diagram (p. 108).

Frau Goebbels, and Hitler's two secretaries, Frau Christian and Frau Junge, were invited into the private suite. There they sat for some hours, drinking champagne and talking. The conversation was of old times and old comrades, of Goebbels' marriage which Hitler had witnessed, in happier days; now the position of the parties was reversed, and the happiness was reversed too. Hitler spoke again of his plans of suicide. National Socialism was finished, he said, and would never revive; death would be a relief to him now that he had been deceived and betrayed by his best friends. A temporary gloom overcame the party; and one of the secretaries left the room. There was a good deal of coming and going, for it was a long session, and there was other business to be done. For part of the time Krebs and Burgdorf and von Below came in and joined the party, and Guensche, the S.S. adjutant, and Fraeulein Manzialy, the vegetarian cook; and for some time Hitler was absent with Frau Junge in an adjoining room, to which other members of the party were also occasionally summoned. He was dictating his will.[15]

Thus, after many years, Eva Braun's position was at last defined. The ambiguity of her status was at last terminated; and when a servant, in a moment of crisis next day, broke the ban on speech with "E.B.," and addressed her as "Gnaediges Fraeulein," she could at last answer, "You may safely call me Frau Hitler." [16]

The reasons which impelled Hitler to this belated ceremony are unknown; but they may be conjectured without great fear of error. It was clearly Eva Braun's wish to be married. She had long been embarrassed by her undefined position at court, and would have welcomed such a solution long ago had Hitler been prepared to countenance it. But Hitler was unwilling. Presumably he wished to avoid the imputation of

[15] This account of the wedding ceremony is taken from the statements of Fraeulein Krueger, Frau Christian, Frau Junge, Zander, Lorenz, von Below; and from the evidence of the certificate.
[16] Karnau.

humanity which the acknowledgment of wife or mistress would entail. At the end, he had not wished for her presence, and when she arrived in Berlin for the last time on 15th April, he had tried, ineffectually, to send her away. But since she had stayed, she was entitled to her reward. Her loyalty had increased her claims to consideration. Hitler had said that only she would remain faithful to him at the end, and she had not failed to justify his intuition. As all others fell away, her devotion became more conspicuous and more regarded. In conversation with his personal adjutants, Hitler contrasted her fidelity with the gross treachery of Goering and Himmler in whom he had trusted,[17] Signal devotion deserves signal recognition; and there is no doubt what recognition she most desired,—the status which would separate her from all other women of the court and would entitle her to that honour which she now most affected, of sharing in the ritual death of the Fuehrer. It was an easy request; at this last hour there was little danger of misinterpretation; and it was granted.

Meanwhile, in the intervals of the social gathering which followed the wedding, Hitler was continuing the succession of business which preoccupied him throughout this active night. He had sent for his secretary, Frau Junge, and was dictating two documents: his personal and his political testaments, which should be his final appeal to posterity and the textual basis of the Nazi myth.

Since this was clearly their purpose, these documents are extraordinarily interesting; for in this last advertisement of the Nazi movement, designed as a dignified valediction to the world and a message to later generations, there is nothing but the old hollow claptrap, the negative appeal, the purposeless militarism, of the Revolution of Destruction; the protestations of innocence, and the recriminations of failure.

The political testament is in two parts; the first general,

[17] Von Below.

the second particular. "It is untrue that I, or anybody else in Germany, wanted war in 1939. It was wanted and provoked exclusively by those international politicians who either came of Jewish stock, or worked for Jewish interests. After all my offers of disarmament, posterity cannot place the responsibility for this war on me. . . ." The mind goes back from the testament to *Mein Kampf*, from the epitaph to the prospectus of the Nazi Party, from the disclaimer of responsibility for defeat to the promise of glorious victory. Then comes the cry of despair. "After a six-years' war, which in spite of all setbacks will one day go down in history as the most glorious and heroic manifestation of a people's will to live, I cannot forsake the city which is the capital of this state. Since our forces are too small to withstand any longer the enemy's attack on this place, and since our own resistance will be gradually worn down by an army of blind automata, I wish to share the fate that millions of others have accepted and to remain here in the city. Further, I will not fall into the hands of an enemy who requires a new spectacle, exhibited by the Jews, to divert his hysterical masses. I have therefore decided to remain in Berlin, and there to choose death voluntarily at the moment when I believe that the residence of the Fuehrer and Chancellor can no longer be held. . . ." Then the valediction to those forces on which the Nazi Party had relied is coupled with a sidelong stab at the force which he charged with failure: "In future may it be a point of honour with German Army officers, as it already is in our Navy, that the surrender of territory and towns is impossible, and that, above all else, commanders must set a shining example of faithful devotion to duty until death." In the first world war, Hitler was a soldier; and when it failed, he blamed the politicians for betraying the soldiers. In those days he could not praise the German General Staff highly enough. "The organisation and leadership of the German Army was the mightiest thing that the world has ever yet seen." In the second world war he was

a politician; when it failed, he blamed the soldiers for betraying the politicians, and all for betraying him.

After the generalities, the particulars. The second part of
the political testament, like the first, is stronger in recrimination and negation than in positive statement. "Before my
death," it begins, "I expel from the Party the former Reich
Marshal, Hermann Goering, and withdraw from him all the
rights conveyed upon him by the Decree of 29th June 1941
and by my Reichstag speech of 1st September 1939. In his
place I appoint Grand Admiral Doenitz as Reich President
and Supreme Commander of the Armed Forces."

It was now clear what had been decided behind the locked
doors of the Fuehrerbunker after the news of Himmler's
treachery had been brought. The question of the succession
was at last resolved. Since the politicians had betrayed him,
and the Army had betrayed him, and the S.S. had betrayed
him, a sailor should succeed. The Navy, if its operations had
not always been spectacular, at least was always Nazi. "In
future may it be a point of honour with German Army
officers, *as it already is in our Navy* . . ." In that phrase
Hitler had found the solution to the problem which had so
long seemed insoluble.

The next paragraph is in form like its predecessor. It con-
cerns the other arch-traitor. "Before my death I expel from the
Party and from all his offices the former Reichsfuehrer S.S.
and Reich Minister of the Interior, Heinrich Himmler. In his
stead I appoint Gauleiter Karl Hanke as Reichsfuehrer S.S.
and Chief of the German Police, and Gauleiter Paul Giesler
as Reich Minister of the Interior.

"Goering and Himmler, by their secret negotiations with
the enemy, without my knowledge or approval, and by their
illegal attempts to seize power in the state, quite apart from
their treachery to my person, have brought irreparable shame
on the country and the whole people."

Having disposed of the traitors and appointed his own and

their successors, Hitler then dictated the government which they should accept. "In order that the German people may have a government of honourable men who will continue the war by all methods," he usurped the privilege of his successor and appointed his own nominees to nineteen cabinet offices. Apart from Doenitz, who was to be Reich President, Supreme Commander of the Armed Forces, Minister of War, and Commander-in-Chief of the Navy, the most interesting appointments are those of Goebbels as Reich Chancellor, Bormann as Party Chancellor, and Seyss-Inquart, the Austrian quisling and oppressor of Holland, as Foreign Minister. Thus Ribbentrop, the second Bismarck, was at last dropped from the position he had so unskilfully occupied. Another who was silently omitted was Albert Speer. He was succeeded as Armaments Minister by his deputy, Saur. To the end a certain favour was accorded to the erring Benjamin of the court; his transgressions were passed over in silence, and he was displaced not in anger but in pain. Field-Marshal Schoerner, on whose unbroken Army Group the defence of Bohemia might yet depend, was appointed Commander-in-Chief of the Army. In the general change, one name at least remains constant,—the Minister of Finance, Count Schwerin von Krosigk. In the great crises of his time he could boast of the achievement of the abbé Sieyès: *J'ai survécu*.

To this new government, imposed by testament, Hitler then dictated his orders. Though some of them, such as Bormann and Goebbels, had come to Berlin of their own will, wishing not to desert the capital but to fall there with their Fuehrer, nevertheless they must obey his orders and survive to carry on the Nazi administration, the Nazi war, the Nazi myth. Finally (so this strange document ends) they must "above all else, uphold the racial laws in all their severity, and mercilessly resist the universal poisoner of all nations, international Jewry."

Hitler's personal will is a shorter, less grandiose document;

jeden einzelnen verpflichtet, immer dem gemeinsamen
Interesse zu dienen und seine eigenen Vorteile dem-
gegenüber zurückzustellen. Von allen Deutschen,
allen Nationalsozialisten, Männern und Frauen
und allen Soldaten der Wehrmacht verlange ich, daß
sie der neuen Regierung und ihren Präsidenten treu
und gehorsam sein werden bis in den Tod.

Vor allem verpflichte ich die Führung der
Nation und die Gefolgschaft zur peinlichen Ein-
haltung der Rassegesetze und zum unbarmherzigen
Widerstand gegen den Weltvergifter aller Völker,
das internationale Judentum.

Gegeben zu Berlin, den 29. April 1945, 4.00 Uhr.

HITLER'S WILL

(Last page of his "Political Testament," showing his signature. Below
are the signatures of four witnesses, viz: Dr. Joseph Goebbels, Martin
Bormann, Wilhelm Burgdorf, and Hans Krebs.

it is the testament not of the revolutionary genius, the angel of destruction, but of the Austrian petty-bourgeois, the picture-going host of Obersalzberg, the husband of Eva Braun. It explained his marriage, disposed of his property, and announced his impending death.

"Although during the years of struggle I believed that I could not undertake the responsibility of marriage, now, before the end of my life, I have decided to take as my wife the woman who, after many years of true friendship, came to this town, already almost besieged, of her own free will, in order to share my fate. She will go to her death with me at her own wish, as my wife. This will compensate us for what we both lost through my work in the service of my people.

"My possessions, in so far as they are worth anything, belong to the Party, or if this no longer exists, to the State. If the State too is destroyed, there is no need for any further instructions on my part.

"The paintings in the collections bought by me during the course of the years were never assembled for private purposes, but solely for the establishment of a picture gallery in my home town of Linz on the Danube.

"It is my most heartfelt wish that this will should be duly executed.

"As executor, I appoint my most faithful Party comrade, Martin Bormann. He is given full legal authority to make all decisions. He is permitted to hand over to my relatives everything which is of worth as a personal memento, or is necessary to maintain a petty-bourgeois standard of living;[18] especially to my wife's mother and my faithful fellow workers of both sexes who are well known to him. The chief of these are my former secretaries, Frau Winter, etc., who helped me for many years by their work.

"My wife and I choose to die in order to escape the shame

[18] The German phrase is "Zur Erhaltung eines kleinen buergerlichen Lebens."

of overthrow or capitulation. It is our wish that our bodies be burnt immediately in the place where I have performed the greater part of my daily work during the course of my twelve years' service to my people." [19]

At four o'clock in the morning the two documents were ready for signature. There were three copies, for delivery was uncertain, and such important documents must not be lost to posterity. After Hitler had signed them, the political will was witnessed by Goebbels, Bormann, Krebs, and Burgdorf. The personal will was witnessed by Goebbels, Bormann, and Colonel Nicolaus von Below, Hitler's Luftwaffe adjutant, who was summoned for this purpose as one who had been a member of his personal *entourage* for the last eight years.

After the signature, Hitler retired to rest. But for Bormann and Goebbels there was still work to do. Both had been present at that secret conclave which had met after the announcement of Himmler's treachery, and at which, we must presume, the question of this succession and its attendant problems had been faced and resolved. Both, according to Hitler, had wished, or stated a wish, to remain and die in Berlin. Both had been ordered by Hitler to survive and carry on the Nazi administration. Each now had a decision to make: which of these two voices to obey.

Martin Bormann was an unromantic man. Neither statesman nor soldier, neither prophet nor priest, neither champion nor devotee, he loved one thing only, power; and the power

[19] At the time of their discovery and first publication, the authenticity of Hitler's testaments was doubted by the writer of a letter to the *Daily Telegraph*, and others, who referred to un-German characteristics in the typescript. These characteristics are not in the original documents, but were introduced into the photographic reproductions printed in the newspapers by sub-editors who wished to restore the blurred lettering. The argument therefore has no basis in fact. In fact, the authenticity of the documents has been established without the possibility of doubt by a mass of internal and circumstantial evidence, expert scrutiny of the signatures, and the testimony of those who knew of them, including one of the signatories of the Personal Testament (von Below), and the secretary who typed both documents (Frau Junge).

that he loved consisted not in its outward semblance, its trappings and deference, nor in its material rewards, but in its reality, in the quiet assurance of its exercise. Under Hitler he had enjoyed that assurance; now that Hitler had resolved to die, what hope had he of continuance? He did not really wish to die, he had always given his voice for survival and escape; but if he were to survive, how could he retain the power he loved? He was himself a cipher, dependent entirely on his master. There were only two possibilities of his survival as the "Brown Eminence" behind the Throne. Either he must himself succeed, or the successor must be one who would still make use of his indispensable services. Whether Bormann ever hoped personally to succeed, we cannot say; but it is improbable. His gifts were those of the secretary, not of the ruler: of Father Joseph, not of Cardinal Richelieu; and Hitler doubtless considered him, like Himmler, "too inartistic" to be the Fuehrer of Germany. If then he was to be not successor, but adviser to the successor, it was essential to him that the appointed successor should be a man who would make use of his services. This Goering would certainly never do, and Goering had therefore been displaced. To make doubly sure, Bormann had recently taken, or now took, an additional precaution. He sent to his trusted servants in Obersalzberg a telegram of unmistakable significance. "The situation in Berlin," it read,[20] "is more tense. If Berlin and we should fall, the traitors of 23rd April must be exterminated. Men, do your duty! Your life and honour depend upon it!" This telegram was duly delivered to the commandant of the fortress where Goering was imprisoned; but the commandant refused to recognise the authority of Bormann, and Goering was spared from that form of death.

[20] The text of this telegram is given by Koller (1st May) as having been received "yesterday" (*i.e.* 30th April); but since the text has been vouched for by Zander, who left the Bunker on 29th April, it must have been sent earlier. Frau Christian knew of the telegram; she did not know whether Hitler had authorised it.

It was equally certain that Himmler would never employ Bormann as his adviser; Himmler already had too many eager competitors for that office. But the danger of Himmler's succession had also been averted by the events and decisions of this eventful and decisive night. The chosen successor was now Doenitz. Doenitz was not a politician, but a sailor. He was also a Nazi. He had no political experience, but was devoted to Hitler and the ideals of Hitler. He would certainly need a good Nazi adviser, who understood the mysteries and was experienced in the habits of government and administration. What advice Bormann had given about the succession, if he was consulted, we do not know; but there can be little doubt that the nomination of Doenitz was welcome to him, and Hitler's testamentary command that he should not die but live fell, in such circumstances, on open and appreciative ears. Under Doenitz, Bormann decided that his duty lay in obedience; obeying, he might still wield the authority without which life would hold no sweetness for him.

Goebbels was a very different character. As the intellectual of the Party, the substance and justification of his life lay not in the power that he wielded, nor in the rewards that he drew from it, but in the myth of which he was the prophet, and which he alone could lucidly and cogently express. To him survival meant the survival not of his person, but of the myth; and with his clear understanding, he had realised that the survival of the one meant the annihilation of the other. Hitler himself had realised this important psychological truth, and was himself adopting the course which he had forbidden to his prophet. But why should Hitler thus monopolise all the virtue of the Party? If, by his death, he was to go down to history as the leader, was there not room, by his side, for the true follower? If the God of Destruction was to immolate himself in his ruined heaven, should not the priest of destruction do the same, in his ruined shrine—less magnificently of course, less obtrusively, as befitted his junior status? Survival in such circumstances would be not only an anti-climax, but a logical inconsistency.

In all his last actions, speeches, and writings, Goebbels had borne witness to this philosophy. When Bormann had advised flight, he had protested that he would stay. In the last days, the Bunker had rung with his tedious oratory. Hobbling about his room, or clasping the back of a chair like a rostrum, he had denounced the treacherous survival of Goering, and glorified, in the name of future historians, the great and fertile example which would be set by a well-staged death.[21] In his letter to his stepson, which Hanna Reitsch had carried out of the Bunker, Goebbels had expressed the same philosophy. "Germany will outlive this terrible war," he had written, "but only if it has examples by which to guide its reconstruction." By "reconstruction" he meant, of course, the reconstruction not merely of German industry or independence or greatness, but of Nazism; and his statement, thus interpreted, has a profound psychological truth. After any great defeat there are always men who will say that the prime need is to continue the administration. They can adduce good arguments in support of this view, which is convenient to the victors. But if it is not merely survival under a different system, but the revival of a defeated ideology that is required, this is a short-term view, and will fail, as Marshal Petain discovered, and those who supported him. The revival of a myth requires not continuity but a gesture; even if that gesture is suicide.

After witnessing Hitler's two testaments, Goebbels therefore withdrew to his own apartment, and there composed his personal apologia in the form of an "Appendix to the Fuehrer's Political Testament."

[21] Hanna Reitsch's account of Goebbels' behaviour in the Bunker, like all her accounts, is highly-coloured by personal bias and an incorrigible love of rhetoric; but basically it is probably true. At any rate the sentiments correspond with those expressed by Goebbels in his letter to his stepson, Harold Quandt (of which the text survives), and in his *Appendix*, of which Hanna Reitsch knew nothing.

"The Fuehrer has ordered me," he wrote, "should the defence of the Reich capital collapse, to leave Berlin, and to take part as a leading member in a government appointed by him.

"For the first time in my life I must categorically refuse to obey an order of the Fuehrer. My wife and children join me in this refusal. Otherwise,—quite apart from the fact that feelings of humanity and loyalty forbid us to abandon the Fuehrer in his hour of greatest need,—I should appear for the rest of my life as a dishonourable traitor and common scoundrel, and should lose my own self-respect together with the respect of my fellow citizens; a respect I should need in any future attempt to shape the future of the German nation and State.

"In the delirium of treachery which surrounds the Fuehrer in these most critical days of the war, there must be someone at least who will stay with him unconditionally until death, even if this conflicts with the formal and (in a material sense) entirely justifiable order which he has given in his political testament.

"In doing this, I believe that I am doing the best service I can to the future of the German people. In the hard times to come, examples will be more important than men. Men will always be found to lead the nation forward into freedom; but a reconstruction of our national life would be impossible unless developed on the basis of clear and obvious examples.

"For this reason, together with my wife, and on behalf of my children, who are too young to speak for themselves, but who would unreservedly agree with this decision if they were old enough, I express an unalterable resolution not to leave the Reich capital, even if it falls, but rather, at the side of the Fuehrer, to end a life which will have no further value to me if I cannot spend it in the service of the Fuehrer, and by his side."

It was half-past five in the morning when Dr. Goebbels put his signature to this, the last of his famous broadsheets addressed to the German nation. At least we must admit that at the end he was not deserted by the psychological acumen of his mind, the Latin clarity of his expression.

Thus the night of 28th/29th April, like the afternoon of 22nd April, was a time of formidable decisions. The day which followed was occupied by their execution. The first business was the despatch of Hitler's testaments to his successors. At about eight o'clock in the morning General Burgdorf sent for Major Willi Johannmeier, Hitler's Army adjutant, and told him that an important mission had been entrusted to him. He was to carry a copy of the Fuehrer's political testament out of Berlin, through the Russian lines, and deliver it to Field-Marshal Schoerner, the newly appointed Commander-in-Chief of the Army. With him would go two other messengers, bearing similar documents, S.S. Strandartenfuehrer Wilhelm Zander, Bormann's personal adviser, representing Bormann, and Heinz Lorenz, the official of the Propaganda Ministry who had brought to the Bunker the news of Himmler's treachery, as representative of Goebbels. These two men would receive separate instructions. As an officer of the Wehrmacht, a soldier with a distinguished fighting record and a reputation for bravery and resourcefulness, Johannmeier was charged to escort the party on their difficult journey through the enemy lines. Burgdorf then gave to Johannmeier a copy of Hitler's political testament. With it was a covering letter from Burgdorf to Schoerner, written in his own hand:

DEAR SCHOERNER,—Attached I send you by safe hand the Testament of our Fuehrer, who wrote it today under the shattering news of Himmler's treachery. It is his unalterable decision. The Testament is to be published as soon as the Fuehrer orders it, or as soon as his death is confirmed. All good wishes and *heil Hitler*.—Yours, WILHELM BURGDORF.

Major Johannmeier will deliver the Testament.

Schoerner at least would understand, if he received the letter, that Hitler, like Julius Caesar, had died with *Et tu Brute* on his lips.

About the same time, Bormann summoned his adviser Wilhelm Zander, and gave him similar instructions. He was to take copies of the Fuehrer's will to Admiral Doenitz. When Zander heard this, his heart sank. A half-educated, stupid, but honest man, in these last days, he had looked with a philosophical eye upon the history of the past twelve years; he had seen his own part in that history in a new and clearer perspective; and he had come to a decision. An idealist, as he assured himself, who had joined the Party long ago, and served it steadily, abandoning his comfortable business in Italy not to refresh himself with the perquisites, but to bow at the altar of the new God, he had learned at last, and too late, whither idealism leads its uncritical devotees. Now, when the true consequences had become apparent to him, Zander had seen that there was no turning back. It was too late to change. He had dedicated his life, and could not recover it; and now by an inversion of his former idealism, he only wished, by a silent death, to end a wasted life and expiate the illusions which it was too late to shed. A week ago, when the convoy of planes and trucks had carried the fugitives from the Party Chancellery to Obersalzberg, he had refused to go. He was determined to share in Berlin the doom of Nazism. Now, on the eve of this great event, he was ordered out to begin again, without guidance or purpose, his half-wasted life. All this he explained to Bormann, and explaining, begged to be excused. Bormann went to Hitler and described the hitch that had interfered with their plans. Returning, he told Zander that his objections had been overruled. It was the Fuehrer's order; he must go. Thereupon he handed him his papers,—copies of Hitler's personal and private testaments, and the certificate of the marriage of Hitler and Eva Braun. To cover these documents Bormann scribbled a short note to Doenitz in which, as in all his last communications, he expressed his bitterness at the failure of the relieving army.

DEAR GRAND ADMIRAL,—Since all divisions have failed to arrive, and our position seems hopeless, the Fuehrer dictated last night the attached political Testament. *Heil Hitler.*—Yours, BORMANN.

Meanwhile Johannmeier had found Lorenz and had told him that a special mission awaited him. Lorenz went into the general dining-passage in the outer part of Hitler's Bunker for breakfast; there he met Zander, who gave him a similar message, and advised him to go to Goebbels or Bormann at once. Lorenz reported to Goebbels, and was told to go to Bormann and then return. From Bormann, Lorenz received copies of Hitler's personal and political testaments. On his return, Goebbels gave him the Appendix which he had himself composed. Lorenz was told to take these documents and escape to Doenitz's headquarters, or elsewhere in British or American territory. Ultimately they were to be taken to Munich, the cradle of the Nazi movement, there to be preserved as documents of the Heroic Age. With an eye to history, Goebbels had attached his own manifesto to this set of papers; it was not to generals or admirals that he appealed, but to posterity.

The rest of the morning was spent in hurried preparation for the journey, and at about noon the three men, Lorenz, Zander, and Johannmeier, accompanied by a corporal called Hummerich, left the Bunker. They were an ill-assorted, ill-equipped party, and their mission showed every sign of hasty improvisation. Neither food nor money nor papers were issued to them; each took what he could find as his *viaticum*. Lorenz had reported to Hitler and taken his leave, but Hitler had said nothing to him, only shaken hands in silence. Zander had no time to say goodbye to Bormann, and when he telephoned to do so, he was merely asked angrily why he had not left and ordered to start at once. Their dress was equally miscellaneous: Johannmeier and Zander were in military and S.S. uniform respectively; Lorenz in plain clothes. They left the Chancellery through the garages in the Hermann Goering Strasse, and worked their way westward through the Tiergarten and Charlottenburg towards Pichelsdorf, at the north end of the Havel Lake. Johannmeier and Hummerich went ahead; Lorenz and Zander followed, directed by hand signals. On their way they had to penetrate three Russian rings thrown round the centre of the city, the first at the Victory Column, the second at the Zoo station, the third before Pichelsdorf. Between four and five in the afternoon they reached Pichelsdorf, where a battalion of Hitler Youth was holding the bridge against the expected arrival of Wenck's army. There the battalion commander accommodated them in his bunker and they slept till night. At ten o'clock that night, after consultation with the battalion commander, they took two boats and pushed out into the lake, heading southwards for the Wannsee bridgehead, held by units of the German Ninth Army. In the early hours of 30th April they landed independently, Johannmeier on the Wannsee bridgehead, Lorenz and Zander on the Schwanenwerder Peninsula. There they remained, resting all day in underground bunkers; and in the evening they reunited, and sailed together to the Pfaueninsel, an island in the Havel. From the Wannsee bridgehead Johannmeier had been able to send a radio message to Doenitz, informing him of their position and asking that an airplane be sent to fetch them. On the Pfaueninsel Johannmeier and Zander obtained civilian clothing and disposed of their uniforms. There too they were overtaken by three other men, who had come, like them, from the beleaguered Reich Chancellery.

For in the morning of 29th April, when the three bearers of Hitler's testament left the Bunker, all telephone communication between Berlin and the outside world had ceased; the balloon upon which the radio-telephone to the Combined General Staff had depended had been shot down, and a conversation between Krebs and Jodl had died unfinished. The adjutants and A.D.C.'s of the generals at court no longer had any functions to perform. This being so, three of them, Major Baron Freytag von Loringhoven, adjutant to General Krebs, Rittmeister Gerhardt Boldt, his A.D.C., and Lieut.-Colonel Weiss, adjutant to General Burgdorf, decided to escape, if possible, from the Chancellery and go to join the still awaited army of General Wenck. They studied their maps; they applied to their generals; and their generals promised to seek permission from Hitler.

At midday on 29th April the usual situation conference was held in the Bunker. It was attended by Hitler, Bormann, Goebbels, Krebs, Burgdorf, Hewel, Voss, von Below, Freytag von Loringhoven, and Boldt. Krebs reported the latest news. The Russians had advanced in Grunewald, in Charlottenburg, at the Anhalter railway station; from the other fronts there was silence. Of Wenck there was no news. The supply of ammunition dropped from the air during the night was inadequate; and not all the containers had been found in the debris of Berlin. After the conference, General Burgdorf asked whether Hitler would allow the three officers to make an attempt to reach Wenck's army. Hitler agreed, and the three officers were summoned and given their orders. They were to find General Wenck and to tell him to hurry; for the Chancellery would soon have fallen. In the course of the afternoon, Freytag von Loringhoven, Boldt, and Weiss took their leave and left the Bunker. They followed the route of their predecessors, and with the help of a guide from the Hitler Youth reached the bridge at Pichelsdorf early on the morning of 30th April. Thence they sailed down the Havel in a folding-boat to the Wannsee Peninsula and the Pfaueninsel, where they overtook the three bearers of the testament. At the Reichsportfeld they had already been overtaken by yet another fugitive from the Bunker, by Colonel Nicolaus von Below, Hitler's Luftwaffe Adjutant, the last man to leave the Fuehrerbunker before the death of Hitler.

Colonel von Below had served in the Fuehrer's *entourage* for eight years and was by now a familiar, if junior, member of the court. Thanks to this personal connexion, he had been invited to participate in the wedding reception on the morning of 29th April and to witness Hitler's personal testament. But although he had received from Hitler, at his own request, a phial of poison, he had no ambition to participate in the final act; and when, after the midday conference, he heard the Fuehrer approve the departure of Freytag von Loringhoven, Boldt, and Weiss, he reflected that he too was an adjutant who had no further functions to perform in the doomed and isolated Reich Chancellery. The example of the other adjutants encouraged him. Evidently it was not compulsory to stay in the Bunker. Krebs and Burgdorf had stated that they would stay and die, but they had let their adjutants go; might not Hitler do the same? And in spite of the public vows of suicide witnessed, or at least recorded, by Hanna Reitsch, three men had already left the Bunker that morning, three more were preparing to leave, and both Hewel and Voss had discreetly assured von Below that they saw no reason to contemplate such drastic action, but intended, if they could, to escape.

At the afternoon conference at four o'clock, von Below heard from Krebs that the situation was as before, only worse. Then he approached Burgdorf and asked whether he too might not be permitted to escape. Burgdorf replied that this was a matter for the Fuehrer to decide. Von Below went to Hitler, and put his request to him. Hitler agreed at once. He seems to have agreed to everything that day: 29th April, it seems, was like 23rd April, when he had forgiven Speer. Both were days of calm after a crisis of decision. But Hitler had another reason for allowing von Below to leave the Bunker. He wished to send yet another document out of the Bunker, to add, as it were, a postscript to his testament. He told von Below that he must seek to reach the headquarters of the

Combined General Staff, now at Ploen in Schleswig-Holstein, and to deliver a document to Field-Marshal Keitel. He was to be ready to start after the evening conference.

This conference began at ten o'clock that night. It was attended by Hitler, Goebbels, Bormann, Krebs, Burgdorf, Hewel, Voss, von Below, and General Weidling, the commandant of the city. General Weidling described the military situation in Berlin which had deteriorated according to expectation. The Russians had advanced in the Saarlandstrasse and the Wilhelmstrasse, almost as far as the Air Ministry. West of Berlin they had penetrated from the north into the streets between the Bismarckstrasse and the Kantstrasse, and from the south into the northern border of the suburb of Grunewald and the Reichsportfeld; only a small German force was still holding a bridgehead on the Havel at Pichelsdorf—the Hitler Youth detachment which had forwarded the two parties of fugitives on their way. On the other fronts Weidling described other Russian successes; the advance was universal. The Russians would reach the Chancellery by 1st May at the latest. Now or never, said Weidling, the troops in Berlin might seek to break through the Russian ring and escape from Berlin. Hitler replied that this was impossible. Retreat was barely possible for individual fugitives; for larger units of soldiers, battle-weary, ill-armed, and without ammunition, it was hopeless. With these words the subject was closed. As always, Hitler's word was final.

After the conference, von Below sent for his batman, Heinz Matthiesing,[22] whom he ordered to prepare himself for the journey. Then he took his official leave. Hitler shook hands with him, but, as with Lorenz, in silence. Von Below then said goodbye to all the others in the Bunker. General Krebs asked him to greet his wife for him, if possible, and gave her address; he also handed him a letter to General Jodl. In this Krebs in-

[22] Matthiesing has been interrogated, and his story used to check and confirm that of von Below.

formed Jodl that the situation in Berlin was desperate; [23] the encirclement of the city was complete, arms and ammunition were lacking, supplies dropped from the air were inadequate, it was no longer possible to land in Berlin, nothing had been heard of Wenck, and relief by his army was no longer expected. Resistance in Berlin could only last a few days. The Fuehrer expected other fronts to fight on to the last man.

Hitler's postscript was handled to von Below by Burgdorf; it was addressed to Keitel, and was Hitler's valediction to the German Armed Forces. In it (if von Below has correctly reconstructed it) Hitler stated that the fight for Berlin was now drawing to its close, that he intended to commit suicide rather than surrender, that he had appointed Doenitz as his successor, and that two of his oldest supporters, Goering and Himmler, had betrayed him at the end. Then he turned to the achievements of the Armed Forces, which his strategy had led to destruction. The Navy he praised; by its high morale it had wiped out the disgrace of 1918, and it could not be blamed for its defeat. The Luftwaffe he excused; it had fought bravely; it was Goering who had failed to maintain its initial supremacy. But the Army,—when Hitler considered the Army he saw there two nations: the common soldiers, to whose ranks he had once belonged, who trusted in him and in whom he still trusted, and the generals who had misdirected this great weapon, who had resisted his strategy, undermined his policy, and conspired against his person. In his last message to the world he could not omit, once again, to utter his hatred of that Army General Staff which he had once considered the mightiest thing the world had ever seen. "The people and the Armed Forces," he wrote (according to von Below's version of the letter [24]), "have given their all in this long and

[23] According to von Below. (The original text was destroyed.)

[24] The original text of this document was also destroyed, and it is given here as reconstructed by von Below. On internal evidence, Below's version seems genuine.

hard struggle. The sacrifice has been enormous. But my trust has been misused by many people. Disloyalty and betrayal have undermined resistance throughout the war. It was therefore not granted to me to lead the people to victory. The Army General Staff cannot be compared with the General Staff in the first world war. Its achievements were far behind those of the fighting front." The letter ended with a repetition of the now futile dream of the Pan-Germans, the ultimate, the only positive and consistent message of *Mein Kampf*: "The efforts and sacrifices of the German people in this war have been so great that I cannot believe that they have been in vain. The aim must still be to win territory in the East for the German people."

At midnight on the night of 29th/30th April von Below and his batman left the Chancellery. They followed, with variations, what was by now the classical route, by the Hermann Goering Strasse, through the Brandenburger Tor, up the Charlottenburger Chaussee, to the Tiergarten railway station; then by the Kantstrasse, under Russian fire, and the Masuren Allee to the headquarters of the Hitler Youth, whence a guide led them by the Reichstrasse to the Reichsportfeld. There they found Freytag von Loringhoven, Weiss, and Boldt; and following them to the bridgehead at Pichelsdorf, thence, in the next evening, they sailed, like their predecessors, down the Havel and landed on the western bank between Gatow and Kladow.

Chapter Seven

THE DEATH OF HITLER
(30TH APRIL–1ST MAY)

WHEN VON BELOW left the Bunker, Hitler was already preparing for the end. During the day the last news from the outside world had been brought in. Mussolini was dead. Hitler's partner in crime, the herald of Fascism, who had first shown to Hitler the possibilities of dictatorship in modern Europe, and had preceded him in the stages of disillusion and defeat, had now illustrated in a signal manner the fate which fallen tyrants must expect. Captured by partisans during the general uprising of northern Italy, Mussolini and his mistress Clara Petacci had been executed, and their bodies suspended by the feet in the market-place of Milan to be beaten and pelted by the vindictive crowd. If the full details were ever known to them, Hitler and Eva Braun could only have repeated the orders they had already given: their bodies were to be destroyed "so that nothing remains"; "I will not fall into the hands of an enemy who requires a new spectacle to divert his hysterical masses." In fact it is improbable that these details were reported, or could have strengthened an already firm decision. The fate of defeated despots has generally been the same; and Hitler, who had himself exhibited the body of a field-marshal on a meat-hook, had no need of remote historical examples or of a new and dramatic instance, to know the probable fate of his own corpse, if it should be found.[1]

[1] It has often been stated, by those whose imagination is stronger than their memory, that Hitler's decision was affected by the fate of Mussolini. An account of the table-talk of the prisoners at Nuremberg, ascribed to the chief psychiatrist at the trial and printed in the *Sunday Express*, 25 August

In the afternoon, Hitler had had his favourite Alsatian dog, Blondi, destroyed. Professor Haase, his former surgeon, who was now tending the wounded in his clinic in Berlin, had come round to the Bunker and killed it with poison. The two other dogs belonging to the household were shot by the sergeant who looked after them. After this, Hitler gave poison-capsules to his two secretaries for use in extremity. He was sorry, he had said, to give them no better parting gift; and praising them for their courage he had added, characteristically, that he wished his generals were as reliable as they.[2]

In the evening, while the inhabitants of the two outer bunkers were dining in the general dining-passage of the Fuehrerbunker, they were visited by one of the S.S. guard, who informed them that the Fuehrer wished to say good-bye to the ladies and that no one was to go to bed till orders had been received. At about half-past two in the morning the orders came. They were summoned by telephone to the Bunker, and gathered again in the same general dining-passage, officers and women, about twenty persons in all. When they were assembled, Hitler came in from the private part of the Bunker, accompanied by Bormann. His look was abstracted, his eyes glazed over with that film of moisture which Hanna Reitsch had noticed. Some of those who saw him even suggested that he had been drugged; but no such explanation is needed of a condition upon which more familiar observers had often commented. He walked in silence down the passage and shook hands with all the women in turn. Some spoke to him, but he said nothing, or mumbled inaudibly. Ceremonies of

---

1946, even quotes Goering as saying: "You remember the Mussolini incident? We had pictures of Mussolini dead in the gutter with his mistress, and hanging in the air upside-down. They were awful! Hitler went into a frenzy, shouting, 'This will never happen to me!'" A glance at the dates disposes of this romance. Goering saw Hitler for the last time eight days before Mussolini's death. Goering may have seen pictures of Mussolini's body in captivity; Hitler never. Such is the value of unchecked human testimony, on which, however, much of written history is based.

[2] Frau Junge.

silent hand-shaking had become quite customary in the course
of that day.[3]

When he had left, the participants in this strange scene
remained for a while to discuss its significance. They agreed
that it could have one meaning only. The suicide of the
Fuehrer was about to take place. Thereupon an unexpected
thing happened. A great and heavy cloud seemed to roll away
from the spirits of the Bunker-dwellers. The terrible sorcerer,
the tyrant who had charged their days with intolerable melodramatic tension, would soon be gone, and for a brief twilight
moment they could play. In the canteen of the Chancellery,
where the soldiers and orderlies took their meals, there was a
dance. The news was brought; but no one allowed that to
interfere with the business of pleasure. A message from the
Fuehrerbunker told them to be quieter; but the dance went
on. A tailor [4] who had been employed in the Fuehrer's headquarters, and who was now immured with the rest in the
Chancellery, was surprised when Brigadefuehrer Rattenhuber,
the head of the police guard and a general in the S.S., slapped
him cordially on the back and greeted him with democratic
familiarity. In the strict hierarchy of the Bunker the tailor
felt bewildered. It was as if he had been a high officer. "It was
the first time I had ever heard a high officer say 'good evening'," he said; "so I noticed that the mood had completely
changed." Then, from one of his equals, he learned the reason
of this sudden and irregular affability. Hitler had said goodbye, and was going to commit suicide. There are few forces
so solvent of class distinctions as common danger, and common relief.

Though Hitler might already be preparing for death, there
was still one man at least in the Bunker who was thinking of
life: Martin Bormann. If Bormann could not persuade the
German armies to come and rescue Hitler and himself, at least

[3] Von Varo.
[4] W. O. Mueller.

he would insist on revenge. Shortly after the farewell ceremony, at a quarter-past three in the morning of 30th April, he
sent another of those telegrams in which the neurosis of the
Bunker is so vividly preserved. It was addressed to Doenitz
at Ploen; but Bormann no longer trusted the ordinary communications, and sent it through the Gauleiter of Mecklenburg. It ran:

DOENITZ!—Our impression grows daily stronger that the divisions in the Berlin theatre have been standing idle for several days.
All the reports we receive are controlled, suppressed, or distorted
by Keitel. In general we can only communicate through Keitel.
The Fuehrer orders you to proceed at once, and mercilessly,
against all traitors.—BORMANN.[5]

A postscript contained the words: "The Fuehrer is alive, and
is conducting the defence of Berlin." These words, containing
no hint of the approaching end,—indeed seeming to deny its
imminence,—suggest that Bormann was reluctant even now
to admit that his power would soon be over, or must be
renewed from another, less calculable source.

Later in the same morning, when the new day's work had
begun, the generals came as usual to the Bunker with their
military reports. Brigadefuehrer Mohnke, the commandant
of the Chancellery, announced a slight improvement: the
Schlesischer railway station had been recaptured from the
Russians; but in other aspects the military situation was un-
changed. By noon the news was worse again. The underground railway tunnel in the Friedrichstrasse was reported in
Russian hands; the tunnel in the Vossstrasse, close to the
Chancellery, was partly occupied; the whole area of the
Tiergarten had been taken; and Russian forces had reached
the Potsdamer Platz and the Weidendammer Bridge over the
river Spree. Hitler received these reports without emotion. At

[5] In the German text the name of Keitel is represented by his code-
name, "Teilhaus."

about two o'clock he took lunch. Eva Braun was not there; evidently she did not feel hungry, or ate alone in her room; and Hitler shared his meal, as usually in her absence, with his two secretaries and the cook. The conversation indicated nothing unusual. Hitler remained quiet, and did not speak of his intentions. Nevertheless, preparations were already being made for the approaching ceremony.

In the morning, the guards had been ordered to collect all their rations for the day, since they would not be allowed to pass through the corridor of the Bunker again; and about lunch-time Hitler's S.S. adjutant Sturmbannfuehrer Guensche, sent an order to the transport officer and chauffeur, Sturmbannfuehrer Erich Kempka, to send 200 litres of petrol to the Chancellery garden. Kempka protested that it would be difficult to find so large a quantity at once, but he was told that it must be found. Ultimately he found about 180 litres and sent it round to the garden. Four men carried it in jerricans [6] and placed it at the emergency exit of the Bunker. There they met one of the police guards, who demanded an explanation. They told him that it was for the ventilating plant. The guard told them not to be silly, for the plant was oil-driven. At this moment Hitler's personal servant, Heinz Linge, appeared. He reassured the guard, terminated the argument, and dismissed the men. Soon afterwards all the guards except those on duty were ordered to leave the Chancellery, and to stay away. It was not intended that any casual observer should witness the final scene.

Meanwhile Hitler had finished lunch, and his guests had been dismissed. For a time he remained behind; then he emerged from his suite, accompanied by Eva Braun, and another farewell ceremony took place. Bormann and Goebbels were there, with Burgdorf, Krebs, Hewel, Naumann, Voss, Rattenhuber, Hoegl, Guensche, Linge, and the four women, Frau Christian, Frau Junge, Fraeulein Krueger, and Fraeulein

[6] A jerrican is a German petrol-can containing 4½ gallons.

Manzialy. Frau Goebbels was not present. Unnerved by the approaching death of her children, she remained all day in her own room. Hitler and Eva Braun shook hands with them all, and then returned to their suite. The others were dismissed, all but the high-priests and those few others whose services would be necessary. These waited in the passage. A single shot was heard. After an interval they entered the suite. Hitler was lying on the sofa, which was soaked with blood. He had shot himself through the mouth. Eva Braun was also on the sofa, also dead. A revolver was by her side, but she had not used it; she had swallowed poison. The time was half-past three.[7]

Shortly afterwards, Artur Axmann, head of the Hitler Youth, arrived at the Bunker. He was too late for the farewell ceremony, but he was admitted to the private suite to see the dead bodies. He examined them, and stayed in the room for some minutes, talking with Goebbels. Then Goebbels left, and Axmann remained for a short while alone with the dead bodies. Outside, in the Bunker, another ceremony was being prepared: the Viking funeral.

After sending the petrol to the garden, Kempka had walked across to the Bunker by the subterranean passage which connected his office in the Hermann Goeringstrasse with the Chancellery buildings. He was greeted by Guensche with the words, "The Chief is dead."[8] At that moment the door of Hitler's suite was opened, and Kempka too became a participant in the funeral scene.

While Axmann was meditating among the corpses, two S.S. men, one of them Hitler's servant Linge, entered the

[7] The method of death chosen by Hitler and Eva Braun has been reported identically by Fraeulein Krueger and Frau Junge (who had it from Guensche) and Frau Christian (from Linge), and by others who heard it from the same sources. It is also described by Axmann, who personally inspected the bodies. Kempka, who carried out the body of Eva Braun, unblanketed, observed no signs of blood.

[8] "Der Chef ist tot." Hitler's personal servants referred to him as "der Chef."

room. They wrapped Hitler's body in a blanket, concealing the bloodstained and shattered head, and carried it out into the passage, where the other observers easily recognised it by the familiar black trousers. Then two other S.S. officers carried the body up the four flights of stairs to the emergency exit, and so out into the garden. After this, Bormann entered the room, and took up the body of Eva Braun. Her death had been tidier, and no blanket was needed to conceal the evidence of it. Bormann carried the body into the passage, and then handed it to Kempka, who took it to the foot of the stairs. There it was taken from him by Guensche; and Guensche in turn gave it to a third S.S. officer, who carried it too upstairs to the garden. As an additional precaution, the other door of the Bunker, which led into the Chancellery, and some of the doors leading from the Chancellery to the garden, had been hastily locked against possible intruders.

Unfortunately, the most careful precautions are sometimes unavailing; and it was as a direct result of this precaution that two unauthorised persons in fact witnessed the scene from which it was intended to exclude them. One of the police guards, one Erich Mansfeld, happened to be on duty in the concrete observation tower at the corner of the Bunker, and noticing through the opaque, sulphurous air a sudden, suspicious scurrying of men and shutting of doors, he felt it his duty to investigate. He climbed down from his tower into the garden and walked round to the emergency exit to see what was afoot. In the porch he collided with the emerging funeral procession. First there were two S.S. officers carrying a body wrapped in a blanket, with black-trousered legs protruding from it. Then there was another S.S. officer carrying the unmistakable corpse of Eva Braun. Behind them were the mourners—Bormann, Burgdorf, Goebbels, Guensche, Linge, and Kempka. Guensche shouted at Mansfeld to get out of the way quickly; and Mansfeld, having seen the forbidden but interesting spectacle, returned to his tower.[9]

After this interruption, the ritual was continued. The two corpses were placed side by side, a few feet from the porch, and petrol from the cans was poured over them. A Russian bombardment added to the strangeness and danger of the ceremony, and the mourners withdrew for some protection under the shelter of the porch. There Guensche dipped a rag in petrol, set it alight, and flung it out upon the corpses. They were at once enveloped in a sheet of flame. The mourners stood to attention, gave the Hitler salute, and withdrew again into the Bunker, where they dispersed. Guensche afterwards described the spectacle to those who had missed it. The burning of Hitler's body, he said, was the most terrible experience in his life.[10]

Meanwhile yet another witness had observed the spectacle. He was another of the police guards, and he too came accidentally upon the scene in consequence of the precautions which should have excluded him. His name was Hermann Karnau. Karnau, like others of the guard who were not on duty, had been ordered away from the Bunker by an officer of the S.S. Escort, and had gone to the Chancellery canteen; but after a while, in spite of his orders, he had decided to return to the Bunker. On arrival at the door of the Bunker, he had found it locked. He had therefore made his way out into the garden, in order to enter the Bunker by the emergency exit. As he turned the corner by the tower where Mansfeld was on duty, he was surprised to see two bodies lying side by side, close to the door of the Bunker. Almost at the same instant they burst, spontaneously it seemed, into flame.

[9] This account is given independently by Kempka and Mansfeld, who agree. Kempka mentions the incident when a guard (*i.e.* Mansfeld) collided with the procession in the porch and was dismissed by Guensche. Some of the details were accidentally noticed by Schwaegermann.

[10] Fraeulein Krueger, Frau Junge.

Karnau could not explain this sudden combustion. He saw no one, and yet it could not be the result of enemy fire, for he was only three feet away. "Possibly someone threw a match from the doorway," he suggested; and his suggestion is essentially correct.

Karnau watched the burning corpses for a moment. They were easily recognisable, though Hitler's head was smashed. The sight, he says, was "repulsive in the extreme." Then he went down into the Bunker by the emergency exit. In the Bunker he met Sturmbannfuehrer Franz Schedle, the officer commanding the S.S. Escort. Schedle had recently been injured in the foot by a bomb. He was distracted with grief. "The Fuehrer is dead," he said; "he is burning outside"; and Karnau helped him to limp away.

Mansfeld, on duty in the tower, also watched the burning of the bodies. As he had climbed the tower, after Guensche had ordered him away, he had seen through a loophole a great column of black smoke rising from the garden. As the smoke diminished, he saw the same two bodies which he had seen being brought up the stairs. They were burning. After the mourners had withdrawn, he continued to watch. At intervals he saw S.S. men come out of the Bunker and pour more petrol on the bodies to keep them alight. Some time afterwards he was relieved by Karnau, and when Karnau had helped him to climb out of the tower, the two went together to look at the bodies again. By now the lower parts of both bodies had been burned away and the shin-bones of Hitler's legs were visible. An hour later, Mansfeld visited the bodies again. They were still burning, but the flame was low.

In the course of the afternoon a third member of the police guard sought to watch the spectacle of the burning bodies. His name was Hans Hofbeck. He went up the stairs from the Bunker and stood in the porch; but he did not stay there. The stench of burning flesh was intolerable and drove him away.

Late that night Brigadefuehrer Rattenhuber, the head of

the police guard, entered the Dog-bunker where the guards were spending their leisure, and spoke to a sergeant of the S.S. Escort. He told him to report to his commanding officer, Schedle, and to pick three trustworthy men to bury the corpses. Soon afterwards Rattenhuber returned to the Dog-bunker and addressed the men there. He made them promise to keep the events of the day a holy secret. Anyone talking about them would be shot. Shortly before midnight Mansfeld returned to duty in the tower. Russian shells were still falling, and the sky was illuminated by flares. He noticed that a bomb crater in front of the emergency exit had been newly worked upon, and that the bodies had disappeared. He did not doubt that the crater had been converted into a grave for them; for no shell could have piled the earth around it in so neat a rectangle. About the same time, Karnau was on parade with the other guards in the Vossstrasse, and one of his comrades said to him: "It is sad that none of the officers seems to worry about the Fuehrer's body. I am proud that I alone know where he is."[11]

That is all that is known about the disposal of the remnants of Hitler's and Eva Braun's bodies. Linge afterwards told one of the secretaries that they had been burned, as Hitler had ordered, "till nothing remained"; but it is doubtful whether such total combustion could have taken place. 180 litres of petrol, burning slowly on a sandy bed, would char the flesh and dissipate the moisture of the bodies, leaving only an un-recognisable and fragile remainder; but the bones would with-stand the heat. These bones have never been found. Perhaps they were broken up and mixed with the other bodies, the

[11] In their narratives of the burning of the bodies, Karnau and Mansfeld agree on facts, but differ on dates and times. Both mistake the date. Mansfeld's times are correct where they can be checked, while Karnau's are hope-lessly erratic. If Mansfeld is reliable throughout, the bodies were set alight at about 4 P.M. (this is almost certainly correct), and were still burning at 6:30; Rattenhuber's orders for burial were given "late at night"; and the bodies had been buried by 11 P.M.

bodies of soldiers killed in the defence of the Chancellery, and the body of Fegelein, which were also buried in the garden. The Russians have occasionally dug in that garden, and many such bodies have been unearthed there. Perhaps, as Guensche is said to have stated, the ashes were collected in a box and conveyed out of the Chancellery. Or perhaps no elaborate explanation is necessary. Perhaps such investigations as have been made have been somewhat perfunctory. Investigators who left Hitler's engagement-diary unobserved in his chair for five months may easily have overlooked other relics which were more deliberately concealed. Whatever the explanation, Hitler achieved his last ambition. Like Alaric, buried secretly under the river-bed of Busento, the modern destroyer of mankind is now immune from discovery.

While these last rites and pieties were being observed by guards and sentries, the regents of the Bunker were busy with more practical matters. Having set the bodies alight and paid their last summary respects, they had returned to safety underground, there to contemplate the future. Once again, as after Hitler's first leave-taking, a great cloud seemed to have been lifted from their spirits. The nightmare of ideological repression was over, and if the prospect before them remained dark and dubious, at least they were now free to consider it in a businesslike manner. From this moment nobody seems to have bothered about the past or the two corpses still sizzling in the garden. That episode was over, and in the short space of time remaining they had their own problems to face. As the tragically-minded guard observed, it was sad to see everyone so indifferent to the Fuehrer's body.

The first evidence of the changed atmosphere in the Bunker was noticed by the secretaries, who had been dismissed during the ceremony, but who now returned to their stations. On arrival they learned the details from Guensche and Linge; but it was not from such second-hand information only that they knew that Hitler was dead. Everyone, they observed, was smoking in the Bunker. During Hitler's lifetime that had been absolutely forbidden; but now the headmaster had gone and the boys could break the rules. Under the soothing influence of nicotine, whose absence must have increased the nervous tension of the past week, they were able to consider the administrative problems which the Fuehrer had left them to face.

First, there was the succession. With Hitler's death, the centre of power had moved automatically from the Bunker to the distant headquarters of the new Fuehrer in Schleswig-Holstein. It was mortifying to Bormann, who for so long had given orders and exercised authority in the name of Hitler, to admit that now he had no position at all, unless Doenitz should confirm his appointment as Party Minister in the new government. On the other hand it was improbable that any copy of Hitler's will had yet reached Doenitz, who was therefore unaware not only of Hitler's death, but also of his own right of succession. It was clearly Bormann's duty to inform the new Fuehrer of these facts by telegram; and it is interesting to notice the ambiguous manner in which this was done.

After Hitler's death, Bormann sent the following telegram to Doenitz:

GRAND ADMIRAL DOENITZ:
In place of the former Reich-Marshal Goering the Fuehrer appoints you, Herr Grand Admiral, as his successor. Written authority is on its way. You will immediately take all such measures as the situation requires.

BORMANN.

The important and relevant fact that Hitler was already dead was not mentioned. It seems as if Bormann wished to prolong yet a little longer the authority which he loved but could no longer legally exercise.

The arrival of this document caused something like consternation at Ploen. The appointment was entirely unexpected.

Only two days before, Doenitz had gone to Himmler and offered his support to him as Hitler's most obvious successor, and Himmler was even now preparing his government. Now the position was suddenly reversed. "Not Himmler but Doenitz!" exclaimed the astonished Schwerin von Krosigk, who as usual had backed the wrong horse, though his genius for survival guaranteed his own appointment in either event. Doenitz himself was not only surprised but mortified. Almost alone among the Nazi leaders, he had entertained no ambitions of the succession, and now the succession had been thrust upon him. Ever since his appointment to the command of the northern area, Doenitz had been in a nervous state; on receipt of this telegram, says one of his *entourage*,[12] his condition became obviously worse. Nevertheless, since it was the Fuehrer's order, no one thought of disobeying it. There was no coup, no question. Himmler's cumbrous bodyguard, which seemed to dominate the whole headquarters, stood idle, while Himmler, reluctantly abandoning his hopes of supreme power, offered to serve under Doenitz; and Doenitz, reluctantly assuming his new responsibility, replied thus by telegram to the Fuehrer whom he supposed still alive:

My Fuehrer!—My loyalty to you will be unconditional. I shall do everything possible to relieve you in Berlin. If Fate nevertheless compels me to rule the Reich as your appointed successor, I shall continue this war to an end worthy of the unique, heroic struggle of the German people.—Grand Admiral Doenitz.

What was Bormann's purpose in thus concealing the fact of Hitler's death, while covering himself by authorising Doenitz to assume responsibility? To speculate deeply on human motives is an unprofitable undertaking; but in this instance one thing at least is certain. Bormann was determined, one way or another, to reach Ploen. He was already considering alternative means of making that journey. It therefore

[12] Julius Weitmann, Press Referent at Doenitz's headquarters.

seems probable that he intended, if possible, himself to be the
first bearer of the news. Thus, having reduced to a minimum
the period of his temporary eclipse, he might hope, by his
personal presence at the decisive moment, to reinforce his
claim to continued authority.

Bormann's first plan for such a journey consisted of a mass
escape through the Russian lines; and at first the survivors of
the court were told to be prepared for such an attempt in the
darkness of the coming night. But such a mass escape would
certainly be dangerous and might fail;—Hitler had already
declared it impossible on the previous day, when the situation
was less desperate than now;—and in the course of the afternoon another, less hazardous possibility suggested itself. Since
Goebbels and Bormann were, by virtue of Hitler's will, members of the new government, might not the Russian military
authorities recognise their status, and, if they offered surrender, send Bormann to Ploen to have it ratified by Doenitz?
Bormann would thus be sent to Ploen by the Russians as a
privileged envoy, would join the new government, and would
take up his position as one of the rulers of the new Reich. Such
a hope seems ridiculous to us; but in the fools' paradise of
Nazism nothing seemed ridiculous. It was certainly no more
ridiculous than the political plans of Himmler, or of Schellenberg, or of Ribbentrop, or of Schwerin von Krosigk, all of
whom assumed the possible survival of a Nazi, or at least a
semi-Nazi government; and it did not seem ridiculous to
Bormann.

This project of a treaty with the Russians was worked out
in the course of a long conference in the evening of 30th
April. Bormann and Goebbels were there, with Krebs, Burgdorf, and Axmann; possibly also Mohnke. Contact was made
with the Russian headquarters by wireless, and a messenger
was then sent to enquire whether Marshal Zhukov would
receive a representative of the German Government. The
reply was favourable; and at midnight Krebs himself set out

from the Bunker carrying a letter from Goebbels and Bormann. In this letter they informed Zhukov of Hitler's death, and quoted, as their authority for writing, the positions to which they had been appointed by Hitler's will. They authorised the bearer, General Krebs, to negotiate an armistice or truce, pending the decision of the new Fuehrer, Admiral Doenitz.[13]

For the rest of the night, and throughout the following morning, Goebbels and Bormann awaited the return of Krebs and the answer to their letter. At eleven o'clock in the morning no reply had been received; and now at last Bormann decided, or agreed, to inform Doenitz that his reign had begun. Even so, he still avoided an explicit admission of Hitler's death. His laconic telegram was more concerned with his own position. It ran:

GRAND ADMIRAL DOENITZ,—The Testament is in force. I will join you as soon as possible. Till then, I recommend that publication be held up.—BORMANN.

With this brief and not entirely satisfactory communication, Doenitz had, for the time, to be content.

At noon, or soon afterwards, Krebs returned to the Bunker from Marshal Zhukov's headquarters. The reply which he brought was not satisfactory. It demanded unconditional surrender, and the delivery of all persons present in the Bunker. There was clearly no question of privileged status, no possibility of an accredited journey to Schleswig-Holstein. Another meeting was held in the Bunker, and it was decided to send a message to the Russian headquarters that the negotiations were closed. There was now no alternative. The mass escape must be attempted.

At quarter-past three, a third and last telegram was sent to Doenitz to supplement the meagre messages of Bormann. It was signed by Goebbels. Having now no personal ambitions,

[13] Frau Christian, Fraeulein Krueger.

Goebbels, unlike Bormann, had no need of the ambiguities and reticences of policy; he could afford to be explicit. His telegram was as follows:

GRAND ADMIRAL DOENITZ—
Most secret—urgent—officer only.
The Fuehrer died yesterday at 1530 hours. Testament of 29 April appoints you as Reich President, Reich Minister Dr. Goebbels as Reich Chancellor, Reichsleiter Bormann as Party Minister, Reich Minister Seyss-Inquart as Foreign Minister. By order of the Fuehrer, the Testament has been sent out of Berlin to you, to Field-Marshal Schoerner, and for preservation and publication. Reichsleiter Bormann intends to go to you today and to inform you of the situation. Time and form of announcement to the Press and to the troops is left to you. Confirm receipt.—GOEBBELS.

On receiving this telegram, Doenitz assumed the burdens, but also the rights, which they conferred. These included the right to accept or to reject advice from the ministers of his predecessor, and the right to choose his own government. He decided not to accept the ministers imposed upon him by telegram (for he had not received, and never did receive, the full list contained in the testament), and not to wait for Bormann's arrival before making an announcement. At half-past nine in the evening, Hamburg Radio warned the German people that "a grave and important announcement" would be made; then, heroically accompanied by strains from Wagner's operas and the slow movement of Bruckner's Seventh Symphony, came the news of Hitler's death, fighting to the end against Bolshevism. At 10.20 Doenitz himself announced both Hitler's death and his own succession. The Fuehrer, he said, had fallen "this afternoon"; he had died fighting "at the head of his troops." Both statements were untrue, for Hitler had fallen yesterday, not today, and since Doenitz had never been informed of the manner of his death, any account of it was necessarily speculation. The former inaccuracy was probably a mere error; the latter was probably designed. Had Doenitz known, and said, that Hitler had committed suicide, how would the troops have received such a statement? Might they not have felt that they had been betrayed, that the Fuehrer had deserted his post, and that their oaths of loyalty to him had been dissolved by his desertion? Such had been the attitude of Koller and of Jodl on 22nd April, when Hitler had announced his intention of suicide, and such, on this same day, was the attitude of General Weidling. Weidling had arrived as usual in the Bunker and had been told that "the Fuehrer had committed hara-kiri"; he had returned to his command-post in disgust and released his soldiers from their oaths. As the new Fuehrer, who regarded the soldiers' oaths to his predecessor as still binding them to him,[14] Doenitz could not afford such consequences. If he was to negotiate a successful peace with the West, the support of the Armed Forces must strengthen him in negotiation; and therefore, though he had no knowledge, he no doubt thought it most prudent to suppose that the Fuehrer had died a soldier's death.

Meanwhile, in the Bunker, Bormann and his colleagues were planning the details of the mass escape which was to bring them to deliverance and himself to power. Not all of them, for there were some who had by now given up all hope of life, or all interest in it, and who preferred, as Zander would have preferred, to meet their end now in the ruined Chancellery. Among these was Goebbels. His decision had long been taken; he had published it in his Appendix to the Fuehrer's testament; his wife had received a last decoration from the Fuehrer; and now the time of fulfilment had arrived. After sending his last telegram, Goebbels retired to his own apartments in the Bunker, with his wife and family. A few friends visited them

[14] This was the argument adopted by Doenitz in his broadcast to the German people on the evening of 1st May. Owing to the interruption of communications it was physically impossible for him to exact a new oath of loyalty from the Army.

to take their leave, among them Axmann and Kempka. Then
they prepared themselves for the end. This time there was no
Wagnerian drama; Goebbels did not attempt to compete with
his master. As a tribal chief, Hitler might enjoy a spectacular,
symbolic funeral; but Goebbels, as a secondary figure, would
follow him, at a decent interval, unobtrusively to the shades.
He had worked out his formula; the answer was nought; and
self-annihilation was the logical consequence of his ideological
nihilism. First, the six children were poisoned; Dr. Haase, the
former court surgeon who had disposed of the dogs, is said to
have disposed of them too, but that is uncertain. Then, in the
evening, Goebbels called his adjutant, Guenther Schwaegermann. "Schwaegermann," he said, "this is the worst treachery
of all. The generals have betrayed the Fuehrer. Everything is
lost. I shall die, together with my wife and family. You will
burn my body. Can you do that?" Schwaegermann promised
to do so, and Goebbels took leave of him, only pressing upon
him a silver-framed photograph of the Fuehrer from his
writing-desk. Frau Goebbels also said goodbye. Then
Schwaegermann sent Goebbels' driver and S.S. orderly to
fetch petrol for the burning; for the grotesque scene of yesterday was to be re-enacted on a smaller stage. Shortly afterwards (it was now about half-past eight in the evening)
Goebbels and his wife walked through the Bunker. At the
foot of the stairs they passed Schwaegermann and the driver,
Rach, who were standing there with the petrol; but they
passed them without a word and walked up the stairs into the
garden. Almost immediately, two shots were heard; and when
Rach and Schwaegermann reached the garden, they found the
two bodies lying dead on the ground. The S.S. orderly, who
had shot them, was standing by. Obediently, they poured four
cans of petrol over the bodies, set it alight, and withdrew. It
was a perfunctory cremation, and the charred bodies were
found next day by the Russians; no attempt had been made to

destroy or to bury them. On the way back through the Bunker, Rach and Schwaegermann met Brigadefuehrer Mohnke, who ordered them to set the Bunker on fire. They emptied one remaining can of petrol in the conference room, and set it alight. Then they left the Fuehrerbunker; for it was nine o'clock, and the mass escape from the New Chancellery was due to begin.[15]

In the Bunker of the New Chancellery a disorderly group of Party officials, soldiers, and women were gathered together. They were under the general command of Bormann; yet, as one of the participants said, "There was never any real command; they all ran around like chickens with their heads off." [16] When they were all assembled, the order of their exodus was described to them. They were to move in a succession of compact groups, through vaults and tunnels, into the underground station in the Wilhelmsplatz. Thence they would walk along the tracks of the underground railway as far as the Friedrichstrasse station, where they would regain the surface. In the Friedrichstrasse they would attach themselves to the remains of Mohnke's battle-group, which had been defending the Chancellery area, and with its aid they would attempt to force a way over the river Spree, and through the Russian lines, in a north-westerly direction. Once in the north-western suburbs of Berlin, individuals would make their way, as best they could, to German headquarters or to personal safety.

Such was the plan; the execution was different. It was eleven o'clock before the party was ready to move. They left, as planned, in groups. The first group included Mohnke, Guensche, Hewel, Admiral Voss, Hitler's pilot Baur, the three secretaries, and the cook. The rest followed at intervals, in four or five other groups. Bormann was in one of the central groups; in his pocket he carried the last copy of Hitler's

[15] This account is based largely on the statement of Schwaegermann supplemented by statements of Axmann and Kempka.
[16] W. O. Mueller.

private testament,[17] he intended to take it to Schleswig-Holstein as the certificate of his claims. When the last group left the Chancellery, there were still three men left behind. They were General Krebs, General Burgdorf, and the commander of the S.S. Bodyguard, Hauptsturmfuehrer Schedle. These preferred to stay and to shoot themselves when the Russians entered the Chancellery; and it is most probable that they are now dead. Schedle was wounded in the foot, and could hardly have escaped had he wished. When the others left the Chancellery, flames were rising from the deserted Fuehrerbunker,—the funeral flames of Dr. Goebbels.[18]

Arrived at the Friedrichstrasse station, the first group of fugitives emerged into the street and found a formidable and bewildering prospect before them. Everywhere the ruins of Berlin seemed to be in flames, and shells were falling all around. Nevertheless, this group kept together. Creeping forward by devious tunnels, they reached the river Spree and crossed it by an iron footbridge running parallel to the Weidendammer Bridge; then, pushing gradually ahead, they reached the Charité hospital and paused there, while their leaders, Mohnke and Guensche, looked for the groups which should have followed them. It was in vain. No other group had been able to advance beyond the river Spree.

The groups behind them had also regained the open air at the mouth of the Friedrichstrasse station; but there all cohesion had been lost in the confusion they had found, and the mem-

[17] Statement by Bormann to Axmann, reported by Axmann. The document must have been the single copy of the private testament which is unaccounted for.

[18] It must have been between the exodus of the main party and the capture of the Chancellery by the Russians on 2nd May that an incident took place which was described at Nuremberg (on 26th June 1946) by Hans Fritzsche. As the only high official left in Berlin, Fritzsche had collected the remaining government employees in the ruins of his office, and had prepared (in defiance of Hitler's orders to fight on) to offer capitulation to Marshal Zhukov. "When I was sending the emissary to cross the battle-line, Hitler's last adjutant, General Burgdorf, appeared and wanted to shoot me in fulfilment of Hitler's orders."

bers made their way as individuals along the blazing Friedrichstrasse to the Weidendammer Bridge. At the north end of the
bridge was an anti-tank barrier; and beyond this no one could
pass for heavy Russian fire. Drawing back therefore to the old
Admiral's Palace at the south end of the bridge, they waited
till the arrival of a few German tanks offered hope of forcing
the barrier. Gathering round the tanks, they moved forward
again,—a miscellaneous group including Bormann, Stumpfegger, Axmann, Kempka, Beetz (Hitler's second pilot), Naumann, Schwaegermann, and Rach. Some of these passed the
barrier with the leading tank and reached the Ziegelstrasse,
about three hundred yards ahead; but there a *Panzerfaust*,
falling upon the tank, caused a violent explosion. Beetz and
Axmann were wounded; Kempka was knocked out and temporarily blinded; Bormann and Stumpfegger were thrown to the
ground, perhaps unconscious, but escaped injury. The advance
was frustrated, and the parties retreated once more to the
bridge.

Defeated in their attempt to advance as a group, each individual now sought only to save himself. Kempka succeeded in
crossing the river by a footbridge, and after hiding for a whole
day among Yugoslav women in a railway arch, while the
Russians celebrated the fall of Berlin in their midst, he was
captured by the enemy; but escaping, swam the Elbe and
achieved instead an American captivity. Of Beetz nothing has
been heard; he probably perished or fell silently into Russian
hands. As for the rest, Bormann, Naumann, Schwaegermann,
Axmann, Stumpfegger, Rach, and one other kept at first
together, following the tracks of the railway line to the
Lehrter station. There they divided, and while Bormann and
Stumpfegger walked eastwards along the Invalidenstrasse
towards the Stettiner station, the others went westwards
towards Alt Moabit. These walked separately, and were soon
divided. Schwaegermann and Rach escaped, the former into
American captivity; Naumann also escaped. But Axmann,

coming upon a Russian patrol, turned back and followed in the direction in which Bormann and Stumpfegger had gone. Before long he overtook them. Behind the bridge, where the Invalidenstrasse crosses the railway line, he found both of them lying outstretched on their backs, with the moonlight on their faces. Stopping for a moment, he saw that both were dead; but Russian fire prevented closer examination. There were no obvious wounds, no sign of a shattering explosion. Presumably they had been shot in the back. Axmann continued on his way alone, and ultimately escaped to join the relics of his Hitler Youth, which survived for six months in a secret fold in the Bavarian Alps, until he too was captured and told his tale.[19]

Meanwhile the first group, which had passed the river Spree, had fared ultimately no better. Leaving the Charité hospital, they had made their way northwards along the Friedrichstrasse and the Chausséestrasse to the Maikaefer Barracks. There the fire of a Russian tank drove them underground, and when they emerged, some hours later, Admiral Voss was no longer with them; he had been captured by the Russians.[20]

[19] These incidents have been described by Axmann, Kempka, and Schwaegermann. The account of the death of Bormann rests on the evidence of Axmann only; but since Axmann's account (apart from accidental errors of time) has proved accurate in other particulars, it is probably correct here also, unless he is deliberately lying to protect Bormann. After consideration of all other evidence on the subject, I have decided to accept this statement as being at least consistent with all available information, although the evidence of a single witness can never be final. Rattenhuber, when he arrived in the cellar in the Schoenhaeuser Allee, told the rest of the party that Bormann had been killed in the Friedrichstrasse; but this is probably a variant of the mistake made by Kempka, who assumed (wrongly) that Bormann had been killed in the tank explosion which has been mentioned. Axmann's account up to his own separation from Naumann, etc., is confirmed by Schwaegermann.

The account given at Nuremberg by Bormann's counsel, who attempted to show that Bormann had perished in the tank explosion, is incorrect. It is based only on the second-hand report of Rattenhuber (which cannot be checked) and the supposition of Kempka (who, since he was blind and unconscious, was not an accurate observer). The evidence of Axmann and Schwaegermann, though available, was evidently overlooked.

[20] According to information from Frau Jodl, December 1945.

The remainder of the party moved purposelessly eastwards, gathering and shedding stragglers as they went, to the Schoenhaeuser Allee. There they all took refuge in a cellar. Mohnke, Guensche, Baur, and Hewel were there, and the four women; and Rattenhuber, who had been carried wounded to join them. It was their last refuge. In the afternoon of 2nd May, the Russians arrived at the cellar and demanded immediate surrender. Resistance was impossible, and the party gave themselves up. The four women were allowed to go free, and three of them ultimately reached the British and American zones.[21] When they left the cellar, Rattenhuber, Hewel, Guensche, and Mohnke had all stated their determination to commit suicide, which they may well have done, although the Russian communiqué reported the capture of Rattenhuber; for Russian captivity can have offered little hope to such men. Baur was captured alive, but seriously wounded.[22] Of the other characters who had known the secrets of the Bunker, and who have not been mentioned in this account of the exodus, Hoegl was killed at the Weidendammer Bridge; Linge was captured by the Russians.[23]

Thus ended, in total failure, the attempted escape from Berlin. With it ended the hopes of Bormann to participate in the new government and to give it a link of continuity with the old; and the last chance of delivering to Doenitz the testament of Hitler.

For meanwhile the three other bearers of that treasured document were making but slow progress in their westward

[21] Frau Christian, Frau Junge, and Fraeulein Krueger. Fraeulein Manzialy became separated from the party soon after leaving the cellar.

[22] The Russian communiqué of 6th May mentioned the capture of Baur and Rattenhuber. Information from Frau Baur, obtained in October 1945, showed that Baur was then in a Russian military hospital, recovering from the amputation of a leg.

[23] He was seen and recognised in a group of Russian prisoners by Fraeulein Krueger and Frau Christian. The Russians have not been able to comply with requests for the identification of Rattenhuber, Baur, and Linge; but by now there is little that they could add to the story, although Rattenhuber (if alive) would know about the burial of Hitler's and Eva Braun's bodies.

journey. We left them on the Pfaueninsel, an island in the
Havel lake, on the night of 30th April. There they waited all
the next day, vainly hoping that Doenitz would send a plane
to fetch them; but no plane arrived. During the following
night the Russians bombarded the island, and the four men,
Johannmeier, Lorenz, and Zander, with their companion
Hummerich, seized a canoe and paddled out into the lake to
avoid the fire. Finding a small yacht at anchor, they took
refuge in it; but the yacht had no sails, and they dared not
move in any other way lest the Russians should see them
from the shores; for a munition ship lay blazing on the Havel,
shedding a bright light over the water. As they waited on the
stationary yacht, a three-engined Junkers 52 seaplane alit upon
the water—the plane, no doubt, sent by Doenitz to fetch
them. From their position they could only see the shadow of
the plane upon the water and hear the roar of the engines.
They determined to reach the pilot. Zander set out towards it
in a boat; Lorenz and Hummerich followed in another boat;
and Johannmeier remained on the yacht, signalling to the
plane with his pocket-lamp. Their efforts were unavailing.
Zander and Lorenz drew up alongside the plane and sought to
speak with the pilot; against the roar of the engines they
shouted that Major Johannmeier was with them, and the pilot
told them to bring him out. At that moment Zander upset his
boat, and the efforts of his companions were diverted to his
rescue; the Russians began to shell the plane; and while the
emissaries returned to fetch Johannmeier, the pilot took fright
and flew away. He returned to Doenitz and reported that he
had failed to find the party. By such a narrow margin did
Johannmeier and his companions fail in their mission.

The party spent another day on the Havel, sometimes on
the Pfaueninsel, sometimes on the yacht; then, before dawn
on 3rd May, they set out again, and landing at the Wannsee
swimming-bath made their way to Potsdam and Brandenburg,
crossed the Elbe at Parey, between Magdeburg and Genthin,

and passed ultimately, as foreign workers, into the area of the Western Allies. By this time the war was over; Doenitz had surrendered; and they easily convinced themselves that their mission had now no purpose or possibility of fulfilment. Zander made the long journey to Bavaria, and there, having hidden his documents in a trunk deposited in the village of Tegernsee, he cast off, or sought to cast off, all the traces and associations which bound him to his disastrous past. He changed his name, his identity, his status; his few friends let it be known that he was dead; and he began an altogether new life under the name of Wilhelm Paustin. Johannmeier went to his family's home in Iserlohn, in Westphalia, and buried his documents in a bottle in the back garden. Had the fate of the papers depended upon these two men, they would never have been found by the Allies; for one was too proud, too courageous to yield the truth, the other had too successfully withdrawn from human cognisance. It was the garrulous journalist, Lorenz, whose vanity and indiscretion led accidentally to the discovery of these important documents.

Nor was von Below more successful in delivering his documents. In the early morning of 1st May, he, with his batman Matthiesing, had landed on the west bank of the Havel. Thence they pursued their way westwards, hiding in remote forests by day and moving by night. In a few days he too gave up hope of fulfilling his mission, and in a lonely wood he burned the documents which he was to have delivered to Keitel and Jodl. A few days later, in a hut near Friesack, von Below and Matthiesing met a sergeant-major from their old office in Berlin. His name was Pardau, and he had escaped from the cellar in the Schoenhaeuser Allee when Mohnke and the rest had been captured. Pardau told the story of the death and burning of Hitler and Eva Braun; then they parted. Von Below made his way to Bonn University, there to begin a new life as a law student; Matthiesing to his home near Osnabruck; both ultimately into British captivity.

Freytag von Loringhoven, Boldt, and Weiss also continued their journey; though having no papers to deliver, their escape interested only themselves. After parting from Johannmeier and his party on the Pfaueninsel, they had rejoined the Wannsee garrison only in time to see the whole garrison captured or destroyed in an attempt to break out; for their ammunition was exhausted. Only Freytag von Loringhoven and Boldt escaped; and that night, while hiding in a slit-trench in a wood, Boldt tried to commit suicide by taking an overdose of morphine. Freytag von Loringhoven forced him to vomit the whole dose, and thus saved his life. Thereafter they moved westward, dodging Russian patrols, and swimming rivers, till they parted, in western territory, into western captivity.

Thus, with the scattering of the disciples after Hitler's death, ended the last days in Berlin. The Fuehrer was dead; his testament was lost; his companions were killed or captured, or wandering as anonymous fugitives in the forests of central Germany. The old centre of power had dissolved without a trace; and a new centre had arisen in Schleswig-Holstein that had no other continuity with the old than the text of the two telegrams which informed Doenitz of his appointment, and the sinister, ever-present shadow of the disappointed Himmler.

For if Doenitz had accepted with chagrin the unwelcome appointment, it was with even greater chagrin that Himmler learned of his failure to gather the inheritance. All his plans had now failed; his brief moment of recovered certainty was past; the purpose had once again gone out of his life. He had sold his soul to the Devil,—he had lapsed from the faith and forgotten the unconditional terms of his loyalty,—and now he had not been paid the price. Though he went to Doenitz and offered to serve under him, it was without relish, and without assurance of acceptance. Between him and Doenitz there was no common idiom, except political insufficiency. As Himmler's secretary explained, "in the Grand Admiral's

purely military circles, Himmler's political approach to the
Western Powers was not understood." That night Himmler
contemplated resignation—he did not know that Hitler had
already dismissed him, and did not dream that Doenitz might
dismiss him; he even contemplated suicide.

Himmler did not commit suicide,—at least not yet. To the
unrealist everything is possible, and that night an absent spirit
returned from the north to reawaken his sleeping fantasies. It
was Schellenberg. To Schellenberg the situation presented no
difficulty at all; everything would turn out well if only it were
left to him. Wherever he went, he saw only evidence of the
importance attributed to himself and to his political opinions.
Had not Doenitz "on the strength of my original suggestion"
dismissed Ribbentrop and appointed the good Schwerin von
Krosigk as his successor? Did not Schwerin von Krosigk ask
Schellenberg for his collaboration? Did not everyone seem to
listen attentively to his large and subtle views on the Northern
Question and the Czech Problem? Did not Keitel and Jodl
plainly regard him as "the most experienced in foreign affairs"?
Schellenberg offered himself as an envoy to Sweden, or to
General Eisenhower. Everything now seemed possible to him;
why then should Himmler despair? Himmler agreed not to
despair. Indeed, if Schellenberg is to be believed, he joined in
the universal admiration of Schellenberg's genius. Within a
few days (we learn from this partial source) they had "a short
but significant talk together, the gist of which was, 'If only I
had listened to you sooner,' and 'Perhaps you are the first
German to be permitted to do something for his poor country
again.' " As Samuel Butler says, "the advantage of doing one's
praising for one's self is that one can lay it on so thick, and
exactly in the right places."

Nor were Schellenberg and Himmler alone in their strange
and irresponsible optimism. The air of Schleswig-Holstein was
after all still the gaseous air of Nazi Germany, which had
generated so many fantastic notions in the heads of those who

had become acclimatised to it. Just as Bormann expected to wield authority under Doenitz, so Ribbentrop, though dismissed, did not despair of future political influence. The day after his dismissal, he drafted a document for submission to Doenitz in which he suggested that an independent German government in Schleswig-Holstein might obtain Allied recognition and serve as the nucleus of a new "national and national-socialist" Germany.[24]

Narrow-minded and fanatical though he was, Doenitz at least had some of the ordinary common sense of the practical man. If he was politically ignorant, at least he was not politically silly. When he surveyed the legacy which had been thrust upon him, at first he trembled to contemplate it. He ordered elaborate proofs to be made of the legality of Hitler's, and therefore of his own authority; he ordered an examination, upon oath, of all the clerks responsible for the reception and decoding of the last telegrams from the Bunker, to be sure of their authenticity; and while these measures of justification were in progress, he prepared to modify the commitments which he had accepted. Like all conservatives, he intended to rely, in this critical posture of defeat, on a ministry of non-political specialists. Hitler's will, or rather the short abstract of it which he had received by telegram, imposed upon him a government including Bormann, Goebbels, and Seyss-Inquart. Doenitz knew nothing of the fate of Goebbels and Bormann; but not even Hitler's will could force upon him such Nazi notorieties. The telegram informing him of his appointment had authorised him to take at once "all such measures as the situation requires"; on the assurance of that authority he had already appointed Schwerin von Krosigk as his Foreign Minister: and now, on the same assurance, he decided to ignore the later, more inconvenient order. At the same time he resolved gradually to disburden himself of the compromising Nazis who still surrounded him, and in particular of Himmler.

[24] This draft was among documents captured at Flensburg.

On 2nd May, Doenitz moved his headquarters from Ploen to Flensburg, on the Danish frontier. With him, as an unofficial member of the new government, went Albert Speer. Now that Hitler was dead, Speer was able to carry out the plan he had so long projected but which, in the Fuehrer's lifetime, he had not ventured to execute. On 3rd May, the speech which he had recorded at Hamburg was at last broadcast to the German people, who now, after years of abstract slogans and political mythology, heard the sane voice of the technocrat telling them not to despair, not to let political disillusion breed practical apathy, but to keep famine at bay and the life of the nation undestroyed. They must repair the railways, "in so far as the enemy allows or orders it"; industry and trade must continue; agricultural work must go on, and the producers of food must have first claim to fuel and power for production and distribution. If the "biological substance" of the German people was to be saved, this at least was a more practical means of saving it than the complacent political virtuosity of Schellenberg.

At the same time Doenitz sent Admiral von Friedeburg to Field-Marshal Montgomery with the first offer of surrender.

Himmler also moved his headquarters to Flensburg.[25] In spite of all the omens which, to a more sensitive observer, might have portended his decline, he had now recovered from his momentary depression and was more confident than ever. His huge bodyguard was undiminished; a retinue of staff cars followed him around; high S.S. officers jostled cumbrously about him; one of them, Pruetzmann, once head of the infelicitous Werewolves, was now liaison officer with Doenitz. In incautious conversation with his indiscreet subordinates, Himmler mentioned his ambition: he would be Prime Minister of a defeated Germany, under Doenitz;—and perhaps not always under Doenitz either, for Doenitz, he hinted, was old,

[25] The above account of Himmler's last days at Flensburg is based mainly on statements by Ohlendorf, Juettner, von Woyrsch, and von Herff.

while he himself had many years of life and power ahead of him. Meanwhile he was painfully eager to impress upon Doenitz his own indispensable gifts, and begged his friends to represent to the new Fuehrer, by this or that argument, the advantages of his admission to power. He even anticipated the answer, turning up uninvited at Doenitz's staff conferences. He could not believe that he was unwanted, and embarrassed even the S.S. leaders by his insensitivity to the most obvious hints.

On 5th May Himmler held, at Flensburg, his last staff conference. Like obsolete dinosaurs, moving inappropriately in the wrong geological age, they gathered at his headquarters,—high S.S. and police leaders, Obergruppenfuehrer and Gruppenfuehrer, heads of now defunct organisations, sustained only by portentous titles, the memory of vanished authority, and absurd illusions. Himmler entered, attended by his secretary and his adjutant, and delivered a speech on the political situation. He mentioned that he had been reproved for having negotiated with the Western Powers without the late Fuehrer's authority,—for Ritter von Greim and Hanna Reitsch had arrived in Schleswig-Holstein and discharged upon him their angry rhetoric; but he was indifferent to that now. He still saw political possibilities, he said,—"although I can tell you," says one who heard him, "the possibilities of which he spoke made me clutch my head." He intended to establish a "reformed" Nazi administration in Schleswig-Holstein, which would conduct peace negotiations with the Western Powers as an independent government in its own territory. Then he went into the details of administration which so delighted that strange, bipartite mind. The S.S. head offices were to be dissolved, and their leaders to join Himmler's staff as advisers. The chief of the ordinary police, Obergruppenfuehrer Wuennenberg, was ordered to continue his duties: policemen detailed for duty in the area of the new "government" were to be selected carefully for their smart and soldierly appearance.

Other tasks and titles were allotted to others of his followers. As for himself, he had no intention of committing suicide, he assured them, or of being killed. On the contrary he was full of plans and vitality. All he wanted now was an interview with Field-Marshal Montgomery. He had plans, he seemed to imply, of bargaining for life and authority with the Western Powers; and he seemed confident that his plans would succeed. When the meeting was over, even the S.S. leaders shook their heads sadly at the illusions of the Reichsfuehrer.

Next day the illusions were clearly exposed. Doenitz wrote a letter to Himmler. It ran:

To the Reich Minister of the Interior,
Reichsfuehrer S. S. Himmler.

DEAR HERR REICH MINISTER,—In view of the present situation, I have decided to dispense with your further assistance as Reich Minister of the Interior and member of the Reich Government, as Commander-in-Chief of the Replacement Army, and as Chief of the Police. I now regard all your offices as abolished. I thank you for the service which you have given to the Reich.[26]

Parallel letters were addressed to Goebbels, whose death was not yet known in Flensburg; to Rosenberg, who still held the ironical title of Minister for the Occupied Territories in the East; and to the Nazi Minister of Justice, Thierack. Bormann, since he had no ministerial post, did not need to be dismissed; he could be ignored. Doenitz had decided to break with the past; he had dismissed the Nazis. Within a week of the death of Hitler, who from his underground bunker, by the mere force and terror of his name, had artificially prolonged its existence, the *detritus* of the Party could be thus easily swept away. Two days later, the instrument of unconditional sur-

[26] It is not certain whether this letter (the text of which was captured in Doenitz's file) was actually delivered to Himmler, or whether (as Ohlendorf states) Doenitz conveyed the news of his dismissal to Himmler in a personal interview. The letter is unsigned, but a manuscript note upon it reads, "To be sent by order of the Grand Admiral."

render was signed at Rheims, and the Thousand-Year Reich was over.

Still Himmler remained. No longer Reichsfuehrer, or High Priest, or Inquisitor, but a purposeless, vacillating, ignorant man who had lost the principle of his life, and yet could not admit his unreality, he hung on in Flensburg, an embarrassment to his successors, an enigma to his now meaningless staff. Still he kept up his pretentious establishment: a staff of 150 men, a radio detachment, an escort of four cars to protect him; but to what end he did not know. Sometimes he consulted his friends for advice. Should he commit suicide? Should he give himself up? Should he go to ground? Perhaps one of the Nazi field-marshals would protect him,—Busch, for instance, or Schoerner. He went to Busch; but after a few days Busch sent him back; and Schoerner was now out of reach. Himmler could not understand that the respect which had once been offered to his power would not extend to his weakness. One day he disappeared again, quite silently; but again he returned. He wrote to Field-Marshal Montgomery, and enquired daily whether a reply had come; but no reply came. Now there was not even Schellenberg to comfort him with false hopes; for Schellenberg was away in Sweden. Himmler asked daily for news of him; "but Schellenberg," says one of his staff, "did not dream of returning. He had made far too many promises to Himmler which he could never fulfil." Himmler had to rely for comfort on the detestable Gebhart; and Gebhart, like everyone else in these last days, thought only of himself. It should be added that Schellenberg did not, of course, ascribe the failure of his ingenious political schemes to any defects in his own conception or handling of them; his complacent nature was proof against such a conclusion. When he looked back, from Sweden, upon his universal failure, his judgment spared his own pride. "It was the indecision of the Reichsfuehrer," he said, "that had ruined everything."

The Reichsfuehrer remained undecided. For another fortnight he led a purposeless life in the outskirts of the Flensburg administration; then one day he left, with his adjutant and his secretary. He was dressed as a common soldier, and for disguise had a patch over his eye. Undecided to the end, he did not even know whither he was going. In fact he walked into a British control post; and there, recognised, stripped, and searched, when the doctor's fingers reached his mouth, and his last chance of determining the manner of his death would soon have gone, he at last made a decision. He bit the poison capsule which was concealed behind his teeth, and was dead in a few seconds.

It was an appropriate death, as appropriate as the barbaric funeral of Hitler and the silent, secondary death of Goebbels; appropriate to his character,—for it was squalid and delayed, —and appropriate to the functions which he could no longer exercise. The terrible high-priest of Hitler, who had once served the altar, expounded the mysteries, and presided over the human sacrifices with such undeviating devotion, having once yielded to doubt, had become a mere wandering shadow, a ghostly sacristan, fitfully haunting the shrine he could no longer tend. Now the god himself had perished; the temple had been utterly destroyed; the faithful had been scattered, or converted; and the suicide of the exiled priest is the natural end of a chapter in history: the history, it seems, of a savage tribe and a primitive superstition.

EPILOGUE

THE original purpose of the enquiry which caused this book to be written was to establish the facts of Hitler's end, and thereby to prevent the growth of a myth; and certainly Hitler's own exploitation of mythology in politics has been sufficiently disastrous for the world to apprehend a repetition. The facts are now clear, and if myths, like the truth, depend on evidence, we are safe. But myths are not like truths; they are the triumph of credulity over evidence. The form of a myth is indeed externally conditioned by facts; there is a minimum of evidence with which it must comply, if it is to live; but once lip-service has been paid to that undeniable minimum, the human mind is free to indulge its infinite capacity for self-deception. When we consider upon what ludicrous evidence the most preposterous beliefs have been easily, and by millions, entertained, we may well hesitate before pronouncing anything incredible.

Therefore, though the facts in this book are confidently asserted, for their original purpose I only timidly prophesy success. Many men saw Nero die; but within a year, several false Neros arose and were believed. In our own history, the Princes were clearly murdered in the Tower, but there were many who afterwards found it convenient to discover their survival. From such discouraging examples we turn with relief to the story of the Greek philosopher Empedocles, who, in the interests of his reputation, plunged secretly down the crater of Mount Etna, confident that his bereaved fellow citizens, remembering his own judicious prophecies, would suppose him translated to Heaven. But the citizens of Girgenti came to no such conclusion. Finding a shoe of the prophet casually ejected by the volcano, they satisfied their curiosity without recourse to miracles. This analogy, if true, is certainly more promising; but it is only fair to add that the Greeks of Sicily, who so creditably disbelieved the impossible, were favoured by a sceptical education and a high standard of living. The Germans have long been without the former; and they are unlikely, for some time, to enjoy the latter.

Nevertheless, I believe that the facts given in this book do belong to the category of the undeniable minimum, of which even the most extravagant myths must take account. Nazism may revive; the ancient froth of Nibelung nonsense, whose exhalations had poisoned German political thought even before Hitler, may well find another vent; a new party may appeal to a myth of Hitler; but if so, it will be to a myth of Hitler dead, not of Hitler living. This is perhaps small comfort; but it is as much as mere truth is capable of supplying. To prevent political myths from arising is the function not of historical enquiry but of practical politics.

Turning aside, therefore, from the inappropriate task of seeking to control the future, we may here consider what further lessons are to be derived from this extraordinary chapter of history. Some of these lessons will already have been apparent in the course of the narrative, but in this epilogue it will perhaps be of value to resume and summarise them; for no one, I think, can have read this account of life in a monkey-house without asking at least two questions to which he may expect an answer: firstly, how did such monkeys succeed in seizing and retaining power; and secondly, how did they so nearly win the war? The first of these questions involves us in a consideration of the nature of dictatorial power.

Thomas Carlyle supposed that power should be entrusted unconditionally to great men, heroes who were laws to themselves, not responsible to the institutions or prejudices of inferior men. When a nation is so fortunate as to breed a great man (he thought), it should not seek to limit the expression of his greatness; it should be happy to forward his design. This doctrine rang musically in German ears, in a time of gloom and defeat, when Germans despaired of political institutions and their own capacity to use them. It was acceptable to Hitler, whom we have seen listening with egotistical relish to readings from Carlyle's *History of Frederick the Great* in the Bunker in Berlin. Hitler, like Carlyle, believed in "historical greatness," which to him was more important than the happiness or survival of a people; and he conceived of himself as a great man,—in which he was surely not mistaken; for it is absurd to suggest that one who made such a stir in the world was of ordinary stature. The Germans accepted him as the Messiah for whom they were waiting, and in the hours of his apparent success they sacrificed their political institutions to him; for they believed not in them, but in the man.

Now this doctrine of Carlyle, which the history of Nazism so aptly illustrates, depends upon two premises of doubtful validity: firstly, that "greatness," or any other merely abstract conception, is desirable; secondly, that the human character is constant,—for a great man can clearly be trusted with absolute power only if his qualities remain "great." The opposite doctrine to this is the doctrine summarised by Lord Acton in his famous aphorism, "Power tends to corrupt, and absolute power corrupts absolutely": the doctrine that power is not merely the effective expression of a fixed character, but can affect and alter the character which exercises it. The history of Nazism suggests that this doctrine is true.

In the early days of Nazism, Hitler showed a political genius which we are in danger now of forgetting, but which it is very important that we should remember. His ultimate purpose was indeed clear to those who did not willingly deceive themselves: he aimed at the destruction of European civilisation by a barbarian empire in central Europe,—the terrible hegemony of a new, more permanent Genghiz Khan: "a new Dark Age," as Mr. Churchill called it, "made more sinister, and perhaps more protracted, by the lights of perverted science." But when we have admitted the bestiality of his ambition, we must admit that he set himself to realise it with political genius. He detected and exploited all the cruel impulses, the irrational beliefs, the atavistic prejudices, the memories and fears of a frustrated people; he discovered a new technique of exploitation; and he used it with skill and daring in the direction of his ultimate aims. His purpose was clear, his policy consistent, his methods various, adaptable, and effective. If the Germans wanted the same results as he, and if Carlyle's theory were correct, they might reasonably suppose (as too many of them did suppose) that the Fuehrer had found the secret of politics, and that institutions which limited or constrained the infallible power of the new Leviathan, the mortal god, were but the idols of a discarded faith, only fit for sacrifice.

In the years 1938–41 Hitler enjoyed his most spectacular successes; and with each success the German people burnt a new sacrifice before him, until, in 1941, he took his own infallibility for granted. With his armies a few miles from Moscow, and himself hailed as the greatest military genius of all time, he no longer felt the need of political skill, of that patience and flexibility which is, after all, merely a recognition of the possibility of weakness or error. In the autumn of 1941, when he demobilised 40 divisions and ordered industry to revert to the production of consumer-goods; in December 1941, when he wantonly declared war on America, that another victim might add splendour to his inevitable triumph; it was clear that he was no longer prepared to make such recognition. Political skill was judged unnecessary and had been discarded; and the institutions which might have corrected him, if he were wrong, had been discarded too.

It is with the recollection of this past history that we should now look at the last days described in this book. In them we see the last, the logical consequences of Carlyle's dream. After

20th July 1944, the opposition of the Army, the last and only opposition in Germany, had been crushed. The power of the Nazis was now so absolute, its institutional channels so utterly destroyed, its divorce from political skill so complete, that we find ourselves examining a new spectacle: a situation in which politics, instead of being a skilful calculation of forces, have become the direct expression of irresponsible power.

The consequences of such irresponsibility are obvious. It is not only that the personal extravagancies of a single corrupted man have unchallenged political effect: that Hitler's formula of *World Power or Ruin* could become a real policy, and his destroying spirit, when the outer world remained firm, could spend itself upon Germany. There are consequences independent of personality. Though dictatorship is sometimes defended as efficient, and under certain conditions may be efficient, real dictatorship is by definition unconditional, and inherently inefficient. Irresponsible power, without elaborate institutions, cannot be centrally exercised, even by a mortal god; it must tend to fall apart into manageable empires in the hands of his equally irresponsible subordinates. Furthermore, such a god, since he is mortal, must die; and there is therefore the problem of the succession. The candidates for the succession will inevitably be those who have contrived, at the moment of his death, to reserve the largest or most effective portion of power. Even those who cannot hope to succeed, must equip themselves to survive under the successor. Behind the façade of unanimity, all dictatorships are to a large extent centrifugal: the rule of a court conceals a political anarchy in which jealous feudatories, with their private armies and reservations of public resources, are secretly bargaining, and may openly fight, for the reversion or preservation of power. In fact, neither courts nor feudalism are nurseries of political intelligence; and therefore the ambitious sometimes ludicrously fail of their ambitions. The satraps of Cromwell, after a brief struggle, sold out to a more traditional authority; and Hitler's *Bonzen* plotted absurdly for a throne to which there could be no possible succession. The characteristics of modern dictatorship,—its careful self-sufficiency, its deliberate intellectual isolation,—reduce still further the likelihood of political intelligence within it: they lead directly to the political and intellectual fools' paradise in which such figures as Goering and Goebbels and Himmler, with their drugs and perfumes, their nihilism and mysticism, their flatterers and astrologers, could determine policy, and such ninnies as Ribbentrop, Schellenberg, and Schwerin von Krosigk could be regarded as experts in foreign affairs. We are reminded of the court-parasites of the Roman Empire, of whom Juvenal wrote: the bad jokes of Fortune,—village pierrots yesterday, arbiters of life and death today, tomorrow keepers of the public latrines.

Nor is it only political intelligence which is killed by the lack of criticism inherent in absolute power; for technical progress, however unpolitical in its aim, is equally dependent upon the free opposition of minds and methods which the uniform patronage of a dictatorship must deny. Now that all German secrets have been disclosed, the decline of German science under the Nazis has become apparent. This book illustrates one instance of it; for how could medicine advance when the direction of studies, the allocation of resources, the judgment of results, and the promotion of merit depended upon corrupt charlatans like Morell and Conti and the crackbrained fanatics of the S.S.? Even in military science the same decline is apparent. Hitler began the war with a group of generals trained to uniform efficiency in the greatest military tradition in the world; he ended it with a handful of obedient nonentities, and himself. The military historians of the future may have something to say about Beck and Halder, Manstein and Rundstedt; it is unlikely that they will waste much time on Keitel and Krebs, or even on Kesselring and Schoerner. What will they say of Hitler himself?

It is customary to laugh at Hitler's strategical genius, which was certainly disastrous for Germany; but here again it is necessary to observe not merely the final issue, but the stages which led to it. Behind the military snobbism of the professional generals, and through the smoke-screen of official servility, it is possible to discern that Hitler's military talents were not really contemptible. The extent of his knowledge, and his amazing grasp of detail, have been universally, if sometimes reluctantly, admitted; his will-power, which ultimately doomed Germany, sometimes achieved results which the professional generals, on purely logistical grounds, thought impossible; [1] and his operational plans have at least the honour of controversy.[2] But Hitler's mind and method were erratic. The intuition which, in politics, chose both Speer and Ribbentrop, in military matters chose both Guderian and Keitel. The correction of criticism, the opposition of both minds and facts, is essential to such a random genius; and it is the disappearance of criticism, not the inherent errors of this thought, which made Hitler's strategy in the end as calamitous as his politics. Those who attended his staff-conferences in the first two years of the war have described his earlier, more patient methods: how he would sit in silence, only now and then asking questions or eliciting opinions, feeling his way warily, and learning

[1] Speer believed that Hitler's intervention in the first Russian winter saved the German armies from greater disaster, and that this incident confirmed Hitler in his belief that all his generals were inept. Certainly Hitler's will-power was extraordinary, and his confidence in it unlimited. His error lay in supposing that faith can move mountains by itself, instead of merely giving the decisive impetus to the spade.

[2] Hitler's critics insist that his strategical successes, such as the battle of France in 1940, were only made possible by the judicious misinterpretations of the Army Command, and that his tactical successes, such as the battle of Kiev in 1941 and the Ardennes offensive in 1944, were strategic blunders. I am not competent to give any judgment in these matters. For some opinions of Halder and Keitel on Hitler's strategy, see above, p. 10, note. Since Halder hated Hitler personally and politically, and despised him militarily (Halder is a military snob, believing that no amateur can ever understand the mysteries of war), his reluctant admissions must be respected.

what he could from the experts whom he wished to despise but secretly feared. But gradually success bred confidence; the propaganda of Goebbels, the sycophancy of Keitel, nourished the self-delusions of unchallenged power; no mind, no fact was allowed to contest the dogmas of strategic genius; [3] and at the end, how different had the conference-table become! Hitler was still there, still the central figure, still the ultimate authority; but a Chinese wall separated him from the outer world of reality. He listened not to other voices, but to echoes of his own; for none of the surviving courtiers dared speak, or even know the truth. He still interested himself in every detail, still moved armies by battalions and regiments; but it was on an imaginary battlefield. He was mounting the impossible Steiner attack, or marshalling the phantom army of Wenck.

Thus, in reading of the last days of Hitler's empire, we must remember that they were the last days, and were different from the first; otherwise we may forget the political lesson that they illustrate. Nevertheless, we should remember that the last days were implicit in the first. Most historical dictators have passed through similar stages of development. Starting with revolutionary power, based on a revolutionary idea which happens to symbolise the mood of a people, they convert it into military power based on success; when the revolutionary promise is betrayed, and the success runs dry, they resort to naked power, based on political expedients and secret police; but since these are inadequate in the long run, the system collapses, or is overthrown. In theory, of course, revolutionary power can become respectable and traditional, and develop along orderly lines, as happened in the Roman Empire; but most of the great modern dictators,—Cromwell, Napoleon, Hitler, Mussolini,—went the other way; and the

---

[3] Hitler's repudiation of inconvenient facts would be incredible, were it not so well attested. According to Halder, Hitler often complained of the "damned objective views" of the Army General Staff.

reason is, I believe, the ultimate inefficiency of dictatorial power, which causes the success to run dry.[4]

These observations will perhaps answer the first question, how power came into the hands of such a set of monkeys; but the answer itself forces upon us another question. If these are the logical consequences of the separation of power from the institutions which should contain it, what forces, in a practical, not a logical world, allowed these merely logical consequences to emerge? Why was there no effective revolt or opposition, once the logical inevitability of their emergence had become plain? It is true the institutions of resistance had been sacrificed, and in the modern world the advantages are on the side of the government; it is true Goebbels sustained the Germans with the promise of miracles and millennia, of secret weapons and diplomatic somersaults; it is true dictatorship kills political intelligence in the governed as well as in the governors; but men are not blind automata; there is still an irreducible residue of common sense; men are after all the agents as well as the victims of governments; and the submission of eighty million men to a clique which was plainly and wilfully driving them to disaster calls for some attempt at explanation.

It is sometimes said that the Allied insistence on "unconditional surrender" frightened the Germans into continued obedience; but if this implies that they would otherwise have revolted, I do not think it is true. Of those Germans who preferred the rule of the Nazis to unconditional surrender, how many would have been inspired to rebellion by an Allied assurance of moderation? Conditions can only be made with

[4] The case of Cromwell is somewhat controversial. His personal character was of course entirely different from Hitler's, and he was never absolute; further, he sought to convert his power from revolutionary to traditional, but found such a change both logically and practically impossible. Nevertheless the basis and nature of his power make it fundamentally similar to Hitler's (more similar than that of Napoleon or Mussolini); and in spite of all differences of circumstance, the same tendency is apparent.

power-holders, or alternative power-holders, otherwise they are not conditions but promises; and what German was influenced by promises after twelve years of Dr. Goebbels? Of alternative power-holders, the Army leaders might perhaps have been ready to bargain; but conditions which included the destruction of the German Army would have seemed no conditions to them; and anyway, even the Army failed in its politics. As for the "democratic opposition," invented by virtuous journalists,—it is a creature as fabulous as the centaur and the hippogriff. No doubt many Germans quietly grumbled about the Nazis and have since claimed to have been their enemies; but in time of war, bargains can be struck only with real political forces, not with whimpering shadows. Who of these "democrats" ever concerted a programme or approached the Allies with concrete proposals? A few high-minded aristocrats, a few disappointed officials and dismayed parsons—were these really more promising than the Schellenbergs and Schwerin von Krosigks? If we wish to explain the docility of the German people, we must look for some other explanation, and find it, perhaps, in that most discouraging German characteristic: the despair of politics.

In thus isolating German characteristics, we must not, of course, fall into the error of racialism. German characteristics do not spring from German blood or climate, but from the habits of thought and traditions of government to which Germans happen to have become accustomed. Now German history is characterised by a record of political failure so continuous as to have become a tradition,—a tradition which in turn perpetuates the record by the appearance of inevitability. Who has succeeded among German politicians? a German may ask himself; and he will answer, Frederick the Great, and Bismarck,—the men of blood and iron. On the other hand, what liberal or popular movements have ever succeeded in Germany? The romantic liberals of 1815–30, vapouring immaturely in provincial universities? the lawyers and businessmen of 1848, theorising solemnly in Frankfurt? the Weimar Republic, silently destroyed from within by Bruening, and then ordered away by the Nazis, without even the show of a revolution? With these and such memories the Germans are easily persuaded that however reason will do for others, only force will succeed with them. The Kaiser indeed failed, but at least he had a run of success, unlike the Weimar Republic; and perhaps he failed for purely technical reasons,—his personal policy, not his cardinal principles were at fault. That at least was Hitler's view, when he spoke of "the fools of 1914–18," and promised to be more successful. Now he has failed even more catastrophically. But at one time he nearly succeeded; and if later "liberal" governments are obvious failures, it may well be that the Germans will look back not to the disastrous failure of Hitler, but to the temporary prosperity and the nearly attained success.

This consistent tradition of political failure in Germany has other consequences besides a despair of reason and a reliance on force; and one of them is the elevation of politics into a mystery. If so few Germans have ever succeeded in politics, a German may say, it is clear that politics are beyond the reach of ordinary men, who will be more profitably and more happily employed in those tasks of commerce and agriculture, of manufacture and industry and military organisation, in which their skill is acknowledged. Thus the political arena is left vacant, and any charlatan who professes to understand the mystery of politics is allowed to enter and to try his hand. Politics in Germany have long taken place in such a vacuum; the real ability of the people has been concentrated on industry or the army; and the direction of industry and the army, for peace or war, has been left to the adventurers who have occupied the neglected political stage. To salve their consciences, the Germans have invented comforting philosophies: the philosophy of Marxism, that all politics are but an immaterial reflexion of social relations, and the philosophy of the technocrats, that politics are quite irrelevant. How fatally untrue those philosophies are has been shown by German history in this war, in which the crazy politics of a fully-developed and therefore calamitous dictatorship have not only controlled German industry and the German army, but have misdirected and ultimately ruined them. The answer to the question, why did the Nazis so nearly win the war? is then, that they did not win the war, or nearly. What nearly won the war was German industry and the German army which, in its early days, the days of its political skill, the dictatorship did indeed foster and serve; what lost it was the unchecked development of the dictatorship, in which the German people acquiesced, even to the end, through a fatal political tradition.

How fatal that tradition was, is clear from one personal history which is described in this book. In these pages, which describe and illustrate so many varieties of human corruption and human lunacy, one figure stands out in extraordinary isolation. Whatever the errors of judgment, and neutrality of conscience, which enabled him to acquire and retain the personal friendship of the most bloodthirsty tyrant in modern history, it is quite clear that in Hitler's court Albert Speer was morally and intellectually alone. He had the capacity to understand the forces of politics, and the courage to resist the master whom all others have declared irresistible. As an administrator, he was undoubtedly a genius. He regarded the rest of the court with dignified contempt. His ambitions were peaceful and constructive: he wished to rebuild Berlin and Nuremberg, and had planned "at the cost of no more than two months' war-expenditure" (as he sadly protested in the dock at Nuremberg) to make them the greatest cities in the world. Nevertheless, in a political sense, Speer is the real criminal of Nazi Germany; for he, more than any other, represented that fatal philosophy which has made havoc of Germany and nearly shipwrecked the world. For ten years he sat at the very centre of political power; his keen intelligence diagnosed the nature, and observed the mutations, of Nazi government and policy; he saw and despised the personalities around him; he heard their outrageous orders and understood their fantastic ambitions; but he did nothing. Supposing politics to be irrelevant, he turned aside, and built roads and bridges and factories, while the logical consequences of government by madmen emerged. Ultimately, when their emergence involved the ruin of all his work, Speer accepted the consequences and acted. Then it was too late; Germany had been destroyed.

NOTE ON SOURCES

THE following is a list of the chief personal sources (excluding captured documents) on which the foregoing account is based:

A. *Personalities in Hitler's Court*

1. SPEER, ALBERT.—Reich Minister of Armament and War Production. In a series of statements and interrogations, Speer has given the completest and most objective account on this subject. He is also a valuable authority on his own policy of opposition to Hitler's plans of "Scorched Earth," a subject on which his statements have been checked and confirmed by subsidiary sources, especially Karl Kaufmann, Gauleiter of Hamburg, and Koller (No. 20 below), and on incidents in Hitler's Bunker on the occasions of his last visits, on 20th and 23rd/24th April 1945. Further details have been given by Speer in the course of his defence at Nuremberg.

2. SCHWERIN VON KROSIGK, GRAF LUTZ.—Reich Minister of Finance. Krosigk's diary, written with an eye to history, records incidents which the writer thought significant during the period 15th April/5th May 1945. See pp. 95 following.

There are numerous subsidiary sources on this subject, which have been used for matters of detail.

B. *Hitler's Relations with Army Leaders*

3. HALDER, FRANZ, Generaloberst.—Formerly (till 1942) Chief of Army General Staff. Halder has given very full, factual, and objective accounts of the whole history of relations between Hitler and the generals, the development of the OKW, etc. These accounts have been supplemented by data from many other generals, including Field-Marshal Wilhelm Keitel (No. 30 below), who believed in Hitler's strategical genius, and a much larger number who did not.

C. *Hitler's Physical Health and Personality*

The following doctors have been interrogated on Hitler's health and physical condition, and on other personal matters:

4. BRANDT, DR. KARL.—Surgeon to Hitler's staff (Begleitarzt) until October 1944.

5. VON EICKEN, PROFESSOR.—Ear, nose, and throat specialist. Attended Hitler in 1935, and again after 20th July 1944.

6. GIESING, DR. ERWIN.—Ear, nose, and throat specialist. Attended Hitler after 20th July 1944.

7. VON HASSELBACH, DR. HANS KARL.—Surgeon, deputy to Brandt (No. 4 above) until October 1944.

8. MORELL, PROFESSOR THEODORE.—Personal physician (Leibartz) to Hitler, whom he last saw on 22nd April 1945.

D. *Himmler and his* Entourage

9. SCHELLENBERG, WALTER.—S.S. Brigadefuehrer, Head of R.S.H.A., Amt VI (Foreign Intelligence). Though nominally subordinate to Kaltenbrunner, Schellenberg had direct personal relations with Himmler, which make him a valuable source. While in Sweden between the end of hostilities and his surrender to SHAEF, Schellenberg compiled a careful diary of the events of the last month of the war, which is very important. He has also been exhaustively interrogated.

10. GEBHARDT, PROFESSOR KARL.—S.S. Obergruppenfuehrer. Himmler's personal doctor and adviser.

11. BRANDT, DR. RUDOLF.—S.S. Standartenfuehrer. Himmler's secretary.

12. GROTHMANN, WERNER.—Himmler's military adjutant.

13. BERGER, GOTTLOB.—S.S. Obergruppenfuehrer. Chief of S.S. Hauptamt and Kriegsgefangenenwesen.

14. OHLENDORF, OTTO.—S.S. Obergruppenfuehrer. Head of R.S.-H.A., Amt III (Sicherheitsdienst), and Ministerialdirektor in Reichswirtschaftsministerium.

15. VON WOYRSCH, UDO.—S.S. Obergruppenfuehrer and General der Polizei.

16. VON HERFF, MAXIMILIAN.—S.S. Obergruppenfuehrer and General der Waffen S.S. Head of Personalhauptamt.

17. JUETTNER, MAX.—S.S. Obergruppenfuehrer. Head of S.S. Fuehrungshauptamt.

18. KALTENBRUNNER, ERNST.—S.S. Obergruppenfuehrer. Head of R.S.H.A. Kaltenbrunner was in south Germany at the end, and is therefore of little direct value for this subject; but he has been thoroughly interrogated, and his reports shed incidental light on many matters.

Of the above, Nos. 10, 14, 15, and 16 were with Himmler in Schleswig-Holstein during the last days; Nos. 11 and 12 were with him when he was captured. Count Folke Bernadotte's book, *The Curtain Falls*, contains some useful information about the personal part played by the author in the last days.

E. *The Dismissal of Goering*

19. GOERING, HERMANN.—Reichsmarschall.
20. KOLLER, KARL.—General der Luftwaffe. Chief of Staff of Luftwaffe. Koller's diary, covering the period 16th April to 9th May 1945, is a detailed record of great value, not only for these events (in which he was the principal intermediary), but also for many other incidents during the period. Koller was with the OKW at Fuerstenburg, and in regular telephone communication with the Bunker. He also, on 8th May, received, and recorded, a first-hand account of events in the Bunker (26th/29th April) from Ritter von Greim.
21. LAMMERS, HANS HEINRICH.—Head of Reichskanzlei. Lammers was present at Goering's conference on 23rd April 1945, and has made a statement and produced documents relevant to this episode.

In addition to these, Speer (No. 1 above) was an eye-witness of certain events in this connexion, and Kaltenbrunner (No. 18 above) has reported a conversation with S.S. Obersturmbannfuehrer Frank, who both took part in Goering's conference and was responsible for his arrest.

F. *Events in the Bunker* (22nd April to 1st May 1945)

22. AXMANN, ARTUR.—Reichsjugendfuehrer. Axmann visited the Bunker on several occasions. He was there on 30th April 1945, and examined the dead bodies of Hitler and Eva Braun. He took part in the escape of 1st May, and claims to have seen the corpses of Bormann and Stumpfegger.
23. VON BELOW, NICOLAUS.—Oberst der Luftwaffe. Wehrmachtattaché (Luftwaffe) at Fuehrer's Headquarters. Was in the Bunker till midnight 29th/30th April. Witnessed Hitler's personal will.
24. BOLDT, GERHARDT FRIEDRICH WILHELM.—Rittmeister. A.D.C. to General Krebs (Chief of Army General Staff). Left the Bunker on 29th April.
25. CHRISTIAN, ECKARD.—General der Luftwaffe. Chef Luftwaffenfuehrungsstab. Was in the Bunker on 22nd and 23rd April, then with OKW at Fuerstenburg. Had contact with the Bunker, and with Ritter von Greim both during and after Greim's stay in the Bunker.
26. CHRISTIAN, FRAU GERDA (*née* DARANOWSKI).—Wife of No. 25. Secretary to Hitler. Left the Bunker on 1st May.
27. FREYTAG VON LORINGHOVEN, BARON, Major.—Adjutant to General Krebs. Left the Bunker on 29th April.
28. JOHANNMEIER, WILLI, Major—Wehrmachtattaché at Fuehrer's Headquarters, assisting General Burgdorf. Left the Bunker on 29th April bearing a copy of Hitler's political testament addressed to Field-Marshal Schoerner.

29. JUNGE, FRAU GERTRUD.—Secretary to Hitler. Left the Bunker on 1st May.

30. KARNAU, HERMANN.—Revier Oberwachtmeister. Guard in Reichssicherheitsdienst, Dienststelle 1, on duty in the Bunker. Left the Bunker on 1st May. Saw the burning of Hitler's and Eva Braun's bodies.

31. KEITEL, WILHELM, Feldmarschall.—Chef OKW. In the Bunker daily till 23rd April; then with OKW at Krampnitz and Fuerstenburg.

32. KEMPKA, ERICH.—S.S. Sturmbannfuehrer. Hitler's personal chauffeur and transport officer. Took part in burning of Hitler's and Eva Braun's bodies. Left the Bunker on 1st May.

33. KRUEGER, FRAUELEIN ELSE.—Bormann's secretary. Left the Bunker on 1st May.

34. LORENZ, HEINZ.—Official of Deutsche Nachrichtenbuero, working in Propaganda Ministry; reported frequently to Bunker, and left it on 29th April, bearing copies of Hitler's personal and political testaments, and Goebbels' Appendix, destined for Munich.

35. MANSFELD (alias SKRZIPCZYK), ERICH.—S.S. Hauptscharfuehrer. Guard in RSD Dienststelle 1, on duty in the Bunker. Witnessed burning of Hitler's and Eva Braun's bodies. Left the Bunker on 1st May.

36. MUELLER, WILLI OTTO.—Tailor, resident in Reich Chancellery. Observed some incidents of interest.

37. MATTHIESING, HEINZ.—Batman to von Below (No. 23 above), whom he accompanied out of Berlin on 29th April.

38. POPPEN, HILCO.—Guard in RSD Dienststelle 1, on duty in Bunker. Left on 1st May.

39. REITSCH, HANNA.—"Flugkapitaen." Test pilot and companion of Ritter von Greim. In Bunker 26th till 29th April.

40. SCHWAEGERMANN, GUENTHER AUGUST WILHELM.—S.S. Hauptsturmfuehrer. Adjutant to Goebbels. Was in the Bunker 22nd April till 1st May. Burnt bodies of Goebbels and his wife and children.

41. VON VARO, BARONESS.—Was casually in second (S.S.) Bunker until 1st May. Was present at Hitler's first leave-taking at 0230 hours on 29th April.

42. ZANDER, WILHELM.—S.S. Standartenfuehrer. Assistant to Martin Bormann. Left the Bunker on 29th April, carrying copies of Hitler's personal and political testaments, and marriage certificate of Hitler and Eva Braun, addressed to Admiral Doenitz.

APPENDIX

THE EXECUTION OF FEGELEIN
(See p. 171.)

THE real causes and circumstances of the execution of Fegelein provide one of the few subjects included in this book upon which final certainty seems unattainable. Both Greim (quoted by Koller) and Reitsch knew of Fegelein's execution, which must therefore have taken place before they left the Bunker (*i.e.* before about midnight on 28th/29th April); but both describe it as the punishment for his attempted escape, and say that it took place immediately after his recapture, which is certainly inaccurate. Reitsch says that Fegelein's absence was first noticed on 27th April, and the evidence from other sources, though never explicit, points to the same date. But it is certain that Fegelein was alive when the news of Himmler's treachery was brought to the Bunker, on the evening of 28th April, and that he was questioned on the subject. Explicit evidence of this has been given by Lorenz and von Below and others, and most sources agree that a day elapsed between the recapture of Fegelein and his execution. It seems necessary and reasonable therefore to agree with Lorenz (who elsewhere proves to be one of the most accurate of witnesses) that Fegelein was degraded in rank for desertion on 27th April, and executed on a second charge connected with Himmler's treachery on the night of 28th/29th April. His execution must then have taken place between the announcement of Himmler's treachery at about 9 P.M. and the departure of Greim and Reitsch soon after midnight.

We are therefore faced with the question, What was this charge, and was it true? No witness has given a clear answer to this question; and it seems clear that the whole matter was deliberately involved in secrecy in the Bunker,—probably because Fegelein's former intimacy with Hitler, Bormann, and Burgdorf, and his relationship to Eva Braun, made the discussion of his supposed apostasy distasteful. According to von Below, however, Burgdorf told him that "Himmler had instigated a plot to hand over Hitler's dead body to the Western Powers," and that Fegelein was implicated in this. Others have also given evidence of a general belief that Himmler had plotted against Hitler's person, and that Fegelein's evidence, on the night of 28th April, proved both this plot and Fegelein's complicity.

Whether Burgdorf actually made this remark to von Below is uncertain; for von Below is very vague on the matter, and he may well have been influenced by the subsequent (and untrue) statements of Schellenberg, which were published while von Below was at liberty. But in any case the statement, as quoted, is incredible. It is quite certain that Himmler never considered any such plot; nor would it have been possible to convey Hitler's body to the Western Powers after 25th April. Nevertheless, it is clear that several S.S. leaders, including Steiner, were talking loosely about the possibility of such a plot, and that Fegelein must have known about such talk; he must also have known about Himmler's meetings with Bernadotte, which were ostensibly for quite legitimate purposes; and it is quite probable that under cross-examination on the night of 28th April he revealed his knowledge of both these facts. Since he had been in confinement since 27th April, and knew nothing of Himmler's treachery, he would not have been aware of the new significance which could now be attributed to such admissions.

It seems most probable to me that this in fact happened; that in the highly-charged atmosphere of the Bunker, and the universal suspicions of treachery, Fegelein's admissions were easily interpreted as knowledge, hitherto treasonably concealed, of an S.S. plot, subsidiary to Himmler's political schemes, and connected with the presumably treacherous failure of the Steiner attack on 21st April; and that Fegelein's absences from the Bunker, culminating in his attempted escape on 27th April, were interpreted as the comings and goings of the indispensable agent between his employer and his victim. In fact, of course, Fegelein was only interested in escaping from the Bunker; but in such an atmosphere

Trifles light as air
Are to the jealous confirmation strong
As proofs of Holy Writ.

INDEX

gram, 138–140; dismisses Goering, 140–141; last efforts to persuade him to leave Berlin, 142; appoints successor to Goering, 151–152; behaviour in the Bunker, 152, 161–163; still obeyed, 168; learns of Himmler's treachery, 169; holds secret conference, 169; orders execution of Fegelein, 170–171; sends Greim from Berlin, 171–173; marries Eva Braun, 174–176; his two testaments, 176–182; settles the succession, 178; nominates new government, 179; holds last military conferences, 191, 192, 193, 199–200; sends last message to Armed Forces, 194–195; farewell ceremonies, 197–198, 200–201; prepares for death, 200–201; suicide, cremation, and disposal, 201–206; nature of his genius and power, 230–233; his strategical genius, 235–236.

Hitler Youth, 110, 143, 162, 190, 191.

Hoegl (SS Staf), 144, 159–160, 200, 218.

Hofbeck, Hans, 204.

Hoffmann (Hitler's photographer), 60, 69, 93, 94.

v. Holstein, Fritz Baron, 36.

Hummerich (corporal), 189, 219.

Isolation, intellectual effects of, 100–101, 233–234.

Japanese, possibly Aryans?, 21–22.

Jesuits, 16–17.

Jews, 18, 177, 179.

Jodl, Alfred (General), 10, 62, 110, 117–118, 120–123, 138, 140, 154, 190, 194, 212, 220.

Johannmeier, Willi (Major), 143, 187, 189–190, 219–220, 245.

Joseph, Father, 183.

Juettner, Max, 158 n., 244.

Junge, Gertrud (Hitler's secretary), 143, 175, 176, 182 n., 200, 218, 246.

Junkers, 8.

Juvenal, 234.

Kaltenbrunner, Ernst, 25, 26, 85, 86, 87, 123, 244.

Kannenberg, Artur (Hitler's butler), 106 n.

Karinhall, 15.

Karnau, Hermann, 203–205, 246.

Kaufmann, Karl, 45, 74, 113 n., 114, 243.

Keitel, Wilhelm (Field Marshal), 10, 11 n., 29, 30, 31, 65, 109, 111, 117, 120–123, 130, 131, 138, 140, 154, 163, 193, 194, 199, 220, 234, 235, 243, 246.

Kempka, Erich (Hitler's driver), 200, 201, 202, 213, 216, 246.

Keppler, Wilhelm, 21 n., 70 n.

Kersten, Felix (Himmler's masseur), 22, 85, 104.

Kesselring (Field Marshal), 111, 119, 173, 234.

v. Kluge, Guenther (Field Marshal), 34.

Koch, Professor, 68.

Koester's Antigas Pills, 66.

Koller, Karl (General), 112, 117, 128–130, 140, 145–147, 153–156, 173, 212, 245.

Krebs, Hans (General), 110, 111, 114, 117, 118, 119, 122, 136, 143, 169, 175, 182, 190, 191, 193, 194, 200, 209–210, 215, 234.

Krueger, Else (Bormann's secretary), 128, 143, 200, 218, 246.

Lahousen, Erwin (Colonel), 24 n., 34.

Lammers, Hans Heinrich, 91 n., 129, 140, 245.

Leibstandarte Adolf Hitler, 72, 89.

Ley, Robert, 79.

Linge, Heinz (Hitler's personal servant), 52, 66, 143, 168, 200, 201, 202, 206, 218.

Lorenz, Heinz, 144, 164, 168, 187, 189–190, 219–220, 246.

Magnus, Professor, 59.

Mansfeld, Erich, 202–203, 204, 205, 246.

v. Manstein, Fritz Erich (Field Marshal), 234.